Complete
First Certificate
Teacher's Book
Guy Brook-Hart

CAMBRIDGE
UNIVERSITY PRESS

CAMBRIDGE
UNIVERSITY PRESS

University Printing House, Cambridge CB2 8BS, United Kingdom

Cambridge University Press is part of the University of Cambridge.

It furthers the University's mission by disseminating knowledge in the pursuit of education, learning and research at the highest international levels of excellence.

www.cambridge.org
Information on this title: www.cambridge.org/9780521698283

First published 2008
9th printing 2013

Printed in China by Golden Cup Printing Co. Ltd

A catalogue record for this publication is available from the British Library

ISBN 978-0-521-69828-3 Teacher's Book
ISBN 978-0-521-69825-2 Student's Book without answers with CD-ROM
ISBN 978-0-521-69826-9 Student's Book with answers with CD-ROM
ISBN 978-0-521-69830-6 Class Audio CDs (3)
ISBN 978-0-521-69827-6 Student's Book Pack (Student's Book with answers, CD-ROM and
                        Class Audio CDs (3))
ISBN 978-0-521-69831-3 Workbook with Audio CD
ISBN 978-0-521-69832-0 Workbook with answers and Audio CD

Contents

Introduction

Who *Complete First Certificate* is for

Complete First Certificate is an enjoyable and motivating topic-based course designed to give a thorough preparation for the revised Cambridge ESOL First Certificate Exam (Common European Framework (CEF) level B2). It is particularly suitable for **teenagers** and **young adults**. It offers:

- stimulating **authentic reading texts** providing training in the reading techniques and strategies needed to deal with exam reading tasks

- listening tasks providing practice with strategies for handling exam listening tasks

- a systematic approach to exam **speaking tasks** providing models for students to follow and **clear outcomes** for improved exam performance

- many opportunities for personalisation with further speaking activities

- a step-by-step approach to writing tasks with **models** to work from and **sample answers**

- comprehensive coverage of all **major grammar areas** tested in the First Certificate Exam. These are supported by work on correcting **common grammar mistakes** made by First Certificate candidates in the exam as revealed by the **Cambridge Learner Corpus** (see below)

- vocabulary input, particularly focusing on and correcting **common vocabulary mistakes** and confusions made by First Certificate candidates in the exam as revealed by the **Cambridge Learner Corpus.**

What the Student's Book contains

- 16 topic-based units of 8 pages each covering topic areas frequently encountered in the First Certificate Exam

- Each unit covers one task from each of the five papers which comprise the exam, so all units contain work on Reading, Listening, Speaking, Use of English and Writing. They also contain **systematic coverage of grammar and vocabulary.**

- Each exam-style task is integrated into a range of classroom work designed to give students the strategies and techniques to deal with exam questions.

- The tasks are all accompanied by **detailed information** about what the task involves and advice about how best to approach it.

- 8 unit reviews covering the grammar and vocabulary encountered in each unit

- A **Grammar reference section** giving clear and detailed explanations of the grammar covered in each unit

- **Writing and Speaking reference sections** containing detailed advice to students on how to approach writing and speaking tasks in the exam, and writing models as examples

- **A complete revised First Certificate Exam** supplied by **Cambridge ESOL**

- A **CD-ROM intended for self-study** with further work and exercises to prepare students for the First Certificate Exam is included in the Student's Book.

The Cambridge Learner Corpus (CLC) ⊙

The Cambridge Learner Corpus (CLC) is a large collection of exam scripts written by students taking Cambridge ESOL English exams around the world. It currently contains over 85,000 scripts and is growing all the time. It forms part of the Cambridge International Corpus (CIC) and it has been built up by Cambridge University Press and Cambridge ESOL. The CLC currently contains scripts from over:

- 85,000 students
- 100 different first languages
- 180 different countries

Exercises in the Student's Book which are based on the CLC are indicated by this icon: ⊙.

What the Teacher's Book contains

- Unit notes for the 16 units of the Student's Book which:
  - state the **objectives** of each unit
  - give **step-by-step advice** on how to treat each part of each Student's Book unit
  - offer a wide range of suggestions for **alternative treatments** of the material in the Student's Book
  - offer a wide range of ideas for **extension activities** to follow up Student's Book activities
  - contain **comprehensive answer keys** for each activity and exercise
  - contain **complete recording scripts**. The sections of text which provide the answers to listening tasks are <u>underlined</u>.

- **16 photocopiable activities**, one for each unit, designed to provide enjoyable recycling of work done in the Student's Book unit, but without a specific exam-style focus. All photocopiable activities are accompanied by detailed teacher's notes outlining:
  - the objectives of the activity
  - a suggested procedure for handling the activity in the classroom.

- **4 photocopiable progress tests**, one every four units, to test grammar and vocabulary taught in the units

- **16 photocopiable word lists** covering vocabulary encountered in the Student's Book. The vocabulary items are accompanied by definitions supplied by corpus-informed Cambridge dictionaries. These lists can be given to students for private study, reference or revision after they have completed the unit, or for reference while they are working on the unit if you prefer. The lists are intended as an extra tool for extending students' vocabulary.
  For suggestions on how to use the word lists, please see page 11.

Other components of *Complete First Certificate*

- **3 audio CDs** containing a wide range of exam-style listening materials, recordings for the **First Certificate Exam** supplied by **Cambridge ESOL** and recordings of different parts of the Speaking test to serve as models for students. The listening material is indicated by a different coloured icon in the Student's Book for each of the CDs.

- A **Student's Workbook** to accompany the Student's Book, with four pages of exercises for each unit. These exercises practise the reading, writing and listening skills needed for the First Certificate exam. They also give further practice in grammar and vocabulary. The Student's Workbook is also accompanied by **an audio CD** containing listening material.

Unit 1 A family affair

There is a photocopiable activity on page 12 for the first day of class in case your students don't have the book yet.

Starting off

This exercise is intended as a warm-up and 'getting to know you' exercise. Encourage students to speak at length. In Speaking Part 1 of the exam, candidates may be asked about their families and family life. This unit provides preparation and practice.

Listening Part 1

❶ *As a warmer* Elicit ideas about the first photograph with the whole class. Possible questions:
- What is happening, and why?
- How do you think the people in the photo are feeling?
- Does the photo show something typical in your country? etc.

Then ask them to work in pairs and talk about the other photos in the same way.

Extension idea Ask students to work in groups and describe what a typical photograph of their families would show them doing.

❷ 🎧 After students have done the first listening task (matching the speakers to the photos), elicit what words or phrases they heard which gave them the answers.

Answers
Photos: Patrick 3   Tracey 2   Vicky 4   Kostas 1

Note: the words/sentences which give answers to questions in the main listening exercises are numbered and <u>underlined</u> for easy reference.

Recording script   CD1 Track 2

Interviewer: How much do you help around the house, Patrick?

Patrick: Not that much really, but that's because my mum doesn't go out to work any more, so she has more time than she used to. I don't have a lot of free time these days because I'm studying for my exams. I mean, my mum does most of the housework, though I used to help more when I was younger – you know, hang out clothes, lay the table, things like that. She's pretty busy, but even so she usually manages to find a bit of time to give me a hand with my studies – she used to be a maths teacher and she knows I'm a bit nervous about the maths

Q1 exam. <u>But I think she really does it for pleasure</u> – she's really good at explaining things, though sometimes I feel I'd just like to get on with things on my own.

Interviewer: Tracey. How often do you all do things together as a family?

Tracey: Oh, all the time, I mean at least once a week at weekends. You see we live in this really old house by the sea, and we've been working on it all year. In fact, we've just finished doing up the kitchen at the back of the house. It's been great fun because we've all been doing it together and I've been learning a lot about DIY, which is really useful. We've made a lot of mess, of course, which we've had to clear

Q2 up and <u>now we're decorating it</u>, so it's looking nicer and nicer. We had lots of really big arguments about the colour, but in the end everyone agreed with me, so I'm really happy because we're doing things the way I want.

Interviewer: Vicky, do you ever do sports with other people in your family?

Vicky: Well, my dad's a fitness fanatic, so he's always running or cycling or doing something

Q3 energetic. I do sporty things with him now and again, more often in the summer though occasionally at other times of the year as well. He's got a few days' holiday at the moment, so he's probably doing something sporty right now. He's always asking me to go out cycling with him, but now I've got a boyfriend and other things to do, so recently I've been spending more time with him than with my dad.

Interviewer: Do you enjoy family celebrations, Kostas?

Kostas: Not much, to be honest. I just feel they go

Q4 on for too long and I'd prefer to be out doing other things with my friends, not sitting around listening to my uncles and aunts and that. Someone is always standing up and giving a speech or singing a song and I've heard all those songs and speeches so many times that

Q4 I've just lost interest. But I don't get annoyed or anything like that. I mean I just wait for things to end and then I go out with my friends. That's what I really like.

❸ 🎧 *Alternative treatment* Before they do the multiple-choice task, ask students to work in pairs and predict the answers, based on what they have already heard when doing Exercise 2.

Answers
1 A   2 C   3 B   4 A

Extension idea Write these headings on the board: *Giving children an education, A common project, Enjoying doing the same things, Family celebrations.* Ask students to match the headings with the photos. Then ask them to discuss this question: Which aspect of family life do you think is the most important?

❹ 🎧 You may need to remind students how to form questions in the present simple. The questions in the book are common mistakes that students make.

Answers
1 How much do you help around the house?
2 How often do you all do things together as a family?   3 Do you (ever) do/play sports with other people in your family?   4 Do you enjoy family celebrations?

Recording script   CD1 Track 3

1   How much do you help around the house, Patrick?

2   Tracey. How often do you all do things together as a family?

3   Vicky, do you ever do sports with other people in your family?

4   Do you enjoy family celebrations, Kostas?

❺ You can elicit possible questions from the whole class from the prompts in the Student's Book before students write them down.

Suggested questions
Where do you go on family holidays? What do you enjoy doing with your family? How does your family spend the weekends? Which member of your family are you most similar to?

❻ *Extension idea* Ask students to change partners and report what they have discovered about the person they interviewed.

Grammar
Present simple and present continuous

❶ You can elicit that continuous tenses are formed using the verb *to be* + main verb + *-ing*.

Answers
2 present simple   3 present continuous
4 present continuous   5 present simple
6 present continuous   7 present continuous

❷ *As a warmer* Students may be familiar with the 'rule' that the present continuous is used for things happening now; ask them to read the sentences and say which of the sentences actually refers to something happening at the present moment (*Answer:* 6).

Answers
2 present continuous 6   3 present continuous 1
4 present continuous 4   5 present simple 5
6 present continuous 3   7 present continuous 7

❸ Remind students that they can use contractions to answer the questions, e.g. 'I am working' ⟶ 'I'm working', 'she has done' ⟶ 'she's done', etc.

Answers
2 work   3 am working, am preparing   4 is coming out   5 are always interrupting   6 am watching
7 is coming, are getting   8 does not do, is always bringing

Extension idea After doing the exercise, ask students to write sentences about themselves or their families illustrating each of these uses of the present simple and continuous.

Reading Part 2

① *As a warmer* Ask students to look at the photos at the bottom of pages 10 and 11. Ask: what do you think these teenagers' parents would say about each of the teenagers in the photos?

- Ask them to work in small groups and make a list of four or five adjectives that parents often use about their teenage children, e.g. untidy.
- Write their adjectives on the board. Ask them which ones are positive and which ones are negative. If there are many more of one than the other, ask them why.

Then move on to the vocabulary exercise in the book.

After doing the exercise, ask them also to copy the adjectives they suggested into the appropriate column.

Answers		
usually positive	usually negative	could be either
hard-working	critical	quiet
mature	fussy	sensitive
tactful	lazy	strict
polite	nervous	talkative
relaxed	rude	
responsible	tactless	
tidy		

② Explain that adjectives beginning with *m* or *p* often take the prefix *im-* (e.g. impossible, immature, impatient), and adjectives beginning with *r* often take the prefix *ir-* (e.g. irregular, irresistible).

> **Answers**
> critical – uncritical, mature – immature,
> polite – impolite, responsible – irresponsible,
> sensitive – insensitive, tidy – untidy

Extension idea Ask students to suggest other examples.

③

> **Answers**
> hard-working – lazy, tactful – tactless,
> polite – rude, quiet – talkative, relaxed – strict

④ Ask students to discuss these two questions in pairs.

⑤ To get them started, elicit a few more ideas from the whole class.

⑥ To encourage skimming skills, you could set students a time-limit, e.g. three minutes. After reading, ask them to compare their answer in pairs.

> **Answers**
> She has a mostly positive attitude. The article suggests that parents' behaviour causes many of the problems with teenage children.

⑦ Use the example given in gap 1: ask students to read and say why *H* is the answer. You can elicit that the text says: 'You'd be very upset.' Why? It says: 'You'd never say that to an adult ...' – ask what would you never say to an adult? Why does it show a total lack of respect?

To help them further, you can tell them that gap 2 is either B or F and ask them to say which is correct and why. (*Answer:* F – the text refers to *any mess*, and F says that the kitchen was sometimes cleaner.)

If you think it's necessary, give them choices for other gaps. Ask them to work in pairs and decide on their answers, giving reasons for them. Note: in the exam, no example is given.

> **Answers**
> **2** F   **3** A   **4** C   **5** B   **6** D   **7** G

⑧ Get students started by eliciting an example from the whole class, e.g. teenagers don't come home at the time they say they will. You can elicit what other complaints were made by parents in the text, though it would be more creative to encourage students to produce their own.

Grammar
Present perfect simple and continuous

① Ask students which sentences are present perfect simple and which are continuous. When they have done the exercise, refer them to the Grammar reference section on page 153 and go through it with them.

> **Answers**
> **1** 1 a, 2 b   **2** 1 b, 2 a   **3** 1 a, 2 b

② Before they do the exercise, elicit why the example in question 1 is continuous (*Answer:* it emphasises the activity). Ask students to check their answers together in pairs and, where they disagree, discuss. Encourage them to look at the Grammar reference section when doing the exercise.

> **Answers**
> **2** have asked   **3** have cleaned   **4** has been playing   **5** have passed   **6** has only been working   **7** have spent   **8** have been cooking

Use of English Part 2

❶ *As a warmer* With their books closed, ask students to brainstorm different household tasks in small groups. Round up the activity by writing the suggestions on the board and then ask students to work in their groups and say which tasks they enjoy doing, which they don't mind doing and which they hate doing, and why.

Then ask them to do the matching exercise in the book.

Answers
2 h   3 d   4 b   5 g   6 f   7 a   8 c

❷ *Alternative treatment* Turn the first question into a class survey by getting students to compile details of who does each task in the family. This can then be developed into a class discussion of any surprising trends, imbalances (e.g. one member of the family doing many more of the household jobs than others), etc. This will then serve as an introduction to the next activity.

❸ If appropriate, ask students if they think housework should be shared equally. Give students two minutes to skim the text for the answer.

Answers
The text does not say who should do housework, but implies that it should be shared equally.

❹

Answers
The four reasons: They say, 'I work long hours', 'my wife's work is less stressful', 'she does it better', and they think their jobs are more important.

❺ In the exam this exercise tests grammar knowledge, collocations, linking words, prepositions and phrasal verbs. Extensive reading outside the classroom is useful preparation for this and other parts of the exam by building up students' knowledge of English. You can help them a lot with this type of exercise, which they will find challenging to start with, by eliciting or guiding them towards the answers, especially for the first few spaces. For example, for the example 0:

- ask them to look at the position of the space in the sentence and say what type of word they need (a verb)

- tell them it's a collocation and ask them what word(s) it will collocate with (*out to work*).

For question 1: what type of word follows *most* and comes before *the + a noun (a noun, a preposition, or an adjective)*?

Ask students to do questions 2–5 in pairs and then round up answers with them.

Ask them to do 6–12 alone and then discuss in pairs when they have finished.

Don't go through the answers until they have done Exercise 6.

❻ Ask students to improve their answers by using the box on page 13.

Answers
1 of   2 doing   3 If/When   4 for   5 that/which
6 so   7 it   8 not   9 mine   10 at   11 is   12 more

❼ *As a warmer* Ask the whole class: do you think you should share the chores equally? Should you share the more unpleasant chores? Should each person do the chore they do best or enjoy most? Ask students to do the task in groups of three or four.

Vocabulary
Collocations with *make* and *do*

❶ ⊙ *As a warmer* Elicit household chores with *make* or *do*, e.g. *make the bed*, *do the ironing*, etc.

Answers
1 do, doing   2 make, do

❷

Answers
1 making, do   2 making   3 doing   4 make, do
5 made   6 make, do

Extension idea If you have class sets of a good learner's dictionary, e.g. the *Cambridge Advanced Learner's Dictionary*, ask students to look up *do* and *make* in the dictionary and find other collocations. Ask them to write them in their notebooks.

Speaking Part 1

❶ Tell students that the aim of the Speaking paper is to see how well they can speak, so they should avoid one-word or very short answers where possible.

② 🎧 Tell students not to worry about writing the names of the towns.

Recording script   CD1 Track 4

Teacher: So, Irene, where are you from?

Irene: I'm from Llanes. It's a small town near Oviedo on the north coast of Spain.

Teacher: And what do you like about Llanes?

Irene: Well, it's quite a quiet place, especially in the winter, but it has wonderful beaches and beautiful countryside. Also, I have a lot of very good friends living there and we have a really good time when we go out together.

Teacher: And you Peter, where are you from?

Peter: Bremen, in northern Germany.

Teacher: And what do you like about Bremen?

Peter: My friends, the shops, the sports centre …

Teacher: Do you come from a large family?

❸ Ask students to briefly discuss this question in pairs first.

❹ If you wish, you can give students two or three minutes to study the questions before they start, to plan how they will answer.

Writing Part 1

❶ *As a warmer* Ask students:
- if they write letters or emails, or chat with people from other countries
- if they enjoy doing this and how it benefits them

- how you can get in contact with students from other countries. (*Suggested answers:* Through educational exchanges, travelling to the country, meeting visiting foreign students, or through internet websites)

Ask students to read the task and make sure they identify the four points they must deal with. Ask them to compare their answers in pairs. In the exam candidates will lose marks if they do not deal with all four points.

② Point out that their email will be 120–150 words, so the notes should be quite brief.

❸ You can point out some features of emails:
- to a friend you can start: *Hello* or *Hi* + name
- you can finish: *Best wishes* + your name.

Ask students if Chiara has included anything which is not asked for in the task in Exercise 1. (*Answer:* Yes: *It's very exciting to hear you're coming to Italy; Let me know when you're coming.*) Remind students that the number of words is limited, so they should just deal with the task, but at the same time make the email sound natural.

❹ Ask students which ways of making suggestions are followed by a verb + *-ing* (*I suggest* … and *How about* …) and which is followed by an infinitive (*it would be a good idea* …).

❺

Extension idea Ask students to write their own sentences suggesting ways of meeting young people in their town or country.

6 Tell students that this task should take them about 40 minutes. If you wish, this can be done for homework.

→ For more on writing emails, you can refer students to page 169 (Writing reference – Part 1).

Sample answer: See the model in Exercise 3 in the Student's Book.

Word lists

In general you should give students the word lists when they have finished, or are near to finishing a unit as reinforcement of vocabulary encountered during the unit.

With a weak or insecure class, you can give them the word lists in advance, but it is always useful to train students to guess the meanings of unfamiliar vocabulary from the context before resorting to a dictionary explanation. They can then use the word lists to check whether their deduction has been correct.

If you wish, you can give out the word lists before students do the final writing task in the unit and ask them to check through the list beforehand to see if they can use any of the vocabulary in the task.

Unit 1 photocopiable activity
The first day   Time: 20–30 mins

This activity provides material for the first lesson, perhaps before students have bought their books.

Objectives

- To formulate questions on work or study
- To ask and answer questions on personal details (work and study) and familiar topics
- To discuss language-learning experiences
- To encourage oral fluency by discussing familiar topics

Before class

You will need one photocopy of the activity page for each student.

In class

1 Tell students they should only formulate questions, not ask or answer them. To get them started, you can elicit questions for the first few prompts in Box A, e.g. *Who do you work for? What are you studying? What do you like and dislike about …? How long have you been working?* etc.

Suggested questions
Do you work or study? Who do you work for?
What are you studying? What do you like / dislike about your job / studies? How long have you been working / studying? Why did you choose that job / subject? What do you hope to do in the future? / Do you have any ambitions for the future? Do you use / speak / need English in your work / studies?

2 When students change partners and ask the questions, encourage them to answer with some details.

3 Students continue with the same partner and ask each other questions to find out the information for Box B. Tell them not to prepare these questions in advance and to try to have a normal conversation. Encourage them to ask follow-up questions.

Suggested questions
How long have you been studying English? Why are you studying English? Where have you studied / been studying? What/Which English exams have you passed? Why are you studying for First Certificate?

4 When students have finished discussing, round up the most useful answers with the whole class.

Extension idea Ask students to work in pairs and write a paragraph describing an idea for learning languages which they find useful. When they are ready, ask them to read their idea to the whole class. This may lead to further discussion.

The first day

❶ Work in pairs. Think of the questions you could ask people about their work or studies to complete Box A below. Examples: *Do you work or study? Who do you work for? What are you studying?*

Box A
Work or study?

• Employer?	• What / studying?
....	....
• What likes / dislikes about job?	• What likes / dislikes about studies?
....	....
• How long working?	• How long studying?
....	....
• Reason for choosing that job?	• Reason for choosing that subject?
....	....
• Professional plans / ambitions?	• Ambitions / hopes for the future?
....	....
• English in your work?	• English in your studies?
....	....

❷ Change pairs. Ask your new partner the questions you have prepared and complete Box A.

Box B
Number of years studying English?
....
Reasons for studying English?
....
Where studied?
....
English exams passed?
....
Reason for studying for First Certificate?
....

❸ Now work in pairs and ask each other (and answer) similar questions in order to complete Box B.

❹ Work in groups of four. Discuss the questions in Box C.

Box C
What is your biggest problem studying English?
What method(s) do you have for learning vocabulary?
What method(s) do you have for studying grammar?
What books have you read in English?
What advice would you give people about reading books in English?
How often do you speak in English? What advice would you give for improving fluency?
How much do you listen to films, radio, etc. in English? What advice would you give for improving listening skills?

Word list

Unit 1

Note: the numbers show which page the word or phrase first appears on in the unit.

amused *adj* (8) showing that you think something is funny

annoy *v* (10) to make someone angry

assume *v* (11) to accept something to be true without question or proof

best-selling *adj* (10) selling in very large numbers

bored *adj* (8) feeling tired and unhappy because something is not interesting or because you have nothing to do

bring up *v* (10) to care for a child until he/she is an adult, often giving him/her particular beliefs

charming *adj* (11) pleasant and attractive

compromise *n* (11) an agreement in an argument in which the people involved reduce their demands or change their opinion in order to agree

counter-argument *n* (11) an argument against another argument, idea or suggestion

countless *adj* (10) very many; too many to be counted

deal with *v* (10)
1 to talk to someone or meet someone, especially as part of your job
2 to take action in order to achieve something or in order to solve a problem
3 to be about or be on the subject of something

desire *v* (10) a strong feeling that you want something

do someone a favour *v* (13) to do something for someone in order to help them

embarrassed *adj* (8) feeling ashamed or shy

energetic *adj* (9) the power and ability to be physically and mentally active

extend *v* (8) to add to something in order to make it bigger or longer

fanatic *n* (9) someone whose interest in something or enthusiasm for something is extreme

firm *n* (9) a company or business

fitness *n* (9) the condition of being physically strong and healthy

give someone a lift *v* (9) to give someone a free ride somewhere, usually in a car

interrupt *v* (9) to stop a person from speaking for a short period by something you say or do

irritate *v* (10) to make someone angry

lack of something *n* (10) not having something or not having enough of something

mature *adj* (10) fully grown or developed

mind your own business *v* (9) used to tell someone in a rude way that you do not want them to ask about something private

on average *n* (13) usually, based on an amount which is calculated by adding some amounts together, and then dividing by the number of amounts

prioritise *v* (11) to decide which of a group of things are the most important so that you can deal with them first

sporty *adj* (9) relating to sports

the key to something *n* (10) the best way of achieving something

upset *adj* (10) worried, unhappy or angry

vital *adj* (11) extremely important

Unit 2 Leisure and pleasure

Unit objectives

- **Reading Part 1:** introduction to task type, training in skimming
- **Writing Part 2:** introduction to writing an article, structuring an article, using adjectives
- **Use of English Part 4:** introduction to task type, writing key word transformations with comparative and superlative structures
- **Listening Part 2:** introduction to task type, identifying the type of information and type of words required
- **Speaking Part 2:** introduction to task type, talking about free time and hobbies
- **Vocabulary:** presenting types of leisure-time activity, some phrasal verbs, adjectives describing feelings
- **Grammar:** adjectives ending in -ed and -ing, comparison of adjectives and adverbs

Starting off

❶ *Alternative treatment* Ask students to cover the text on this page and suggest names for each of the activities in the photographs. They then uncover the text and compare their ideas with the names in the box.

> **Answers**
> 1 riding motorbikes   2 window shopping
> 3 playing computer games   4 clubbing
> 5 doing aerobics   6 playing chess
> 7 playing team sports

❷ 1 Ask students to give details: Where? When? Did they enjoy it, etc.?

2 and 3 Encourage students to give reasons for their answers.

Extension idea 1 Ask students to work in small groups. Tell them to list their leisure-time activities and compare them with the ones in the photographs using questions a–f in 2.

Extension idea 2 If appropriate, ask students to bring photographs from home for the next class showing themselves or their families doing leisure activities, and ask them to talk about why they do them and why they enjoy them.

Reading Part 1

❶ *As a warmer*

- Ask students to look at the photos of Ewan McGregor on page 17 and say what they know about him.
- Ask how many of your class ride motorbikes and how their families felt about them taking up biking. (This is a question you can also perhaps ask to students who don't ride motorbikes.)

❷ Ask them to skim the text for the answers and underline or highlight them. Give them a time limit of three minutes. When they have finished, ask them to work in pairs and summarise the reasons in their own words.

> **Suggested answers**
> His girlfriend left him for someone with a motorbike; he had enjoyed riding a motorbike when he was six; it would allow him to get to places

❸ To help students with multiple-choice questions in a reading text, you can ask them as a class to look at question 1 and:

- locate where it is dealt with in the text
- read that section carefully
- then look at the alternatives and choose the correct answer
- say what words in the text give the correct answer. Point out that there must be something specifically in the text which gives that answer.

Point out that the answers occur in the text in the same order as the questions, so they can work through the questions and the text one by one.

Ask students to work alone through the other questions and then to compare their answers in pairs before rounding up with the whole class.

> **Answers**
> 1 B   2 D   3 B   4 C   5 D   6 A   7 C   8 C

Extension idea Ask students to underline any unfamiliar vocabulary in the text.

- Ask them to work in teams of three. They should choose three words or phrases that they would like to find out the meanings of.
- When they have decided on the words, ask them to read them out and you write them on the board (or they come to the board and write them).
- Tell them that it is a competition and each team has five minutes to try to guess the meanings of the words and phrases on the board from the context.
- At the end of five minutes, get the teams to suggest their definitions. The team whose definition is the closest gets a point, and the team with the most points wins.

❹ *As a warmer* Ask students to brainstorm reasons why teenagers often want a motorbike; ask them to brainstorm reasons why parents often don't want their children to have motorbikes.

Before they do the role play, ask them to work in pairs and give them two or three minutes to prepare roles for either Student A or Student B. Then ask them to change partners and work with someone who prepared the other role.

Vocabulary
Phrasal verbs

❶ Ask students to check their answers by looking at the context in the reading text. Afterwards, ask them to check their answers using a dictionary.

> **Answers**
> 2 a   3 c   4 b   5 f   6 g   7 d

❷

> **Answers**
> 2 sum up   3 start up   4 make up   5 goes out with / is going out with   6 taking up   7 shot off

Extension idea Students work in pairs and write four sentences using phrasal verbs from this section, but leaving a gap where the phrasal verbs should be. They then test another pair by giving them their sentences and asking them to write the phrasal verb in the correct form in the gap.

Grammar
Adjectives with *-ed* and *-ing*

❶ After doing this introductory exercise, go through the Grammar reference section on page 154 (Adjectives with *-ed* and *-ing*) with the class.

> **Answers**
> 1 thrilled, elated   2 exciting

Extension idea Ask students to brainstorm other adjectives they know with *-ed* and *-ing*.

❷ ⊙ Tell students that they should look out for and avoid these mistakes when they are speaking or writing. Tell them they can also correct their classmates if they hear them making a mistake.

> **Answers**
> 2 annoying   3 bored   4 confused
> 5 embarrassing   6 excited

❸ This exercise practises similar skills to those needed for Use of English Part 3 (word formation), where forming adjectives with *-ed* or *-ing* may be tested. However, in the exam a continuous text is used rather than separate sentences.

Make sure that students spell their answers correctly – they can use the base word (e.g. *disappoint*) to check whether *disappointing* has a double or a single *p*. Check also that they drop the final *e* of *amuse* when writing *amusing*.

> **Answers**
> 2 disappointing   3 interesting   4 worried
> 5 exhausting   6 amusing

❹ ⌢ Ask students to listen to the general gist of the story as the recording contains a number of distractors.

> **Answer**   g

> **Recording script**   CD1 Track 5
>
> **Young woman:** The whole experience was amazing actually. I mean, I'd been working really hard, studying, and so I was feeling pretty tired and nervous already, so when my boyfriend suggested I went along with him, I was like shocked like 'No way!' I mean the thought of breaking a bone or something even worse just before an exam was terrifying. But you know he just kept on at me, so for the sake of a bit of peace in the end I said yes. When <u>we were up there in the sky</u> I was just so scared I can't tell you. I just wanted to <u>get out of the plane</u>. I felt trapped, but <u>the only way to do that was to jump, and in fact the jump itself was really exciting</u>. I'd love to do it again. And I didn't break a thing!

❺ ⌢ *Alternative treatment* Before playing the recording again, ask students to work in pairs or small groups and try to remember what adjectives she used for each of these things. They then listen again to check their answers.

> **Answers**
> 2 tired and nervous   3 shocked   4 terrifying
> 5 trapped   6 exciting

❻ Encourage students to use adjectives with *-ed* and *-ing*. If any students have problems, tell them they can talk about someone they know, or give a fictional answer.

Listening Part 2

❶ *As a warmer* Ask students if they play video, computer or online games. Ask them which games they most enjoy. Try to find out if boys/men enjoy different games from girls/women.

Ask students to try to give reasons for their answers. Where possible, ask them to suggest an example.

Suggested answers

1 Positive effects
- They encourage people to be more creative.
- They can distract you from your problems.
- Many of the games are very educational.
- They require imagination to play well.
- People learn to concentrate on tasks.
- They develop many skills, such as hand and eye coordination.
- They teach people how to solve problems.

2 Criticisms
- Young people play computer games instead of being more creative.
- Video games distract young people from their homework.
- People who play these games have less imagination.
- The games are unsociable activities.
- They encourage young people to be violent.
- They are a waste of time. People should spend their time doing something useful.

---

❷ Tell students that in the sentence completion task in Listening Part 2, predicting possible answers is an effective way of improving performance. To get them started, you could elicit that they need an adjective or adjective phrase for question 1. Then perhaps elicit possible answers which will fit the space, e.g. *lazier, more creative, more violent, more imaginative,* etc. Point out that they may need up to three words.

Suggested answers

1 adjective/adjective phrase   2 noun/noun phrase
3 comparative adverb / comparative adjective + noun
4 adjective   5 noun/noun phrase   6 plural noun/ noun phrase
7 personal plural noun   8 comparative adjective
9 verb   10 noun/noun phrase

---

❸ 🎧 After listening, ask them to read their completed sentences carefully to make sure they are grammatically correct and spelled correctly.

Answers

1 more violent   2 crimes   3 less homework
4 better visual   5 driving skills   6 five objects
7 airport security staff   8 more educational
9 make decisions   10 effort

Recording script   CD1 Track 6

Interviewer: And now to video and computer gaming. Many people worry about how these games affect young people and their education. I have in the studio psychologist Sarah Forbes, who has recently written a book about gaming. Sarah, is there any basis behind these worries?

Sarah: Well, people have been suggesting for years that video games and television programmes

Q1 tend to make youngsters <u>more violent</u>, but I'm not sure that these games have really had any negative effect at all. I mean, computer and video games are tremendously popular and the fact that people stay at home playing

Q2 computer games may mean that fewer <u>crimes</u> are being committed. Potential criminals are keeping themselves entertained playing games instead of going out and breaking the law.

Interviewer: So video games are not all bad.

Sarah: Not at all. Of course, you sometimes hear teachers complaining that schoolchildren come to school tired after spending half the

Q3 night gaming and that they do <u>less homework</u> than they used to in the past. And it's true that these days there are lots of things around to distract and entertain young people. But I'm more interested in the positive effects of gaming.

Interviewer: Which are?

Sarah: Well, firstly my research shows that certain
Q4 games give people <u>better visual</u> skills and as a result they are better at managing machines than people who don't play them. Playing computer games seems to be particularly good for old people who react more slowly than young people. When they play computer
Q5 games, their <u>driving skills</u> actually get better.

Interviewer: Interesting. Are there any professions which would benefit from training with computer games?

Sarah: Certainly. We've found that people playing computer games can keep track of as many as
Q6 <u>five objects</u> at any one time on their computer screen. They can also concentrate for longer.

<table>
<tr><td>Q7</td><td>So, people who have to spend their working time examining or inspecting things might find their skills improved by playing computer games – for example <u>airport security staff</u> might do their job better if they were trained with computer games. They spend hours staring at a screen showing the contents of passengers' luggage as it passes through a machine, looking for illegal items.</td></tr>
<tr><td>Interviewer:</td><td>That's true. And what about the teachers' criticisms?</td></tr>
<tr><td>Sarah:</td><td>Well, I think these days there are a lot of interesting things around to distract students from their schoolwork and teachers are finding it harder to compete for their students' attention and enthusiasm. But some educationalists suggest that it's teachers who need to adapt and that computer</td></tr>
<tr><td>Q8</td><td>games can be <u>more educational</u> than a lot of the traditional activities that go on in the classroom. Teachers need to see their value.</td></tr>
<tr><td>Interviewer:</td><td>And that is?</td></tr>
<tr><td>Sarah:</td><td>Well, games players often spend more than a hundred hours working on a game and trying to dominate its complexities. In doing</td></tr>
<tr><td>Q9</td><td>so they gain the ability to <u>make decisions</u> and think more clearly. A hundred hours is a lot of hours and you wouldn't expect your average schoolchild to spend that much time on a school project. By working through these games and eventually winning them, they learn</td></tr>
<tr><td>Q10</td><td>how valuable it is to make a sustained <u>effort</u> in their work.</td></tr>
<tr><td>Interviewer:</td><td>Interesting.</td></tr>
<tr><td>Sarah:</td><td>Yes, and when looked at from that perspective it's hard to argue that computer games are a waste of time and that young people would be better occupied doing something else.</td></tr>
</table>

❹ Extension idea Ask students to prepare a short talk on a leisure activity they feel enthusiastic about. They can, perhaps, prepare this at home using the internet. Ask them to cover the following points (write these on the board):

- how or why they took the activity up
- why they enjoy it
- how the activity benefits them
- any criticisms people make of the activity.

Ask them to give their talk to a small group of students. The students who are listening should take notes and ask one or two questions at the end.

Grammar
Comparison of adjectives and adverbs

❶ After doing the exercise, go through the explanation in the Grammar reference section on page 154 (Comparison of adjectives and adverbs) with them.

> **Answers**
> 2 and 3 harder / cheapest   4 easiest
> 5, 6 and 7 more violent / more educational / most successful   8 better   9 less   10 better

Extension idea Ask students to suggest other examples for each rule.

❷ ⊙ Tell students it's important to look out for and avoid these mistakes when they are speaking and writing. If they notice that they have made a mistake, or they hear a classmate make a mistake, they should correct it.

> **Answers**
> 2 ~~more cheaper~~ cheaper   3 ~~that~~ than   4 ~~more hardly~~ harder   5 ~~as often than~~ as often as   6 ~~the more enjoyable~~ the most enjoyable   7 ~~the less interesting~~ the least interesting   8 ~~more good~~ better

Extension idea Students work in pairs. Ask them to say which sentences they agree with and which they disagree with, and why.

This may be a suitable moment to do the photocopiable activity on page 20.

Use of English Part 4

❶ Since this is students' first encounter with a complex exam task, you may want to follow this procedure.

- Tell students to concentrate on achieving the same meaning.
- Tell them that although the sentences here practise comparison of adjectives and adverbs, questions in the exam may be about a wide range of different grammar and structures.
- Go through the example and the second question with the whole class to give them the idea of how it is done.
- Write their answers to question 2 on the board and count the words they have used (correct answers have two to five words).
- Ask them to do the rest of the exercise in pairs. Tell them to use the Grammar reference section on page 154 to help them.
- If you wish, let them use the clues in Exercise 2 while doing the exercise to give them confidence.

> **Answers**
> **2** is the most enjoyable   **3** one of the easiest
> **4** not as/so interesting as   **5** play tennis so well as
> **6** is the most hard-working   **7** not as/ so cheap as
> **8** more quickly than

❷ You can use these clues and give other clues to guide students to the correct answers. Remind them always to:

- count the number of words (two to five)
- make sure they have used the word given without changing it.

Speaking Part 2

❶ • Tell students that the photos are a starting point for them to speak.

- Ask them to compare them fairly generally, not focusing on small details; compare what is happening in the photos and how people are feeling.
- Tell them to answer both parts of the task.
- In the exam, each candidate will take it in turns to speak for one minute about a different pair of photographs. The candidate who is not speaking will be asked a question at the end about their partner's photographs.

❷ Tell the student who is not speaking not to interrupt and to listen carefully. At the end, ask them:

- Which activity would you prefer to do?
- Which of the activities do you think would be easiest to do?

Writing Part 2 An article

❶ *As a warmer* Ask students if they have ever written an article. If so, what about, where it was published, etc.? Ask them if they enjoy reading articles written by other students, e.g. in college magazines, etc. and why (not). Ask them what sort of articles are most enjoyable.

Point out that it's important to identify who is going to read the article – this will determine what they put in the article and the style they will use.

> **Answers**
> They should underline: *leisure-time activity, How did you get started? Why do you enjoy it so much?* They may also underline *magazine* in the rubric.

❷ Encourage your students to speak for at least a minute.

❸

> **Answers**
> **1** 1 D   2 C   3 A   4 B
> **2** A, C and D
> **3** A and B

Extension idea Elicit from students:

- What are the characteristics of a good article? (*Possible answers:* it must be interesting, tell the reader something they didn't know, be enjoyable to read)
- What would be a suitable style for this article? (*Answer:* neutral or informal)

❹ Tell students the importance of showing a range of vocabulary in their writing.

> **Answers**
> **1** satisfying, relaxing, fascinating, complicated
> **2** creative, useful   **3** competent, successful

❺ Tell students that this task should take them about 40 minutes. If you wish, this can be done for homework.

→ For more on writing articles, you can refer students to page 176 (Writing reference – Articles).

Sample answer: See the model in Exercise 3 in the Student's Book.

Extension idea Collect students' articles, photocopy them and staple them to form a class magazine.

Vocabulary and grammar review Unit 1

Answers

Vocabulary

❶ **2** tactless / insensitive   **3** fussy   **4** talkative / noisy
5 nervous   **6** sensitive   **7** mature   **8** tidy

❷ **2** swept   **3** doing   **4** laid   **5** make   **6** do

❸ **2** make   **3** do   **4** doing   **5** do   **6** made   **7** made
8 making

Grammar

❹ 2 He's doing, he goes   3 is learning   4 I never phone, is always talking, I get   5 are getting   6 isn't coming, he plays

❺ 2 have arrived, have been expecting   3 have spent, has turned up   4 have had / have been having, has been telling, has not told, has seen   5 has lost / has been losing, has been feeling

Vocabulary and grammar review Unit 2

Answers

Vocabulary

❶ 2 started up   3 taking up   4 make up   5 sum up
6 shot off   7 headed off to

Grammar

❷

2 Small towns are ~~more safety~~ *safer* to live in than large cities.
3 Today's the ~~hotest~~ *hottest* day of the year so far.
4 She looks more ~~relax~~ *relaxed* than she did before the exam.
5 Patty is so smart – she's always dressed in the ~~last~~ *latest* fashion!
6 If you study ~~more hardly~~ *harder*, you'll get higher marks.
7 Everest is the ~~higher~~ *highest* mountain in the world.
8 His first day at school was the ~~worse~~ *worst* day of his life.
9 We need to eat ~~more healthier~~ *healthier* food.
10 We should buy this sofa because it's definitely the ~~comfortablest~~ *most comfortable*.

Word formation

❸ 2 exhausting   3 bored   4 disappointed   5 annoying
6 interested   7 surprised   8 exciting

Unit 2 photocopiable activity: Find the person who ...   Time: 30 mins

Objectives
- To formulate and ask personal questions
- To give personal information
- To use comparatives and superlatives accurately in a speaking task

Before class

You will need to photocopy the activity page and cut up the cards so that each member of the class has one of the four cards.

In class

❶ Divide the class into four equal-sized groups, A, B, C and D, and give each person in the group a copy of the card for their group.

❷ Tell them they are going to interview each other and the other members of the class to find out the information needed to complete their card, but first they must formulate appropriate questions.

❸ Students then work together in the same groups to formulate the questions they should ask. For example, to find out who has made the most exciting journey: *Have you ever been on / to ...? What's the most exciting journey you've ever made?* You will have to go round checking, helping and advising.

❹ Students, still in the same group, then ask and answer the questions on the card.

❺ They then form new groups of four with at least one person from each of Groups A, B, C and D. They ask and answer the questions on their different cards.

❻ When they have finished, students return to their original groups, report the information they have obtained and discuss who has had the most exciting journey, who has had the most eccentric teacher, etc.

❼ You may wish to remind them of the sort of language they should be using, e.g. *X's father's job is not as unusual as Y's mother's job. Z's father's job is the most unusual / more unusual than X's mother's job,* etc.

❽ When they have finished discussing, ask a spokesperson from each group to report back the results to the whole class.

Find the person who ...

Group A
Find the person in the group ...

- who has made the most exciting journey. ....
- who spends the most time on the internet. ....
- who has been learning English the longest. ....
- who spends the most time watching television every day. ....
- who can cook the most complicated dish. ....
- who does the most sports. ....

Group B
Find the person in the group ...

- who spends the most time playing online or video games. ....
- who has read the most books in English. ....
- who has the longest journey to class. ....
- who has the most brothers and sisters. ....
- who has had the strangest holiday. ....
- who spends the most time studying each day. ....

Group C
Find the person in the group ...

- who has had the most eccentric teacher. ....
- who has the most unusual ambition. ....
- who had the most interesting weekend last weekend. ....
- Whose family has the most pets. ....
- who watches the least television. ....
- who has the most talented friend. ....

Group D
Find the person in the group ...

- who has done the most dangerous sport. ....
- who has lived in a foreign country the longest. ....
- who speaks the most languages. ....
- who has won the best prize for something they have done. ....
- who does the least housework. ....
- who has spoken in public to the most people. ....

Word list

Unit 2

Note: the numbers show which page the word or phrase first appears on in the unit.

abrupt *adj* (16) describes something that is sudden and unexpected, and often unpleasant

clamber *v* (17) to climb up, across or into somewhere with difficulty, using the hands and the feet

commit *v* (20) to do something illegal or something that is considered wrong

compete *v* (20) to try to be more successful than someone or something else

consistent *adj* (20) always behaving or happening in a similar, especially positive, way

disappoint *v* (19) to make someone feel unhappy because something or someone was not as good as they had expected or because something did not happen

distract *v* (19) to make someone stop giving their attention to something

exhaust *v* (19) to make someone feel extremely tired

fantasise *v* (17) to imagine something that you would like to happen but which is not likely to happen

further afield *n* (17) a long distance away

heap *n* (17) an untidy pile or mass of things

heartbroken *adj* (16) extremely sad, often because a relationship has finished

high-pitched *adj* (17) describes a noise that is high and sometimes also loud or unpleasant

irrelevant *adj* (16) not related to what is being discussed or considered and therefore of no importance

leisure *n* (23) the time when you are not working or doing other duties

make up *v* (17) to invent something, such as an excuse or a story, often in order to deceive

mousy *adj* (16) describes hair which is brown and not special or attractive

on display *n* (16) If something is on display, it is in a place for people to look at.

pile *n* (17) an amount of a substance in the shape of a small hill or a number of objects on top of each other

rush *n* (17) sudden, quick movement

simultaneously *adv* (20) happening or existing at the same time

straw *n* (17) the dried yellow stems of crops such as wheat, used as food for animals or as a layer on the ground for animals to lie on

sum up *v* (16) to describe the important facts about something briefly

triviality *n* (16) something that is not important

urge *v* (16) to strongly advise or try to persuade someone to do a particular thing

venture *v* (17) to risk going somewhere or doing something that might be dangerous or unpleasant

Unit 3 Happy holidays!

Unit objectives

- **Reading Part 3:** studying the questions before the text, locating information
- **Writing Part 2:** introduction to writing a story, using a range of tenses in the narrative, structuring the narrative
- **Use of English Part 3:** introduction to task type, word formation: verbs and nouns to adjectives
- **Listening Part 3:** introduction to task type, working on synonyms to predict how answers may be expressed
- **Speaking Part 3:** introduction to task type, dealing with all the prompts, prompting each other to speak
- **Vocabulary:** confusion between *journey, trip, travel* and *way*; lexis connected with travel and holidays
- **Grammar:** past simple, past continuous, *used to*, past perfect simple and continuous

Starting off

❶ *Alternative treatment* Before doing the task, students work in small groups and:

- cover the text in their books and look at the photographs only
- brainstorm vocabulary they could use to talk about each of the photographs, e.g. for photo 1, *camping, in the mountains*, etc.
- then check their ideas against the vocabulary in the box before doing the task in the book.

Answers

types of holiday	holiday places	holiday activities
a camping holiday	at a campsite	walking and climbing
a beach holiday	at a luxury hotel	meeting new people
a sightseeing holiday	on a cruise ship	sunbathing
a cruise	at a youth hostel	relaxing
backpacking	at sea	visiting monuments
	in the mountains	seeing new places
	in the city centre	
	at the seaside	

❷

Answers
1 Photos: **1** a camping holiday **2** a beach holiday **3** a sightseeing holiday **4** backpacking **5** a cruise

2, 3 and **4** *Students' own answers*

Extension idea Ask students to work in pairs and suggest and describe two more photographs which could be added to the set.

Listening Part 3

❶

Suggested answers
A a sightseeing holiday **B** a cruise, backpacking or a camping holiday **C** a beach holiday or a cruise **D** backpacking or a camping holiday **E** backpacking or a camping holiday **F** a cruise

❷ Tell students that when they listen, they won't hear exactly the same words; thinking of other ways of expressing it will help them to listen for the idea.

Answers
A good food – delicious meals **B** something new – a complete novelty, dangerous – risky **C** did very little – sat around **D** exercise – physical activity, unspoilt – natural **E** friendly – kind **F** in style and comfort – in luxury

Extension idea Ask them to rewrite the sentences in Exercise 1 using vocabulary from the box. They may have to change the form of the word to do so, e.g. Our visit to different cities and islands was luxurious. We visited … in luxury.

❸ In the exam itself, the listening task is not an interview as here, but five separate but related extracts.

Answers
1 B **2** C **3** D **4** A **5** E

Recording script

Interviewer: So, now after that, I'd like to ask each of you a bit more about your holidays. Francesca, what did you particularly like about your holiday?

Francesca: I went on one of those journeys overland to Kenya. Before that I always used to go on family holidays, so really it was <u>a complete novelty</u> for me to be able to go off with a friend and a group of other young people of my own age. I mean, really, on my family holidays we always used to go to the same hotel and lie on the beach and things. This was much more exciting though – going to really strange places and doing lots of things I hadn't done before. But we were well looked after by the driver and the guide so <u>we weren't really doing anything very risky</u>. Otherwise my mum wouldn't have let me go.

Interviewer: Sounds interesting. And what about you, Mike? Why did you choose your particular holiday?

Mike: It was the nightlife we went for really. I went with a couple of my mates, you know, and <u>during the day we just sat around by the pool and were really lazy</u>, unless we made a trip to the beach, which was about twenty minutes away by bus. But after dark we were down at the discos and clubs partying to the small hours.

Interviewer: That sounds like fun! And Sally, what did you like about your holiday?

Sally: My dad used to be a climber and when he was younger, we used to go on climbing holidays together. But this time I went with a couple of my friends, which was great because we were away from the city out in the open air in fabulous <u>natural surroundings</u>. The scenery was amazing, all those big mountain landscapes and we got lots of great photos. And sleeping out under the stars was wonderful. It was a bit tricky at one moment though. We'd just climbed one of the really high peaks and we were on the way down when a storm came. We had to get down quickly or we might have been in trouble. So that was a bit scary. We were carrying pretty big backpacks, so <u>all the physical activity got me quite fit</u> by the end of it.

Interviewer: Sounds a great experience. Now you, Paul. How was your holiday?

Paul: Not my idea of a good time at all, quite honestly. I mean <u>the meals were delicious</u> if you don't mind sitting around with a lot of middle-aged adults in these luxury places. I mean I found it so boring! And my mum and dad dragged me round <u>looking at paintings and sculptures</u>, which I hated. Still there was an upside to it, because that's when I met this Polish girl called Jolanta, while we were walking round one of the museums. She was just as bored as I was, so we left our parents to get on with things and went off for the day together. We had a really great time and we're still in touch.

Interviewer: So, you think you've grown out of family holidays then?

Paul: Pretty much so.

Interviewer: Finally you, Katie. How did you get on?

Katie: It was one of my first non-family holidays too, except for summer camps when I was younger. I went backpacking with some friends round Europe and we took trains and buses everywhere and <u>stayed in these really cheap places</u> with lots of other young people from all over the world who were doing the same sort of thing as us. It was really fun meeting them. I mean, mostly <u>people were so open and kind and wanting to get to know you</u>. I think that's one of the best things about foreign travel – meeting new people. So we've decided to do the same thing again next year.

Interviewer: Fantastic! Now I'd like to ask you all. What do you like about holidays with your friends and what did you use to enjoy about holidays with your families, perhaps when you were younger?

❹ If your students have not had holidays with friends, you can ask them: How do your family decide what sort of holiday to have? What do different members of your family particularly enjoy doing on holiday?

Extension idea Round up opinions by asking the class to vote on which they prefer: holidays with family, or holidays with friends.

Vocabulary

Journey, trip, travel and way

❶ ⊙ If your students all speak the same language, you can ask them how they would translate each of the words into their language.

> **Answers**
> 1 travel 2 journey 3 trip 4 way

Extension idea Ask students to write their own examples to show the differences in meaning.

❷

> **Answers**
> 2 way 3 trip 4 trip 5 travel 6 journey
> 7 trip 8 journey 9 way

❸ Alternatively, you can do the photocopiable activity on page 29, which is quite similar.

Grammar

Past simple, past continuous and *used to*

❶ When students have done the exercise, go through the grammar explanation with them in the Grammar reference section on page 155 (Past simple, past continuous and *used to*).

> **Answers**
> 2 b 3 d 4 a 5 e

❷

> **Answers**
> 2 used to do 3 got, jumped, drove
> 4 used to spend 5 were walking, began
> 6 used to visit, was

Reading Part 3

❶

> **Suggested answers**
> *Advantages:* it's quiet (possibly), you see the countryside, it's safe, you may meet other travellers, trains take you to the city centre, etc.
> *Disadvantages:* you may have to wait a long time for trains, they may be delayed, crowded, you may have to stand up, etc.

Extension idea Ask students to plan a trip round their country for foreign visitors to see the most interesting things and meet people. Ask them to decide on the best means of transport for each part of the trip.

❷

> **Answers**
> *Suggested phrases to underline:* **2** lost something, beginning **3** with an animal **4** was asked to help solve a problem **5** with people, especially nervous **6** saw wildlife **7** was entertained, by another traveller **8** happy to arrive despite a problem **9** without all the correct documents **10** through an area where few people live **11** didn't mind when the train didn't arrive on time **12** witnessed an illegal activity **13** crowded **14 and 15** obtained food, stopped

Extension idea If students study the questions carefully before approaching the texts, they may only need to read the texts once to answer the questions. When they have finished underlining, ask them to work in small groups, and with books closed, see how many of the questions they can remember.

❸ In the exam itself, no example answer is given.

Alternative treatment To make this a communicative classroom activity, you can follow this procedure.

- Divide class into groups of three. Ask one student in each group to read extracts A, D and G, another to read extracts B and E, and another to read extracts C and F. Tell them to find the questions which correspond to their extracts.
- Give them five minutes for this.
- Then tell them to work together and explain which questions correspond to their extract and why (they should quote the words in the extract which support their answers).
- Tell them to discuss any problems, e.g. two students have chosen the same question, or there is a question that no one has found an extract for.

This activity will help students to read all the questions carefully and find evidence in the text to support their answers.

> **Answers**
> 2 C 3 F 4 D 5 G 6 D 7 E 8 F 9 C 10 D
> 11 E 12 B 13 E 14 A or E 15 A or E

❹ To help students talk about memorable journeys, you can write these questions on the board:

When did you make the journey? Who were you with? What happened? How did you feel?

Ask students to think and plan for a minute or two before speaking.

Grammar
Past perfect simple and continuous

❶ To highlight the usefulness of the past perfect tense:
- write the following sentence on the board: *One of the watches had an alarm which ...... went off when the guard left our compartment.*
- ask students: Should I write *fortunately* or *unfortunately* in the space? (*Answer*: It depends, because *'when the guard left'* could either mean when he was leaving – so he heard the alarm, or after he had left – so he didn't hear it. Question 3 will back this up.)

When you have finished these questions, go through the explanation for the past perfect simple in the Grammar reference section on page 155 (Past perfect tenses) with your students.

> **Answers**
> 1 b 2 had left 3 In the first sentence, the guard was no longer in the compartment so he didn't hear the alarm; in the second sentence, he hadn't left but was in the process of leaving so he heard the alarm

❷

> **Answers**
> (extract C) what had happened: she provided me with a letter
>
> (extract E) no one cared that the train had arrived four hours late: no one cared
>
> (extract F) who had got trapped under the seat: I spent the journey trying to rescue my pet monkey; But I'd rescued my pet: I was smiling
>
> (extract G) to make sure we hadn't arrived in Rome: a man got off at every station; to check that nothing had been stolen: a woman took her bag down off the rack

❸

> **Answers**
> 2 had never been 3 had organised 4 arrived, had lost 5 recognised, had never spoken
> 6 had damaged

❹ After answering this question, go through the explanation for the past perfect continuous in the Grammar reference section on page 155 with your students.

> **Answer** a – past perfect continuous

❺

> **Answers**
> 2 had been walking, began 3 had already finished, offered 4 had only been speaking
> 5 got, had been walking

Use of English Part 3

The best general preparation students can have for this exam task is to read extensively to build up their vocabulary. You can point out that there are a number of ways of changing nouns and verbs into adjectives, but there is no general rule to say which way should be used when.

❶ Draw students' attention to spelling changes which occur, e.g. dropping the final 'e' in nature – *natural*; 'y' becomes 'i' as in *luxury* – *luxurious*. In the exam the word must be spelled correctly.

> **Answers**
> nature – natural, danger – dangerous, friend – friendly, comfort – comfortable, luxury – luxurious, risk – risky, nerve – nervous, crowd – crowded, disappoint – disappointed/disappointing, care – careful/careless, wonder – wonderful, dust – dusty, memory – memorable, hunger – hungry, enjoy – enjoyable

Extension idea Ask students to suggest other adjectives formed in the same ways.

❷ In many cases there is more than one correct answer. Encourage students to think of as many possibilities as they can. They will also suggest negative adjectives, so it's worth pointing out that these can sometimes be formed with the suffix *-less*. You can elicit other ways of making them negative (they have seen some in Unit 1), e.g. adding prefixes: *dis-*, *ir-*, *im-*, *in-* and *un-*.

> **Answers**
> educate – educational, educated, uneducated; space – spacious; mass – massive; dirt – dirty; use – useful, useless, used; care – careful, careless, caring; thought – thoughtful, thoughtless; accept – acceptable, accepted; mood – moody; emotion – emotional, emotive; change – changeable, unchangeable, changed, unchanged, changing, unchanging; base – basic

Extension idea Students use English–English dictionaries to explore the differences in meaning between adjectives formed from the same base word, e.g. *thoughtful, thoughtless.* Ask them also to write their own examples.

❸ Tell students to read the whole text fairly quickly before they start to get a general idea of what it's about. In the exam, any type of word is possible – noun, verb, adverb, adjective – but here only adjectives are worked on.

❹ You can get them started by suggesting one or two ideas, e.g. missing your flight or your train; not having the right ticket, etc.

Speaking Part 3

❶ *As a warmer*

- Elicit from your class what the reasons are for organising school trips. (*Possible answers:* To give students wider experiences, to learn a language or learn about a culture, to form stronger relationships with their fellow students, to have some adventure, to have a break from school, to teach things in a practical setting, etc.)
- Put your students in small groups. Ask them to say what school trips they have made, which ones they enjoyed most and which ones they didn't enjoy so much.

Move to the task in the book and elicit vocabulary they may need to complete the task, e.g. museum, adventure holiday, theme park, sightseeing. Then ask them to work in pairs and do the task.

Suggested answers
End-of-year trips: sightseeing, activity holiday in the mountains, a beach holiday, a cruise, a trip to a theme park, visiting a museum or art gallery

Alternative treatment Before they do the Speaking activity in the book (see Exercise 4), ask students to work in small groups and:

- put the pictures in order from **most enjoyable** to **least enjoyable**
- put the pictures in order from **most useful** to **least useful trips for young people**.

❷ 🎧 Before they listen, ask students to predict what benefits the two students will mention about the first two photos. They can then listen to check if they were correct and take notes.

Answers
Sightseeing holiday: you learn about art, architecture and history, other cultures and visit somewhere different

Activity holiday: you have exciting experiences and adventures, and learn to be independent

Recording script CD1 Track 8

Peter:	Shall I start?
Antonia:	OK.
Peter:	I think this first one is a sightseeing holiday.
Antonia:	Yes, that's right.
Peter:	How do you think a sightseeing holiday can benefit students?
Antonia:	I think you can learn a lot from a holiday like this, you know, about art and architecture and history. Things like that.
Peter:	Yes, and also you can visit somewhere very different and learn about other cultures.
Antonia:	Right. What about this photo? It's an activity holiday in the mountains, isn't it?
Peter:	Yes, this one can give students some exciting experiences and adventures.
Antonia:	Yes, and they learn to be more independent because they're away from home and their families.
Peter:	And the third photo? What about that?
Antonia:	It shows people playing on a beach. How do you think students can benefit from a trip to the beach?

❸ 🎧 Point out that it's important to make this task into a natural conversation and so these simple questions will encourage your partner to participate and take turns to say things.

Answers
2 think 3 What about 4 isn't it 5 that

❹ If you did the alternative treatment in Exercise 1, it would be a good idea for your students to change partners at this stage. You can ask them to do this task twice, changing partners to do it a second time after you have given feedback on their performance the first time they did it.

Writing Part 2 A story

❶ It's important that students always analyse the question first to make sure they don't miss any important points. Point out that it's important to identify who will read the story because this will determine the style. Elicit who the readers will be (other students and teachers at the school). Ask what style would be appropriate (informal).

As a warmer Quickly ask your students what is the most memorable journey they have made. Perhaps suggest one yourself, summarising it in two or three sentences. Ask a few of your students to summarise theirs, i.e. where they went and, briefly, why it was memorable.

Alternative treatment as a warmer Before opening their books, ask your students if they ever take part in competitions (or possibly in writing competitions), if they have ever won, and what they think would be a reasonable prize for winning a writing competition. If you wish to develop the discussion, ask them if they think people perform better if they are taking part in a competition. (Why or why not?)

Answers
Suggested phrases to underline: It was a trip I'll never forget; the English-language magazine at your college

---

❷ 🎧 This listening activity is partly intended to stimulate students' imagination for possible trips or journeys they could write about. When they have finished, ask them to say what were the key words or clues which gave them the correct answers, e.g. Jean: the first time I've been anywhere by air.

Answers
1 B   2 C   3 E   4 D   5 A

Recording script   CD1 Track 9

Presenter: Jean

Jean: Just coming to study here is a really big adventure for me. I always lived at home until a couple of months ago when I came here, so to get away from my family just for a few months is out of this world. I mean I miss them but, well, you know. And <u>it's the first time I've ever been anywhere by air</u>, so for me it's all pretty amazing. Especially as I come from a pretty small village in Scotland.

Presenter: Mark

Mark: I can remember a trip I made when I was quite small – I was probably only about eight years old. Anyway, it was one of the first times I'd travelled anywhere without my mum and dad. <u>I was with the other kids from my class and a trip had been organised to a nearby wildlife park</u>. Well, the bus broke down in the middle of it and while we were all sitting inside waiting for the bus to be repaired two lions came incredibly close to the bus. We kids thought it was terribly funny and all screamed with laughter, but I think some of the teachers were pretty scared actually. We could see them so close up!

Presenter: Maya

Maya: For me it has to be something that happened quite recently. My mother's family comes from India and if you count all my uncles and aunts and cousins there are lots of us. In fact I have family living all over the world in lots of different countries. For example, I have an uncle in Canada and a cousin in Kuwait and so on. You name the place, there's probably some uncle or cousin living there. But this is a time when we all got together – nearly forty of us – <u>for my grandma's 80th birthday at her house</u>. People had made a real effort to get there and we had an unforgettable weekend together.

Presenter: Patrick

Patrick: Oh, I can tell you about <u>a trip we made across the River Plate</u> from Buenos Aires to Montevideo on a rather old ferry when <u>a storm came up</u>. I lived there as a child and I was with some friends from school. We'd been invited to someone's house there for a few days during our summer holidays – that's in December, you know. Anyway, it was very rough and we all got quite ill. Luckily, it all blew over in a few hours, but when we got on dry land again, <u>my legs were shaking</u>.

Presenter: Sarah

Sarah: I can tell you about <u>a magical trip</u> we did when I was quite small. I still remember it because it was like one of those things which makes a big impression on you when you're small. Anyway, we all took a train, <u>my mum and dad, various relatives and myself</u> and when we got to the station we walked what seemed a really long way to me. Of course it can't have been very far, but we got to this really nice lake where we had a picnic. Then afterwards we played football together. I'll never forget that day!

❸ Elicit why it's important for articles in college magazines to be interesting (otherwise people won't read them, or won't buy the magazine).

❹ *As a warmer* Ask students to skim the story, then tell their partners if they have ever made a similar journey to this one and get them to give each other details of a similar experience. They then do the exercise.

Remind students of the need to know irregular verb forms in order to be able to do grammar exercises correctly. Refer them to the Grammar reference section on page 168 (Irregular verbs).

Answers
2 had decided   3 had only read   4 had entered
5 had   6 were waiting   7 approached
8 had never felt   9 started   10 managed

❺ Point out to students that they will gain marks in the exam if:

- their writing tasks have a clear structure and are divided into paragraphs
- they use a range of vocabulary – describing their feelings gives an opportunity to use some adjectives they know
- they clearly answer the question – in the sample story there are enough incidents to make this trip very memorable.

Answers
1 Three paragraphs. **Paragraph 1:** where we were going on the trip and how we were feeling; **paragraph 2:** the animals we saw; **paragraph 3:** the puncture and what happened while we waited

2 excited, ancient, noisy, nervous, crowded, fascinating, delighted, thrilled, relieved

3 going to a wildlife park, seeing animals in real life for the first time, the puncture, the monkeys on the bus, his/her classmates' excitement

❻ Tell students that this task should take them about 40 minutes. If you wish, this can be done for homework.

For more on writing stories, you can refer students to page 174 (Writing reference – Stories).

Sample answer: See the model in Exercise 4 in the Student's Book.

Unit 3 photocopiable activity: Perfect holidays   Time: 40 mins

Objectives

- To formulate questions
- To talk about likes and dislikes
- To discuss and solve problems

Before class

You will need one photocopy of the activity page for each student.

In class

❶ *As a warmer* Ask students: What are the advantages and disadvantages of going on holiday with friends rather than your parents? (*Suggested answers:* Advantages: No one tells you what to do, you're free to decide what to do, you can do activities suited to people your age, you enjoy yourself with your friends, you share new experiences which can strengthen your friendship, etc. Disadvantages: cost, you may argue with your friends, etc.)

❷ Ask students to work in groups of three or four. Tell them that each group is going to design the perfect two-week holiday for another group who are going on holiday together.

❸ Tell students they will each have to interview someone from the other group. Before they start, they should work together and decide what questions to ask to complete the questionnaire. You can elicit for the first one: *How do you feel about doing sports on holiday? Do you enjoy doing sports when you're on holiday?*

❹ Ask students to work in pairs with someone from the other group. Students take turns to ask and answer questions on the questionnaire.

❺ When they have finished the interviews, ask students to go back to their original group and:
- compare information
- decide what would be the perfect holiday for all the members of the other group together.

❻ Ask students to tell the other group what holiday they have designed for them. Groups can then discuss whether they like the holiday and anything they would like changed.

Perfect holidays – Customer questionnaire

Name: .... Age: ....

Tastes in holiday activities (*Tick ✓ the boxes which correspond and add a short comment*)

Activities	Enjoys	Doesn't mind	Dislikes	Comment / extra details
Sports in general				
Meeting people				
Sightseeing				
Visiting museums				
Going to the beach				
Doing nothing				
Walking				
Driving from place to place				
Other (please state)				

Preference for holiday location (*Tick ✓ one box which corresponds and add a short comment*)

Location	(✓)	Comment / extra details
Seaside		
Mountains		
Countryside		
City		
Home		
Other (please state)		

Preference for holiday accommodation (*Tick ✓ one box which corresponds and add a short comment*)

Accommodation	(✓)	Comment / extra details
Hotel		
Holiday villa		
Youth hostel		
Camping site		
Home		
Other (please state)		

Taste in food (*Tick ✓ one box which corresponds and add a short comment*)

Type of cooking	(✓)	Comment / extra details
Home cooking		
Fast food		
Smart restaurants		
Other (please state)		

Best and worst holiday (*add details*)

	Location	Type of holiday	Details
Best holiday ever			
Worst holiday ever			

Word list

Unit 3

Note: the numbers show which page the word or phrase first appears on in the unit.

adapt *v* (29) to change something to suit different conditions or uses

bare *adj* (29) If a cupboard or room is bare, there is little or nothing in it.

compartment *n* (29) one of the separate areas inside a vehicle, especially a train

dismantle *v* (29) to take something apart so that it is in many pieces

document *n* (29) a paper or set of papers with written or printed information, especially of an official type

endure *v* (29) to suffer something difficult, unpleasant or painful

epic *adj* (29) describes events that happen over a long period and involve a lot of action and difficulty

excursion *n* (33) a short journey usually made for pleasure, often by a group of people

fake *adj* (29) not real, but made to look or seem real

gust *n* (29) a sudden strong wind

holdall *adj* (29) a small case used for carrying clothes and personal things when travelling

host *n* (30) someone who has guests

in style *n* (27) If you do something in style, you do it in a way that people admire, usually spending a lot of money.

involve *v* (29) If a situation or activity involves something, that thing is a necessary part of it.

luxury *n* (27) great comfort, especially as provided by expensive and beautiful things

mood *n* (31) the way you feel at a particular time

novelty *n* (27) something which has not been experienced before and so is interesting

overnight *adj* (29) for or during the night

packed *adj* (29) completely full

panel *n* (29) a flat, usually rectangular part, or piece of wood, metal, cloth, etc., that fits into or onto something larger

privacy *n* (29) the state of being alone

proclamation *n* (29) a definite statement

route *n* (27) a particular way or direction between places

screwdriver *n* (29) a tool for turning screws, consisting of a handle joined to a metal rod shaped at one end to fit in the cut in the top of the screw

snack *n* (29) a small amount of food that is eaten between meals, or a very small meal

snatch *v* (29) to take hold of something suddenly and roughly

sweaty *adj* (29) covered in sweat or smelling of sweat

unspoilt *adj* (27) An unspoilt place is beautiful because it has not been changed or damaged by people.

wildlife *n* (29) animals and plants that grow independently of people, usually in natural conditions

witness *v* (29) to see something happen, especially an accident or crime

Unit 4 Food, glorious food

Unit objectives

- **Reading Part 2:** scanning, using cohesive devices to help fill the gaps
- **Writing Part 2:** structuring and writing a review, deciding on content, using adjectives to comment
- **Use of English Part 1:** introduction to task type, differentiating between words with similar meanings
- **Listening Part 4:** introduction to task type, identifying and underlining key ideas in questions
- **Speaking Part 4:** introduction to task type, giving and supporting opinions
- **Vocabulary:** confusion between *food*, *dish* and *meal*
- **Grammar:** *so* and *such*; *too* and *enough*

Starting off

As a warmer Ask your students to work alone and write down their five favourite dishes. They must then all walk around the class and find:

- the person whose tastes in food are most similar to theirs
- the person whose tastes in food are most different from theirs.

When they have finished, they should report back to the rest of the class.

They should then sit with one or both of the people they have found in groups of three and answer questions 1–4 in the book.

> **Answers**
> **1**, **2** and **3** *Students' own answers*   **4** *Suggested answers:* healthy ways of eating: photos **2**, **4**; less healthy: photos **1**, **3**

Extension idea Tell students to extend the conversation a little by thinking of two or three other questions they can ask their partner about food and eating habits. As an example, you can suggest: *Who prepares the meals in your house?* or *Do you help at all with the cooking?*

Reading Part 2

❶ *As a warmer* Tell students they are going to read an article about food in a school in the United States. Ask them:
- what they think students in the United States typically eat
- from watching films and TV, how American eating habits are different from eating habits in their own country.

Note: School meals vary round the USA. Many students complain about their quality and go out to fast food restaurants; most US schools have vending machines selling snacks and soft drinks; there is a lot of public discussion about the quality of school food and obesity amongst young people; in some poor districts, school breakfasts are also provided.

> **Suggested answers**
> Benefits: learning to do these things, learning about nutrition, becoming independent, health benefits

❷ Give students three minutes to scan and find the benefits.

> **Answers**
> Students benefit because: they eat what they grow, they eat fresh organic food instead of cheap fast food, they learn about many things connected with what they grow including scientific methods and geography, they learn to cook, they have fun, their attitude to food changes, their diet is healthy which breaks their isolation, they learn to care about each other

❸ Elicit why some of these words and phrases refer to other parts of the text, e.g. in sentence A, who is 'I'? (this must be someone who is speaking about themselves), and 'continue doing so' refers to what? (this must be some activity he has been doing up till now).

> **Answers**
> *Suggested phrases to highlight or underline:*
> **D** One lesson   **E** The problem ... these projects
> **F** These two projects   **G** We ... in this small space   **H** Lessons like this one

❹
> **Answers**
> **2** F   **3** G   **4** C   **5** D   **6** A   **7** B

❺ Encourage students to support their answers with examples, etc. from their own experience.

Vocabulary

Food, dish and *meal*

❶ *As a warmer* ⊙ To highlight the difference, write *lunch*, *eggs* and *mushroom omelette* on the board and ask students which is a meal, which food and which a dish.

❷

> **Answers**
> 2 meals   3 food   4 dishes   5 meal

❸ ⊙ If these are mistakes your students make, you could suggest that they keep a section of their notebooks to note down their typical vocabulary mistakes (many frequent mistakes by First Certificate candidates are dealt with throughout this book). They can then refer to them and revise the differences and corrections easily before the exam.

Note: In question 5, 'ready meals' are pre-cooked meals which you can buy and just heat up in a microwave.

> **Answers**
> 2 ~~meals~~ dishes   3 ~~food~~ dish   4 ~~meal~~ food   5 ~~foods~~ meals   6 ~~food~~ dish   7 ~~dishes~~ meals

❹ *Extension idea* Ask students to describe typical dishes and meals eaten at festivals in their country.

Grammar

So and *such*

❶

> **Answers**
> 2 So   3 such a   4 so   5 such

❷ After students have done this exercise, go through the notes in the Grammar reference section on page 155 (*So* and *such*) with them.

> **Answers**
> a such – examples 1 and 3   b such – example 5
> c so – example 4   d so – example 2

❸ When they have finished, ask students to write four sentences of their own using *so*, *such* and *such a*(*n*).

> **Answers**
> 2 so   3 such a   4 so   5 such an   6 so

❹ ⊙ Remind students to check for these mistakes in their own writing.

> **Answers**
> 2 ~~so much~~ such   3 correct   4 ~~so~~ such   5 ~~so~~ such a   6 ~~such~~ such a   7 correct   8 ~~so~~ such

Listening Part 4

❶ You may have students who know about the Slow Food Movement. Ask them to tell the class what they know.

❷ ∩ You needn't expect your students to come up with all the answers in the range provided below.

> **Answers**
> Purpose: to save traditional dishes, promote healthier ways of eating and living, improve lifestyles, enjoy variety and difference, educate people about food, improve relationships, make people happier

❸ Encourage students to focus on the stem of the question before listening, so they know what they are listening for.

> **Answers**
> *Suggested phrases to underline:* **2** What … is Slow Food   **3** the problem with fast food companies   **4** main aim … to improve   **5** What is the Salone del Gusto   **6** What surprised Valerie   **7** Who … will benefit

Recording script   CD1 Track 10

Interviewer: So, Valerie, what is the Slow Food Movement, can you tell us?

Valerie: Yes. The Slow Food Movement is really a reaction to fast food and our fast modern lifestyles. People have been complaining for years about fast food. You know, people eat too many hamburgers, too many pizzas, and too much fast food in general. It's not just that fast food is bad for health. It's also because we're afraid that traditional dishes will

Q1 disappear. <u>The Movement itself was started by an Italian called Carlo Petrini. He was protesting because a McDonald's had opened near the Spanish Steps – one of the most well-known monuments in the centre of Rome.</u> He felt it was sort of symbolic of the destruction of many valuable traditional things and he was keen to promote healthier ways of eating and living.

Interviewer: So, Slow Food just means healthier food, does it?

Valerie: Not exactly. I think it's more about our lifestyles than anything else. We're always in such a hurry. For many people cooking means rushing into the supermarket, picking up a ready meal and putting it in the microwave. We don't have enough time to take care of ourselves, or enjoy our lives. Slow Food is food that's cooked with care and which we take time to enjoy eating.

Q2 That essentially is what it is: excellent, natural, tasty food that we appreciate.

Interviewer: Fast food companies advertise that their food is healthy as well. How would you answer that?

Valerie: I wouldn't deny it. It may well be true. For me, and for a lot of Slow Fooders, the problem is

Q3 that wherever you sit down for a meal, whether it's in Tokyo, Milan or Cape Town, the food you're given is too similar. It makes eating, and life in general, boring. There's just not enough variety. Traditional food isn't going to be lost completely, but we do want as many people as possible to enjoy it and to take the trouble to look for things which are different.

Interviewer: So, let's see if I've understood you. The Movement's main object is to improve the way we live, is it?

Valerie: Exactly that. It's not just about food. It's about
Q4 how we live and finding time to enjoy our lives. We need to take time to enjoy what's around us.

Interviewer: And what does the Slow Food Movement do to promote its ideas?

Valerie: All sorts of things – it's got a gastronomic university, newsletters, and groups in many different countries. It even has its own trade fair, the Salone del Gusto. Producers of
Q5 traditional food come from all over the world to exhibit their food and meet each other. It includes lots of talks and workshops where people can find out more. It takes place in Italy, so most of the participants are Italian. But
Q6 one of the amazing things is just how many of the visitors are from Britain and how much interest there is in Britain for these sorts of things. I mean the British don't exactly have a reputation for good food, but there they were showing their cheeses and oysters and hams alongside the Italians.

Interviewer: So how, in the end, will this Movement be good for us?

Valerie: Well, as I was saying before, it's not just about avoiding poor quality food. Basically, there are two things we would like to see happen which would generally improve our quality of life.

Firstly, I hope that young people will become better educated about food in general. And while I appreciate that working people may be too busy to cook properly every day I also hope that parents will begin to realise just how important it is to take time over food. And if we can make these two things happen, then
Q7 I believe we will start to see differences in what I think really matters most: the way we live together as families! I think if we sit down together and take time to eat, we'll be relaxed enough to talk to each other more. As a result, relationships will improve and life in general, we hope, will become happier.

Interviewer: Valerie Watson, thank you.

Valerie: Thank you.

❹ 🎧 *Alternative treatment* Before playing the recording again: since students have already listened once, ask them to work in pairs and discuss the answers they think they have already. They then listen again to check and complete their answers.

Answers
1 B   2 C   3 A   4 C   5 A   6 B   7 C

❺ *As a warmer* Ask students what they would have less time for if they spent more time cooking and eating.

Grammar
Too and *enough*

❶

Answers
2 too many   3 too much   4 enough   5 too
6 enough   7 enough

❷ After doing this exercise, go through the notes in the Grammar reference section on page 156 (*Too* and *enough*) with your students.

Answers
a too – example 5   **b** too – examples 1, 2 and 3
c enough – example 7   **d** enough – examples 4 and 6

❸ After doing this exercise, ask students to write four sentences using *too*, *too many*, *too much* and *enough*.

Answers
1 too many, enough   **2** enough   **3** enough
4 too   **5** too

❹ 🔘 Remind students to look out for and correct these mistakes when they are speaking and writing.

❺ To make this exercise more enjoyable, encourage students to exaggerate their complaints and to give details. You can follow up by asking them to change pairs and give an account of the birthday party and why it was such a disaster.

This may be a suitable moment to do the photocopiable activity on page 37.

Speaking Part 4

❶ 🎧

> **Answers**
> Magda answers question 3, Miguel answers question 4

Extension idea Ask students if they agree with Magda and Miguel.

Recording script CD1 Track 11

1

Magda:	I think it depends what you mean by fast, because if you prepare a salad quickly, that's definitely good for you, but if you eat hamburgers and pizzas and things, that's probably quite unhealthy.
Teacher:	And Miguel, what do you think?
Magda:	I think Magda is right, but I'm sure that if you only eat hamburgers sometimes, that's OK. It's when you eat things like hamburgers and pizzas all the time that it can be a bit unhealthy.
Magda:	Yes, it's important to have a balanced diet.
Miguel:	That's right. And eat plenty of fruit and vegetables.
Magda:	I agree.

2

Miguel:	… I think it's a very good thing because we all sit down together and discuss what we've been doing during the day. And we exchange opinions and make plans and it feels very good, because we are spending time together although we are all very busy.
Teacher:	And Magda, do you agree?
Magda:	Yes, very much so. And also, I think people take more trouble to cook well when they are going to cook for several people than when they are cooking just for themselves, so in fact people eat better.

❷ Elicit why it's important to give longer answers, use their own words, etc. Point out that they will get marks for range of vocabulary and range and appropriacy of grammar.

> **Answers**
> 1 False 2 True 3 True

❸ *Alternative treatment* As a whole-class activity. Ask one of the questions to one student, e.g. *Maria, do you think that fast food is bad for you?* Maria answers and then asks someone else in the class: *Do you agree with me?* The next student answers and then asks someone in the class: *Do you agree with me?* until the subject is exhausted. Then another question is chosen. This way the class have to listen carefully to the opinions expressed as well as offer their own.

Extension idea Ask students to write two or three questions of their own on the subject and to ask these also.

Use of English Part 1

❶ *As a warmer* Ask students what things are important when choosing a restaurant to eat at:
- when you're celebrating something important
- when you want a quick meal at midday.

Give students two minutes to skim the text.

> **Answers**
> The surroundings, the service, the food, the price

❷ Elicit why B is the correct answer in the example, i.e. *went* requires *to*, *proved* and *tested* have wrong meanings. Elicit answers for questions 1–3 with the whole class.

> **Answers**
> 1 C 2 D 3 A 4 B 5 C 6 B 7 A 8 B 9 D 10 A 11 D 12 C

③ *Alternative treatment* If they come from the same town, ask students to work in small groups and recommend a restaurant to each other for:

- a night out with friends
- a romantic occasion
- a big family celebration.

Ask them to try to reach agreement.

Writing Part 2 A review

① *As a warmer* Ask students:

- how they find out if a book is worth reading, a video game worth buying, a film worth seeing or a restaurant worth visiting
- if they ever read reviews and if so where they read them.

Ask them to recommend publications or websites for reading reviews (in their own language).

> **Suggested answers**
> 2 yes 3 maybe 4 yes 5 no 6 maybe 7 maybe 8 yes 9 yes 10 yes

② *Alternative treatment* Ask students to write their own plan for the review in Use of English Part 1.

> **Answers**
> 2 yes – paragraph 1 3 yes – paragraph 2 4 yes – paragraph 3
> 5 no 6 yes – paragraph 2 7 no 8 yes – paragraph 4
> 9 yes – paragraph 3 10 no (although the text says 'a short walk from our workplace', the writer does not say where it is located)

③

> **Suggested answers**
>
> | the waiters | the interior | the food | the price |
> |---|---|---|---|
> | friendly | airy | delicious | reasonable |
> | informative | cosy | fresh | |
> | | modern | satisfying | |
> | | | tasty | |
> | | | wonderful | |

④ *Alternative treatment* Tell students they will play a game.

- Ask them to work in groups of three to think of the most unusual and interesting adjectives for each category.
- As a class they then compare adjectives. The most interesting wins five points for the group. The second most interesting wins three points, and the third one point.
- If other students think an adjective is not appropriate for the category, they can ask the students who suggest it to justify it. If they can justify it, then it can score. Otherwise it must be abandoned

⑤ Ask students to work alone to write their plans and note down their ideas.

⑥ When they have finished discussing, get feedback from the class on the vocabulary they can use.

⑦ Tell students that this task should take them about 40 minutes. If you wish, this can be done for homework.

→ For more on writing reviews, you can refer students to page 175 (Writing reference – Reviews).

Sample answer: See the model in Use of English Part 1.

Vocabulary and grammar review Unit 3

Answers

Vocabulary

① 2 trip 3 travel 4 way 5 journey
6 way 7 trip 8 journey

Word formation

② 2 comfortable 3 disappointed
4 natural 5 hungry 6 crowded
7 noisy 8 unfriendly 9 quieter
10 enjoyable

Grammar

③ 2 I had lost 3 used to travel to work 4 when/while she was (still) studying / while (still) studying
5 had never met 6 used to be more

Vocabulary and grammar review Unit 4

Answers

Vocabulary

① 2 food/meal 3 dish 4 food
5 dish 6 meal/food 7 meal
8 food

Word formation

② 2 convenience 3 healthy
4 organisations 5 encourage
6 balanced 7 disappeared
8 repetitive 9 choice 10 easily

Grammar

❸ **2** slowly enough for us to **3** was so full/crowded (that) **4** such delicious food (that) **5** cook well enough **6** such a long time / so much time

---

Unit 4 photocopiable activity: The college canteen Time: 40–50 mins

Objectives

- To increase fluency in a speaking task
- To use functional language: making complaints, asking for advice, offering solutions, justifying opinions
- To use vocabulary related to diet and food in context

Before class

You will need to photocopy the activity page and cut up the role cards separately to hand to students, but make sure that every student or pair of students has a copy of the handout (Exercises 1–3).

In class

❶ Give students a copy of the handout and do Exercise 1. Get feedback from the whole class.

> **Suggested answers**
> What is wrong with the menu: lack of variety, lack of choice, no fresh vegetables or fruit, boring or unimaginative main course, cheap ingredients
> How it could be improved: more choice, fresh ingredients, more interesting dishes, etc.

❷ Move on to Exercise 2. Elicit if the first complaint is reasonable and if so, what can be done about it, e.g. more supervision from teachers. Ask students to work through the other complaints.

❸ Ask students to work in pairs. Give one role card to each pair of students and ask them to prepare their roles together. There are five role cards, so be prepared to have some groups of six or seven by having groups with two Student Representatives and two Catering Assistants. You will need to have extra copies of these cards in this case.

❹ Ask students in pairs to discuss what they are going to say, and how they are going to say it (e.g. how to make a complaint, suggestion, etc.). Encourage them to think of extra ideas and justifications for their opinions.

❺ Put students in groups of five (or six or seven) to do the role play. Tell the student with the role of College Director to act as chair, direct the meeting and make sure that everyone has a chance to speak, and try to reach a solution. Give students about ten minutes to do the role play.

❻ When they have finished, ask someone from each group to summarise what they decided.

❼ As a class, discuss which group achieved the best solution.

Extension idea Ask students to work in pairs and write a short notice – about 60–80 words – to put on the college noticeboard summarising the decisions made at the meeting. You can write the following on the board as a suggestion for starting the notice:

Meeting about College Canteen At this morning's meeting about the college canteen, we decided …

When students have finished, pin their notices on the classroom noticeboard and let the class read each of them.

The college canteen

❶ Work in pairs and study the menu. What do you think is wrong with it? How could it be improved?

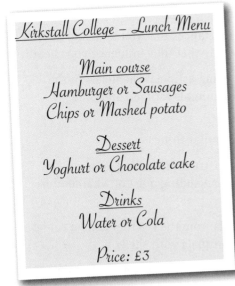

Kirkstall College – Lunch Menu

Main course
Hamburger or Sausages
Chips or Mashed potato

Dessert
Yoghurt or Chocolate cake

Drinks
Water or Cola

Price: £3

❷ Read this email from the college Catering Manager to the Director. Which do you think are reasonable complaints and what can be done about them?

Dear Director,

The situation in the college canteen is not satisfactory at present and unless I receive more support from the college authorities, I will be unable to continue providing a service here. The problems are as follows:

- Students do not clear their tables after eating. Also, they are frequently noisy and unruly.
- Many bring their own food and do not eat the food provided by the canteen.
- Several complain about lack of variety on our menu, but when I offer alternatives no one chooses them, or they complain that I'm not offering the usual menu.
- Some students are demanding a vegetarian menu, but unless you give me more money I cannot offer this.

Could you please look into these problems and let me know what you intend to do about them.
Best wishes,
Catering Manager

❸ Work in groups of five or more. The Director has called a meeting to discuss the problems with the school canteen. Study the role card your teacher will give you. Hold a meeting to discuss the problems.

✂ -

College Director

You are prepared to support any solution which makes everyone happy, except you do not have any more money to spend on the canteen. You are holding the meeting to listen to all the suggestions and complaints, and if the other people at the meeting can reach an agreement, you will be in favour of it. Make sure that everyone at the meeting has a chance to express their point of view.

✂ -

Catering Manager

You don't think students should be allowed to eat food they bring from home in the college canteen: the students are not paying for the facilities and it makes more work for your staff. Also, because students are bringing food from home instead of eating college food, you are finding it hard to make money running the canteen. You would like to provide a more varied menu, but you will have to raise the price, or be given extra money by the college.

✂ -

Catering Assistant

You are annoyed that students do not clear their tables after use. Also they are noisy and sometimes unruly, which you find stressful. You would like students to be more respectful and the college authorities to provide more supervision.

✂ -

Student Representative

You think students should be allowed to use the canteen if they bring food from home. Otherwise, they have to eat it in the corridors or in the garden, which is not possible when it's raining. You would like more variety on the menu, but not at a higher price. You think lunchtime is a time for students to relax and have fun, so complaints about noise are not reasonable.

✂ -

Vegetarian Students' Representative

You want the canteen to provide a variety of healthy food and not cheap fast food. You would be prepared to pay extra for it. You think it's very important that students learn to eat a healthy diet and that some information about nutrition should also be provided. You think the canteen should be for everyone, not just students who want to eat hamburgers and sausages.

Word list

Unit 4

Note: the numbers show which page the word or phrase first appears on in the unit.

aim *v* (35) to intend

airy *adj* (41) with a lot of light and space

attitude *n* (35) a feeling or opinion about something or someone, or a way of behaving that is caused by this

bunch *n* (35) a group of people

cage *n* (39) a space surrounded on all sides by bars or wire, in which animals or birds are kept

combination *n* (40) the mixture you get when two or more things are combined

cosy *adj* (41) comfortable and pleasant, especially (of a building) because small and warm

curriculum *n* (35) the group of subjects studied in a school, college, etc.

diet *n* (34) the food and drink usually eaten or drunk by a person or group

edible *adj* (34) suitable or safe for eating

experimental *adj* (35) experiencing and observing different methods or situations in order to discover what the result will be

feature *v* (40) to include someone or something as an important part

flavour *n* (40) how food or drink tastes, or a particular taste itself

funds *n* (34) money needed or available to spend on something

historic *adj* (38) important or likely to be important in history

ingredient *n* (35) a food that is used with other foods in the preparation of a particular dish

initiative *n* (35) a new action or movement, often intended to solve a problem

isolated *adj* (35) feeling unhappy because of not seeing or talking to other people

nutrition *n* (35) the substances that you take into your body as food and the way that they influence your health

organic *adj* (35) not using artificial chemicals in the growing of plants and animals for food and other products

range *n* (35) a set of similar things

recipe *n* (35) a set of instructions telling you how to prepare and cook food, including a list of what food is needed for this

seafood *n* (40) animals from the sea that can be eaten, especially fish or sea animals with shells

supply *v* (35) to provide something that is wanted or needed, often in large quantities and over a long period of time

talkative *adj* (37) talking a lot

tasty *adj* (36) describes food which has a strong and very pleasant flavour

tuition *n* (34) teaching, especially when given to a small group or one person, such as in a college or university

value for money *n* (40) If something is value for money, it is good quality or there is a lot of it so you think the amount of money you spent on it was right.

variety *n* (38) many different types of things or people

warn *v* (38) to make someone realise a possible danger or problem, especially one in the future

❶ **Each of these sentences contains one mistake. Find the mistake and correct it.**

0   When I was 12, we moved to a new house – partly because the old one wasn't ~~enough big~~   *big enough*
    for all of us and partly because there was too much traffic in the area.

1   My cousin Jamie is a really annoyed person when he talks about his job but I'm always
    interested in listening to his stories about his trips around the world.

2   It was such long time since Dawn had seen her grandfather that there was a lot for them to
    talk about.

3   The person I most admire in my family is my mother because she's so supportive person
    and always has enough time to help me.

4   When the twins were too young, we never had enough money to buy them many things.

5   At the age of ten, David had an amazing singing voice but he usually felt very
    embarrassing when he sang in front of other people.

❷ **Choose the correct alternative in *italics* in each of these sentences.**

0   The resort was *much more busy than* / (*much busier than*) / *much busier that* I had
    expected.

1   It was impossible for anyone to sleep well in the hotel because there was *so much noise* / *so
    noise* / *such big noise* from the club opposite.

2   Lying on the beach for hours when it's *too hot* / *too much hot* / *too hot temperature* is bad
    for you.

3   We had a *such* / *too* / *very* beautiful view of the castle from our hotel window.

4   It's *more better* / *much better* / *much more better* going on holiday with your parents
    because they pay for everything.

5   The water was not *too warm* / *enough warm* / *warm enough* to swim in for more than a few
    minutes.

Word formation

❸ **Use the word given in CAPITALS at the end of some of the lines to form a word that fits
in the gap in the same line.**

It was my 18th birthday, so my dad decided to take the family out for what we hoped would be a (0) ...*memorable*... meal. He had chosen a (1) .... restaurant in the town centre where you sit beside a pool in really (2) .... chairs surrounded by exotic plants. In my family we are quite (3) .... when it comes to eating and enjoy trying out new dishes. My preference is for really (4) .... food.	MEMORY LUXURY COMFORT ADVENTURE SPICE
When we saw the size of the menu we were really surprised – it was probably the (5) .... menu I had ever seen and it had so many sections that we found it quite (6)	LONG CONFUSE
Anyway, the waiter was very (7) .... and in the end we each made our (8) .... I asked for a goat's cheese tart which I didn't think looked very (9) .... when I saw it. Anyway, it tasted fantastic. All in all, it was a (10) .... way to spend my birthday.	HELP CHOOSE ATTRACT WONDER

❹ Complete the sentences below by writing one of the words given in each gap.

0 If you want to (a) ....*do*......... something useful, why don't you (b) ......*make*......... dinner instead of just sitting there?

~~make~~   create   ~~do~~   take

1 Every morning, Tess (a) .... the children ready for school. Then she (b) .... all the housework before going off to work.

does   makes   prepares   gets

2 When I go out for a (a) .... I always choose the (b) .... of the day because I know it's usually the freshest thing on the menu.

dish   diet   meal   food

3 For long-distance (a) .... the only way to go is by plane, but for a shorter, business (b) .... I prefer to go by train if possible.

trip   journey   travel   way

4 The TV critic (a) .... his feelings about the programme on global warming by saying he believed many of the so-called facts were (b) .... and it was more fiction than documentary.

started up   made up   took up   summed up

5 My colleagues often accuse me of being (a) .... , and perhaps I do upset people sometimes by what I say. But it's usually because I'm in a new situation and feeling (b) ....

immature   nervous   fussy   tactless

Grammar
Past tenses

❺ Read the text below and for Questions 1–10 choose the correct alternative in italics.

From 2000 to 2005 I (0) (*worked*) / *had worked* / *had been working* as a gossip columnist for a national newspaper. It (1) *had been feeling* / *was feeling* / *felt* like the best job in the world, but after five years I realised the excitement (2) *started* / *was starting* / *used to start* to wear off. When I was a young child, I always (3) *was dreaming* / *used to dream* / *had been dreaming* of going travelling. My parents (4) *used to stop* / *were stopping* / *had stopped* me from taking a year off after leaving school though, because they (5) *had thought* / *thought* / *were thinking* I'd never come back! When I finally (6) *booked* / *was booking* / *used to book* a round-the-world ticket, I (7) *was saving* / *used to save* / *had been saving* the money I needed for more than two years. Less than a week after I (8) *was leaving* / *had left* / *had been leaving* my life in London, I (9) *was standing* / *had been standing* / *had stood* on a fisherman's boat at dawn, sailing down the Ganges River. My adventures (10) *just began* / *were just beginning* / *had just been beginning* and I was happier than I had been for years.

Present tenses

❻ Complete this interview by writing the verbs in brackets in the correct form.

Interviewer: So Jessica, here you are in New Zealand – a long way from home.
(0) ....*Are*............ you ....*having*............ (have) a good time?

Jessica: Yes, fantastic.

Interviewer: How long (1) .... you .... (travel)?

Jessica: Six months, and I'm having the time of my life.

Interviewer: And what (2) .... (be) your best experience since you left home?

Jessica: I think it's what I (3) .... (do) now.

Interviewer: Which is?

Jessica: I (4) .... (learn) to skydive.

Interviewer: Really? (5) .... you .... (like) doing dangerous things?

Jessica: Yes, I guess since I was a small child I (6) .... always .... (want) to push myself and this is a great opportunity.

Interviewer: Any bad experiences since you left home?

Jessica: People warned me about crime and illness but I (7) .... (be) lucky so far – nothing bad (8) .... (happen) to me, and I hope it won't in the next six months.

Interviewer: (9) .... you .... (travel) on your own?

Jessica: Yes, and I (10) .... (love) it. I've met some really great people.

❼ Complete the second sentence so that it has a similar meaning to the first sentence, using the word given. Do not change the word given. You must use between two and five words, including the word given.

0 Espresso coffee is stronger than the other coffees we sell.
   THE
   Espresso is ....*the strongest coffee*........ we sell.

1 In the UK, there are fewer Italian restaurants than Indian ones.
   AS
   In the UK, there aren't .... Indian ones.

2 Generally speaking, we don't eat as much meat as we used to.
   LESS
   Generally speaking, we .... we used to.

3 The new oven isn't as efficient as the old one.
   WORKED
   Our old oven .... the new one.

4 I hate washing-up more than any other job in the kitchen.
   LEAST
   Washing-up is my .... in the kitchen.

5 It's easier to cook pasta than most other dishes.
   ONE
   Pasta is .... to cook.

Unit 5 Studying abroad

Unit objectives

- **Reading Part 3:** identifying main ideas in questions, processing the questions before reading
- **Writing Part 1:** making enquiries, replying to an invitation, common spelling mistakes at FCE
- **Use of English Part 3:** forming nouns from verbs, deciding what type of word is required
- **Listening Part 1:** listening for gist and specific information
- **Speaking Part 1:** talking about studying and educational experiences, giving reasons in answers
- **Vocabulary:** confusion between *find out, get to know, know, learn, teach* and *study; attend, join, take part* and *assist;* words connected with education *term, subject, assignment,* etc.; collocations to give reasons for studying abroad
- **Grammar:** zero, first and second conditionals, forming indirect questions

Starting off

❶ *As a warmer* Before students open their books, ask them to brainstorm benefits of studying abroad. When they have finished, ask them to open their books and look at the photos. Ask which of their ideas is shown in the photos.

Students then do the exercise in the book and compare their ideas with the ideas listed there.

> **Answers**
> 2 b 3 f 4 g 5 d 6 e 7 a 8 c

Extension idea Ask students to say which photos match the sentences 1–8. Note that some photos may match more than one sentence.

❷ If your students are doing this course abroad, ask them what reasons motivated them and what main benefits they are getting from the experience. You can also ask if there are any disadvantages to studying abroad.

❸ You can also ask if the best reasons for studying abroad are academic, i.e. their studies, or the experience of living in another country.

❹ Encourage students to give fairly long answers.

Listening Part 1

❶
> **Answers**
> 2 a 3 g 4 h 5 i 6 c 7 d 8 e 9 b

Extension idea To activate the vocabulary, write the following prompts on the board:

- favourite subject?
- term / enjoy most?
- most difficult course?
- subject / best marks?
- ever done research?
- degree?

Ask students to make questions with these words to ask to others in the class. (Some possible questions: *What's your favourite subject? What was your favourite subject at school? Which term do you enjoy most? Which is the most difficult course you have studied? Which subject do you get the best marks in? Have you ever done any research? What degree would you like to do? What degree are you doing?* etc.)

❷ Although students may need to underline most of the words in a question, this is a useful habit for them to acquire as it:
- makes them think about what each question is asking
- serves as a reminder when they look at the question again.

> **Answers**
> *Suggested phrases to underline:* **2** Who caused the problem **3** What does she like most **4** the main benefit **5** Why is he talking

❸ 🎧 *Exam advice:* Point out to students that in the exam itself there are eight extracts, not all on the same subject.

> **Answers**
> 1 C 2 C 3 B 4 A 5 A

Extension idea 1 Follow up the listening exercise with these questions:

- What, for you, is the best part of learning a language?
- What, for you, is the main benefit of studying English?
- How do you feel about other students copying your work?

Extension idea 2 After doing the listening exercise and the vocabulary exercise which follows, ask students to work in pairs and:

- write one multiple-choice question like those in the exercise and one short monologue or dialogue to go with it. They first read their question and then their monologue/dialogue to the class, who should choose the answer.
- ask them to include one or two of the phrases from the vocabulary exercise in their script.

Recording script CD1 Track 12

1

Will: Actually, at the beginning of term I was a bit lost. You know, I felt that most of the other students knew a lot more about the subject than I did. Listening to them, I got the idea that some of them felt the course was a bit of a waste of time. In my case, I was having problems not just with the language but also with the ideas. But I managed to get over all

Q1 that and I'm happy to say that the course has lived up to expectations and I've made a lot of progress. I mean, we've got an exam next week which I should be feeling a bit anxious about but in fact I'm feeling pretty confident.

2

Mike: Hi, Helena. You're not looking too happy.

Helena: I'm not! Do you know what's happened? We were given an assignment by our course tutor at the beginning of the month and I did lots of research for it in the library, made lots of notes

Q2 and so on. Anyway, this girl, Valerie, who is on the same course as me came round to my flat one day for coffee and while she was there, my mother phoned. I was out of the room for about half an hour and during that time she must have copied all my notes! I was really embarrassed when I found out about what she'd done. It was during a tutorial and when my tutor gave me my mark for the assignment, he said it looked very like an essay Valerie had handed in the week before. I can tell you I was furious, but there was nothing I could say.

3

Hitoshi: So, what are you doing here in Japan?

Maggie: I'm learning Japanese at a language school. I go to classes for just two hours a day, which is good because I learn Japanese from Japanese teachers, and then I'm free to practise it during the rest of the day.

Hitoshi: That sounds a good idea.

Maggie: It is. You see they also organise lots of other
Q3 things for you to take part in after you've finished your language lesson. There are clubs you can join if you're interested and they really are the best part. For example, I'm also doing a karate course taught in Japanese which is great fun. I'm learning something completely different in the language I'm studying and I'm getting to know lots of Japanese people.

Hitoshi: Fantastic!

Maggie: Yes, if you speak a bit of the language, it's much easier to make friends.

4

Sandra: I'm not sure whether I'll study abroad. I've been thinking of going to an Italian university and studying international business for a year. The trouble is partly that if I went, it might make it more difficult for me to get a good degree when I come home. On the other hand, I think the opportunity to live abroad for a year would make it a once-in-a-lifetime experience.

Q4 If I lived in Italy, I'd learn about how Italians live and think. The trouble is I'd have to leave the friends I've got and probably live on my own, and I'm not sure if I'm ready for that.

5

Peter: Now, just a few words, especially for new
Q5 students. First, you're expected to attend all your tutorials once a week and do the assignments which your tutors give you. If for any reason you can't make it to a tutorial, try to let your tutor know. If your tutor has to cancel a tutorial or put it off, he or she'll try to tell you the week beforehand. Also, please remember that this course is largely practical and you have to do one piece of original research during the year. You're allowed to do it in groups, and if you work with other students, you'll probably find it easier. Your tutors will organise you into groups and suggest research unless you prefer working alone.

Vocabulary

Find out, get to know, know, learn, teach and study; attend, join, take part and assist

1 *⊙ Alternative treatment* Ask students to work out the correct answers using a learner's dictionary, e.g. *Cambridge Advanced Learner's Dictionary.*

Answers
2 found out **3** learn **4** learn **5** taught **6** getting to know **7** take part in **8** join **9** attend

❷ Tell students to copy the words into their notebooks and check that they do not confuse them in their writing tasks.

❸

Answers
2 got to know   3 study   4 learnt   5 find out
6 know   7 taught   8 assist   9 joined
10 taken part in

Extension idea Ask students to write three or four sentences using words from the box, but with a space where the word should be. They then pass their sentences to a partner to complete.

Grammar
Zero, first and second conditionals

❶ After students have done the exercise, go through the notes in the Grammar reference section on page 156 (Zero, first and second conditionals) with them.

Answers
1 c   2 b   3 a   4 b   5 a   6 a

❷ *Alternative treatment* Ask students to work in pairs, cover the right-hand column and complete each sentence in any way they like. When they have finished, they compare their ideas with the endings in the right-hand column.

Answers
2 f   3 j   4 g   5 a   6 e   7 c   8 d   9 i (or f)   10 b

❸ Encourage students to give reasons for their answers and to discuss them.

Extension idea Ask students to add two or three more questions of their own to the list and ask these as well.

This would be a suitable moment to do the photocopiable activity on page 47.

Use of English Part 3

❶ The confusion between *advice* (noun) and *advise* (verb) is a common mistake at First Certificate. *Practice* and *practise* have the same distinction in British English (not American).

Answers
2 confidence   3 understanding   4 improvement
5 behaviour   6 advice   7 assistant (assistance)
8 knowledge

❷

Answers
2 entertain   3 feel   4 achieve   5 investigate
6 obey   7 prefer   8 sense

Extension idea Ask students what suffixes they can add to verbs to change them into nouns (looking at Exercises 1 and 2). (*Answers: -ment, -ing, -tion, -ation, -ence (-ent* changes to *-ence), -iour, -ledge,* and *-ise* sometimes changes to *-ice.*)

Ask students to brainstorm other words that change in these ways.

❸

Answers
1 knowledge   2 appreciation   3 interesting
4 difficulty   5 enjoyable   6 communication   7 basic
8 improvement   9 assistance   10 confidence

❹ *Extension idea 1* Ask students which of the things they've suggested they themselves do. You can take this opportunity to discuss your students' general approach to language learning and make suggestions for other things they can do to help themselves.

Extension idea 2 Ask your students if they think having studied one language helps when learning another, e.g. there may be skills you learn which are transferable. You can turn this into a general discussion.

Reading Part 3

❶ *Alternative treatment*

- With books closed, ask students to work in small groups and brainstorm problems students can have when studying abroad. Ask them to discuss which are serious problems and which are not so serious.
- When students open their books, the second question gives students a further opportunity to practise second conditionals.

Suggested problems: strange food, finding somewhere to live, making friends, finding one's way around, not understanding the language

❷ Tell students that in some questions they may have to underline most of the words. You can also point out that success in the exam requires efficient reading techniques. Here the questions are printed before the texts and they should spend time studying and understanding the questions before reading the texts. This will avoid constantly going back and forth between the texts and the questions.

Answers

Suggested phrases to underline: **2** made good progress with a foreign language **3** entertained by a teacher **4** wanted to spend less time studying **5** overcame ... initial difficulties **6** appreciated meeting people ... different countries **7** discouraged ... by problems **8** felt homesick **9** communicating with other students difficult **10** unique experience **11** more attractive to future employers **12** surprised by the country **13** learnt a lot about people **14** and **15** practical working experience

❸

Suggested answers
a 2, 9 **b** 5, 8, (9) **c** 1, 2, 3, 6, 10, 11, 13, (14/15) **d** 4, 5, 7, 8, 9 **e** 3, 6, 8, 9, 12, 13, 14/15

❹ *Alternative treatment* Ask students to work in pairs to find the answers and make the reading exercise a race to see which pair can find all the correct answers first.

Answers
2 E **3** B **4** D **5** A **6** C **7** E **8** A **9** A **10** D
11 E **12** D **13** B **14** B/C **15** B/C

❺ If necessary, elicit the advantages of working versus studying. Working: work experience, earning money, mixing with native speakers, etc. Studying: concentrating on language, mixing with other students, safe environment, etc. Ask students to think of the disadvantages of each. They then discuss.

Speaking Part 1

❶ *As a warmer* Elicit what happens in Speaking Part 1 (this was covered in Unit 1).

Alternative treatment With books closed, ask students to think of questions they might be asked about their education and studies. They then compare with those in the book, and ask and answer them in pairs.

❷ 🎧

Answers
1 biology – he likes science, he wants to study medicine, he has an excellent teacher **2** in her job – she wants to work in business and travel

Recording script CD1 Track 13

Teacher:	Nikolai, which is your favourite subject at school?
Nikolai:	I find biology very interesting. That's because I enjoy all science subjects a lot and if I can get good enough marks in my final exams, I'll study medicine when I go to university. Also, my biology teacher is an excellent teacher, so she makes the subject more ... more enjoyable.
Teacher:	And you, Magda, how do you think you'll use English in the future?
Magda:	Well, it'll help me to find a job, and if my work involves travelling, I'm sure I'll need to speak English. I'd like to work in business, and I think English is essential for that.
Teacher:	Thank you. Nikolai, can you remember your first day at school?

❸ 🎧 You can elicit why the points raised by this exercise (e.g. not to speak too briefly, etc.) are good exam practice.

Answers
2 True **3** True **4** False **5** False

❹ *Note:* In Speaking Part 1 students may be asked a wide variety of questions about themselves, not just about their studies as practised here.

Extension idea Ask each pair of students to give each other feedback on how they performed. The criteria for feedback can be the three points in Exercise 3.

Writing Part 1

❶ *Extension idea*

• Ask students to say what trips would be interesting for students to do in their countries (like the trips to Vancouver or the Rockies).

• You could also ask them what people can learn from travelling abroad rather than from formal study abroad, and what are the relative advantages/ disadvantages of each.

❷

Answers
1 Two months **2** English **3** Pia wants to go to the mountains because she went to Vancouver two years ago **4** She can make friends and speak English

❸ ⊙ These are common mistakes made by First Certificate candidates. Tell your students to copy the mistake and the correct spelling into their notebooks and to check for these mistakes when they do writing tasks.

Spelling mistakes

~~corses~~ courses   ~~begining~~ beginning   ~~wich~~ which
~~excelent~~ excellent   ~~preffer~~ prefer   ~~experence~~
experience   ~~accomodation~~ accommodation   ~~becaus~~
because   ~~oportunity~~ opportunity   ~~foward~~ forward

 When students have finished this exercise, go through
the notes in the Grammar reference section on page
156 (Indirect questions) with them.

> **Answers**
> 2 True   3 True   4 False   5 False

5

> **Answers**
> 1 Can you tell me how much it costs to rent a flat?
> 2 I would like to know what qualification I would
>   get at the end of the course.
> 3 Do you know how far the college is from the city
>   centre?
> 4 I'd like to know if/whether I will have to do a lot
>   of homework.
> 5 Can you tell me if/whether the college has sports
>   facilities?

Extension idea Ask students to formulate four or five
questions starting with the phrases in questions 1–5
(*I would like to know*, etc.) to ask a partner about study
facilities in their home town or city. Students then work
in pairs and take turns to ask and answer the questions.

6 You can ask students to work in pairs and discuss
how they would deal with the points in the
handwritten notes.

- If you decide to give this task for homework, tell
  students they should take 40 minutes to do it, as
  they would have in the exam.
- When students read the exam advice, remind them
  that they must follow the instructions exactly and
  use all the notes or they will lose marks.

For more on writing letters and emails, you can refer
students to page 169 (Writing reference – Part 1).

Sample answer
Dear Caroline,

Thanks for your email suggesting a summer camp in
Australia. Of course I'd love to come. Can you tell me
what dates the camp is, so that I can put them in my
diary? Also, if possible, I'd like to know how much it will
cost because I'll probably have to start saving right away.

As a matter of interest, do you know what subjects
are taught? I'd be really interested in studying English
because I always need to improve it, and perhaps another
subject such as drama or performing arts. I think that
I'd really get to know people and make friends by doing
that.

I like your idea of travelling together afterwards. I'd prefer
to go to the Great Barrier Reef because I love the sea and I
really enjoy diving.

What a great way to spend the summer! I look forward to
seeing you then.

All the best,

Unit 5 photocopiable activity: School problems   Time: 30 mins

> **Objectives**
> - To brainstorm options and give advice
> - To justify personal opinions by describing
>   consequences
> - To use first and second conditionals to describe
>   consequences

Before class

You will need one photocopy of the activity page for each
student.

In class

1 Divide the class into small groups.

2 Tell the groups they work on a panel which gives advice
to people about problems with education and studies
and hand out the activity pages.

3 Tell them they should look at the first problem
(Mario) and the example sentences below. Elicit other
conditional sentences they can make about the three
choices. Point out that by doing this they are suggesting
and discussing possible consequences of each option.

4 Ask them to discuss which of the three choices they
think is best and then decide together what advice to
give Mario.

5 When they have finished, ask them to deal with each of
the other people's problems in turn. They should:

- discuss what choices or options each person has
- make conditional sentences about them to explain
  the consequences of each option they have come up
  with
- decide what the best solution is for each person.

6 Finally, mix the groups and ask students to present and
compare their suggestions for each problem.

Alternative treatment
- Tell half the groups that they are students and
  should think about the problems from a student's
  point of view.
- Tell the other groups that they are teachers and
  should think about the problems from a teacher's
  point of view.

School problems

Dear Panel,

I'm a 17-year-old student from Brazil. I'm really interested in getting a high level of English (at least the Certificate of Advanced English) before I go to university at the end of next year. At the moment I'm doing a First Certificate course in my town, Salvador. At university I hope to study physics and chemistry combined, so I don't know if I'll have time to go to English lessons as well. I don't want to ask my parents to spend a lot of money because they're already paying quite a lot for my education. What do you think I should do? I think I have three choices:

1 Go to a language school in Britain or the USA for two months in the summer holidays

2 Go to Britain or the USA to work for two months in the summer holidays

3 Go to a language school here in Salvador

Looking forward to your advice,

Mario

Examples:
- If Mario goes to a language school in Britain or the USA, it will be very expensive for his parents.
- If he goes to Britain or the USA to work, he may work with other students. He may not learn very much English.

Dear Panel,

I'm 16, very hard-working and I get good marks in class. The trouble is that other students in the class don't like me because I work so hard. Also, they try to copy my work so they can get higher marks themselves. This seems very unfair to me. I don't know what to do because I want to have friends. If I talk to the teachers about the problem, I may make myself even more unpopular. What do you suggest?

Sabina

Dear Panel,

We're not happy with one of our teachers. She arrives late for class, she doesn't prepare her lessons and she gives us low marks in the exams. When we complained to the school director, he just told us to work harder! The trouble is that we've got university entrance exams at the end of the year. What can we do?

Pablo

Dear Panel,

I know this sounds a bit strange. I'm a secondary school teacher and I've been doing this job for over 20 years. The trouble is that I don't enjoy it any more. I find my students difficult to control and I don't think they respect me. Also, at 45, I think I'm a bit old to think about changing jobs. What would you suggest?

Helga

Dear Panel,

My son, Adam, is 17 and very clever. He used to do very well at school. Just recently, he's started going out with a new girlfriend and he's told me that he doesn't want to continue his education next year – he wants to leave school and get a job. I think it's so important to go to college or university and get really good qualifications. I'm really worried. What can I do?

Olga

Wordlist

Unit 5

Note: the numbers show which page the word or phrase first appears on in the unit.

achieve *v* (47) to succeed in finishing something or reaching an aim, especially after a lot of work or effort

appreciate *v* (48) to recognise or understand that something is valuable, important or as described

approach *n* (44) a way of considering or doing something

aspect *n* (49) one part of a situation, problem, subject, etc.

barrier *n* (49) anything that prevents people from being together or understanding each other

bilingual *adj* (49) (of a person) able to use two languages for communication, or (of a thing) using or involving two languages

cancel *v* (45) to decide that an organised event will not happen

challenge *n* (49) something that is difficult and that tests someone's ability and determination

classmate *n* (45) someone who is in the same class as you at school

culture *n* (44) the way of life, especially the general customs and beliefs, of a particular group of people at a particular time

flatmate *n* (45) a person who shares an apartment or flat with another person

fly by *v* (49) If a period of time flies by, it seems to pass very quickly, usually because you are enjoying yourself or very busy.

focus on something *v* (47) to give a lot of attention to one particular subject or thing

frustrated *adj* (44) feeling annoyed or less confident because you cannot achieve what you want

get to know *v* (44) to spend time with someone or something so that you gradually learn more about them

homesick *adj* (48) unhappy because of being away from home for a long period

hospitality *n* (49) when people are friendly and welcoming to guests and visitors

immerse yourself in something *v* (47) to become completely involved in something

independent *adj* (44) not needing anyone else to help you or do things for you

initial *adj* (48) of or at the beginning

intensive *adj* (47) involving a lot of effort or activity in a short period of time

marked *adj* (49) describes a change or difference in behaviour that is very obvious or noticeable

master *v* (47) to learn how to do something well

overhear *v* (45) to hear what other people are saying without intending to and without their knowledge

qualification *n* (45) an official record showing that you have finished a training course or have the necessary skills, etc.

remind *v* (45) to make someone think of something they have forgotten or might have forgotten

research *n* (44) a detailed study of a subject, especially in order to discover information or reach a new understanding

scare *v* (49) to (cause to) feel frightened

theoretical *adj* (49) based on the ideas that relate to a subject, not the practical uses of that subject

unique *adj* (48) being the only existing one of its type or, more generally, unusual or special in some way

Unit 6 The planet in danger

Unit objectives

- **Reading Part 2:** scanning for particular information, using cohesive features in the text, understanding text structure
- **Writing Part 2:** writing an essay: introduction to task type, using linking phrases, planning
- **Use of English Part 1:** making the correct choice from a lexical set
- **Listening Part 2:** practice in predicting the kind of information and type of words required
- **Speaking Part 2:** structuring a short talk (discourse markers)
- **Vocabulary:** environmental problems; confusion between *look, see, watch, listen* and *hear; prevent, avoid* and *protect; reach, arrive* and *get (to)*
- **Grammar:** ways of expressing the future

Starting off

❶ *Alternative treatment* If you think your students can manage, with their books closed ask them to brainstorm environmental problems. Then they open their books to compare and check vocabulary.

> **Answers**
> 1 exhaust fumes from cars and lorries
> 2 construction work
> 3 industrial pollution
> 4 endangered species / threats to wildlife
> 5 destruction of rainforests
> 6 rising sea levels
> 7 water problems
> 8 climate change

❷ & ❸ *Extension idea* Ask students to prepare a short presentation on an environmental problem affecting their country. They will give it to the class or a group of students. Give them five minutes to prepare. Ask them to make notes on:

- the problems
- the causes of the problems
- who is responsible
- how it will affect the country/region in the future
- the solutions.

Then ask them to speak from their notes.

Reading Part 2

❶ *As a warmer* Ask students to name some endangered species. Can they also name some species which are extinct?

❷ Give students three minutes to do this.

> **Answers**
> The gorillas were eating, playing, feeding their children; they watched the tourists, listened to the guide and disappeared into the forest

❸ Tell students that this time they should read the article looking for clues which will help them when they read the missing sentences. Tell them that apart from underlining cohesive features as suggested here, they should pay careful attention to the content of each paragraph and the information before and after each gap.

> **Answers**
> *Suggested phrases to underline:* **3** He, his hairy sleepy friends, back home **4** Despite the climb, watchful **5** Caleb had been doing this for ten years, he still loved the job **6** Then, as the vegetation cleared **7** We followed him along a little path **8** No one felt afraid

❹ Ask students to look at the example (1) first and say why this is the correct answer. (*Answer:* It makes the connection between the writer looking at the map in London and him now feeling near the heart of Africa.) Remind students that in the exam no example is given.

> **Answers**
> 2 C 3 B 4 H 5 E 6 D 7 F 8 A

❺ *Extension idea* Ask students to work in pairs and decide:

- (if appropriate) What would be a good trip to make in your country or region if you wanted to see wild animals? What animals could you see?
- If friends were going to visit your country or region to see beautiful countryside and landscapes, where should they go? What would they see?

Vocabulary
Look, see, watch, listen and *hear*

❶ ⊙ Before doing the exercise, ask students to work in pairs and explain the difference in meaning between the sets of words. If they speak the same first language, ask them how each of the words is translated. Then ask them to do the exercise.

❷ If these words present a problem for your students, tell them to copy them into their notebooks and, when they are speaking or writing, to pay special attention to make sure they are using the words correctly.

> **Answers**
> **2** watching **3** hear **4** looking at **5** see
> **6** watching **7** listening to **8** hear

Extension idea Ask students to write their own sentences to illustrate the differences between *look*, *see*, *watch* and *listen* and *hear*.

Listening Part 2

❶ Before students discuss the questions, elicit what each photo shows. Ask if anyone has visited a rainforest. If so, ask them to describe the experience.

> **Suggested answers**
> To make land for farming, to sell the wood, to exploit oil and other resources; to preserve habitats, species and ways of life; forest fires

❷ To replicate exam conditions, you can give students 45 seconds to do this task. Then they can compare their ideas in pairs.

> **Suggested answers**
> **1** a time / noun phrase **2** verb – learn (?)
> **3** adjective **4** verb + *-ing* / verb phrase **5** noun – receptionist, guide (?) **6** noun **7** percentage
> **8** comparative adjective – hotter (?) **9** a place
> **10** noun / verb + *-ing*

❸ 🎧 Remind students that:

- they will hear the recording twice
- the words they hear will probably not be the same as the words given in the notes
- the words they write in the gaps must be words they have heard
- they need to check carefully that the words fit grammatically.

> **Answers**
> **1** summer vacation **2** educate visitors **3** relevant work **4** maintaining paths **5** guide **6** farming (land) **7** seventy % / 70% / per cent **8** warmer
> **9** (living) in zoos **10** buying furniture

Recording script CD1 Track 14

Interviewer: So, here I am at the Anona Biological Reserve in Costa Rica and I'm talking to Sylvia Welling, who's a volunteer here. Sylvia, how did you come to work on this project?

Sylvia: Well, it's quite a long story. I'm studying biochemistry at university back in England and I heard about this project from another student on the course. I'm just doing this in my
Q1 summer vacation, so really I've only been here for a few weeks – since the beginning of July in fact. I'll probably be here till the end of September, then I have to go back to university.

Interviewer: So, what's your role here? Are you here to protect the rainforest?

Sylvia: No, not at all. This one's already protected. No trees are being cut down here. It's a really interesting and beautiful place as a matter of fact. It's full of rare animals and plants and it's incredibly peaceful. The main object of the
Q2 project I'm on is to educate visitors and show them how special this place is. At the same time, I'm learning a lot about it too. Hopefully I'm going to work as a researcher when I finish my degree, so it seemed a good idea to come here while I had the chance.

Interviewer: So you're actually here to learn rather than work?

Sylvia: Well, yes, partly, but as I was just saying
Q3 I really came here to get some relevant work experience. I mean I want to be able to show future employers that I've been doing something connected with biochemistry in my free time. And also I hope in my own small way that I'm doing something useful.

Interviewer: So what's your job here?

Sylvia: I do whatever I'm asked to do. We spend
Q4 part of our time maintaining paths through the forest so that visitors can walk around it without getting lost and without doing much damage. It means I have a great time visiting really remote parts of the forest where the only things you hear are things like animals, the wind in the trees, and the rain. And it rains quite a lot here, believe me!

Interviewer: So you know the forest quite well by now, do you?

Sylvia: Q5	I'm getting to know it better and better because I also spend time acting as a <u>guide</u> for people who come to see the forest. I take them on a walk and point out special trees and animals and explain a bit of how the place works to them. Then hopefully they go home with a feeling of how wonderful and important rainforests are.
Interviewer:	And what do you see as the main dangers facing rainforests now and in the future?
Sylvia: Q6 Q7	The main problem is that in other parts of the world forests like these are being cut down or <u>burnt</u> to create more <u>farming</u> land. As a result, plants and wildlife are becoming endangered or dying out. If things continue like this, by the year 2050, <u>70 per cent</u> of the world's rainforests will have disappeared. I think that's pretty worrying.
Interviewer:	It is.
Sylvia: Q8	And it's going to have really drastic consequences for the rest of the planet. I mean, forests absorb carbon and this prevents global warming. If we carry on cutting down forests, climate change will become even more extreme, making the world <u>warmer</u> and leading to rising sea levels, and so on.
Interviewer:	But Sylvia, in spite of all these worries, what are the pleasures of coming to a place like this?
Sylvia: Q9	For me, one of the greatest pleasures is seeing all the animals that live here, the frogs and birds and monkeys and insects and all the other creatures which are threatened with extinction. You know, the danger is that in forty or fifty years' time these animals will only be <u>living in zoos</u>. They just won't exist in the wild and that will be a real shame.
Interviewer:	And what can visitors like myself do when we get home?
Sylvia: Q10	Well, you could look closely before <u>buying furniture</u> – make sure it isn't made of wood taken from the rainforests. And also tell your friends about these wonderful places and how important it is to protect them.
Interviewer:	Sylvia Welling. Thank you.

❹ **Extension idea** Tell the class they will role play being 'volunteer workers' and 'tourists' visiting the rainforest project. Divide the class into equal numbers of each.

- Ask the 'tourists' to work in small groups and think of three or four questions they want to ask the 'volunteers' about the rainforest.
- Ask the 'volunteers' to work in small groups and think of three or four interesting things they'd like to tell the 'tourists' about the rainforest.
- Then put them together in groups of four (two volunteer workers and two tourists) and tell them (1) to ask and answer questions and give information, and (2) decide together what they can all do to protect rainforests when they get back home.

Grammar
Ways of expressing the future

❶ & ❷

Answers		
name of tense	example(s)	uses
future simple future	won't exist will only	d
continuous	be living	b
future perfect	will have disappeared	a
'going to' future	it's going to have I'm going to work	c e

❸ Before doing this exercise, go through the notes in the Grammar reference section on page 157 (Ways of expressing the future) with them.

> **Answers**
> 2 I'm going to take part in   3 We're going to spend   4 will have risen   5 she's going to study   6 will change   7 will remember us   8 It's going to make

❹ This activity can be done in larger or smaller groups as required.
- If your students come from the same area, ask them to discuss their predictions and try to agree.
- If your students come from different areas, at the end ask them to decide whose area sounds as if it will be the best to live in in 20 years' time.

Extension idea Ask students to present the results of the questionnaire to another group of students, or to the whole class.

This would be a suitable moment to do the photocopiable activity on page 55.

Use of English Part 1

❶ *As a warmer* Ask students if there is a lot of air pollution where they live. Elicit the dangers of air pollution. (*Possible answers:* It causes health problems, it damages buildings, it causes acid rain, it leads to global warming, etc.)

❷

> **Answers**
> Car fumes, aerosols and aeroplanes (air pollution);
> Earth getting darker, reduce the growth of some crops,
> oceans cooler, less rain forms, changing weather
> patterns

❸ Start perhaps by focusing on the example (0). Write on the board:

$$Scientists \begin{Bmatrix} tell\ us\ that \\ inform\ us\ that \\ claim\ that \\ instruct\ us\ that \end{Bmatrix} \begin{matrix} the\ Earth\ is \\ getting\ darker. \end{matrix}$$

- You can then elicit why *claim* is the correct answer and point out that *tell*, *inform* and *instruct* require an object.
- Draw their attention to the meaning of *claim: to say that something is true or is a fact, although you cannot prove it and other people might not believe it (Cambridge Advanced Learner's Dictionary)* and elicit why this meaning is suitable (it's quite recent and surprising information which people may find hard to believe, especially in the context of global warming).

You can then point out key techniques of discarding wrong alternatives, and looking at both the grammatical context and the meaning.

> **Answers**
> 1 B   2 A   3 D   4 D   5 A   6 C   7 A   8 B   9 D
> 10 A   11 C   12 B

Vocabulary
Prevent, avoid and *protect; reach, arrive* and *get (to)*

❶ ⊙

> **Answers**
> 1 prevent   2 arrived

❷ Tell students to pay special attention when they use these words in their speaking and writing. They should check that they are using the word with the correct meaning and correct any mistakes they make.

> **Answers**
> 2 reach / get to   3 gets / arrives   4 prevents
> 5 arrived   6 avoid   7 protect

Extension idea Ask students to write four of their own sentences as examples for the vocabulary.

Speaking Part 2

❶ ***Extension idea*** Ask students to think of other useful vocabulary they could use with the photos.

> **Answers**
> First photo: countryside, natural surroundings, picking up rubbish, litter; second photo: pollution, exhaust fumes, noise, public transport

❷ 🎧 Point out that it's important for students to show how much vocabulary they know, but that if they don't know a word, they should find other ways to express the idea.

> **Answers**
> picking up rubbish, countryside, litter, pollution

Recording script   CD1 Track 15

Teacher: In this part of the test, I'm going to give each of you two photographs. I'd like you to talk about your photographs on your own for about a minute, and also to answer a short question about your partner's photographs.

Magda, it's your turn first. Here are your photographs. They show people doing things to protect the environment. I'd like you to compare the photographs, and say how important these activities are for protecting the environment. All right?

Magda: Yes. Well, the first picture shows two young people who are picking up rubbish from the countryside. I think they're probably doing it at the weekend, and they're picking up plastic bags and other litter. In the other picture we can see a man going to work by bicycle, not by car. I think both these ways of protecting the environment are important. In the first picture I suppose they're cleaning up a mess made by other people, but it's also important to avoid causing pollution ourselves, and I think that's what's happening in the second photo. If we don't protect the environment the world may soon become too hot and unpleasant and many animals and plants will disappear and become extinct.

Teacher: Thank you.

---

❸ 🎧 Ask students which phrases in the box are useful:

- for referring to the photos. (*Answer:* The first picture shows … , In the other picture we can see … , In the first picture … , I think that's what's happening in the second photo …)

- when you're not sure about something. (*Answer:* I think they're probably … , I suppose … , I think that's what's happening in the second photo …)
- for answering the second part of the question – how useful these activities are for protecting the environment. (*Answer:* It's essential to … , It's important to …)

> **Answers**
> Magda uses these phrases: The first picture shows … , I think they're probably … , In the other picture we can see … , In the first picture I suppose … , It's important to … , I think that's what's happening in the second photo …

Extension idea Ask students to work in pairs and, speaking, complete the sentences in the box talking about the photos. They can repeat, approximately, what Magda says, or say something different.

4 Each student should speak for about a minute to answer their question. Tell the student who is not speaking to listen and, when their partner has finished, to give them feedback on what they did well and how they could improve their answer.

Writing Part 2 An essay

1 *As a warmer* Ask students: Are you optimistic or pessimistic about the future of our planet? Why?

> **Answers**
> *Suggested phrases to underline:* giving your opinion, Our children will live in a worse environment than we do

2 Students may note down the same or different reasons for their opinions, depending on whether they agree with each other.

3 This is one possible structure for the essay. It would also be possible to produce a 'balanced essay' where ideas in favour of the statement are balanced with ideas against the statement and in the final paragraph the writer expresses his/her opinion.

4 *Alternative treatment* Ask students to quickly look back through the unit for useful vocabulary. You can round up and write the vocabulary on the board.

5 ***Extension idea*** Ask students to find synonyms of these words in the sample essay:
- cause (make, lead to)
- damage (harm, destruction).

Elicit why it's useful to use synonyms (it produces a varied style, it demonstrates range of vocabulary).

6

> **Answers**
> **2** this reason   **3** The first   **4** result
> **5** The second aspect   **6** Consequently
> **7** In my opinion   **8** Unless we do so

7

> **Answers**
>
> | expressing consequences | introducing your opinion | organising ideas logically |
> | --- | --- | --- |
> | Consequently | In my opinion | The first is |
> | As a result | I believe | Finally |
> | Because of this | I feel | Firstly |
> | For this reason | I think | In addition |
> | | | Lastly |
> | | | The second (aspect) is |

8 If short of time, students can do these steps at home.

9 Tell students that this task should take them about 40 minutes. If you wish, this can be done for homework.

→ For more on writing essays, you can refer students to page 177 (Writing reference – Essays).

> **Suggested answers**
> Scientists have given many warnings about the effects of human activity on the environment and I believe that unless we take drastic action, it is very likely that there will be dramatic changes in the environment over the next 50 years.
>
> I think there will be three major changes. Firstly, as a result of air pollution, global temperatures will rise and this will lead to drier, hotter summers and warmer winters. A further consequence may be more frequent natural disasters such as floods and hurricanes.
>
> The second change will be a rise in sea levels. This will mean that people living near the coast will lose their homes and have to move to new areas.
>
> Finally, we are destroying so many natural habitats such as rainforests that many species of animals and plants will become extinct. Consequently, the world will lose a lot of its diversity.
>
> I believe that unless we take urgent action to prevent these things from happening, the future for the environment will be disastrous and future generations will criticise us for the damage we have done.

Vocabulary and grammar review Unit 5

Vocabulary

❶

	¹r	e	²s	e	³a	r	c	h	
			u		s				
			b		s				
			j		i				
			e		g				
			c		n		⁴m		
			t		m		a		⁵t
		⁶d	e	g	r	e	e		
			n		k				r
		⁷n	o	t	e	s			m

❷ 2 study 3 teaching 4 join, get to know 5 attend 6 take part in

Word formation

❸

verb	noun
obey	obedience
practise	practice
prefer	preference
achieve	achievement
understand	understanding
know	knowledge
qualify	qualification

Grammar

❹ 2 study abroad, you will become / you'll become 3 she would not attend / wouldn't attend 4 look after my book 5 knew the answer, I would / I'd 6 he was not so tired / wasn't so tired

Vocabulary and grammar review Unit 6

Vocabulary

❶ 2 destruction 3 pollution 4 habitats 5 extinct 6 warming 7 change 8 acid 9 rising

❷ 1 B 2 D 3 A 4 B 5 C

Grammar

❸ 2 will probably be 3 will have changed 4 will be living 5 will play 6 will be doing 7 is going to be 8 will be 9 won't have cooked 10 will help

Unit 6 photocopiable activity: In 30 years' time   Time: 20 mins

Objectives
- To use future tenses to discuss future predictions
- To give reasons to justify answers and opinions

Before class

You will need one photocopy of the activity page for each group.

In class

❶ Explain the following rules.

- Students should work in groups of three to five. Each group will need a dice and counters.
- Students should take turns to throw the dice and move their counters.
- When they land on a square with a statement, they should speak for at least 20 seconds to say whether they think the prediction will happen or not in 30 years' time and give reasons for their answer.
- If they speak for 20 seconds, they should move their counter forward two spaces.
- If they speak for less than 20 seconds, they should stay where they are.
- If they land on a square where someone has already spoken, they should go forward one space.
- The winner is the first person to reach Finish.

❷ To get them started, elicit some ideas about what students could say if they landed on square number 3 by asking: *Do you think the world will be warmer in 30 years' time? Yes? No? If you think it will be warmer, why?* and get some ideas (which you can note on the board if you like). You can then give a possible answer as an example, e.g. *I think the world will be warmer because we're not doing enough to control pollution at the moment, we're driving too many cars, ice in the Arctic and Antarctic is melting and people are cutting down trees and forests so there will be more carbon in the atmosphere and they say that in 30 years' time the world will be one or two degrees warmer.*

Tell students they should try to give similar answers when they land on squares.

Unit 6 photocopiable activity

In 30 years' time

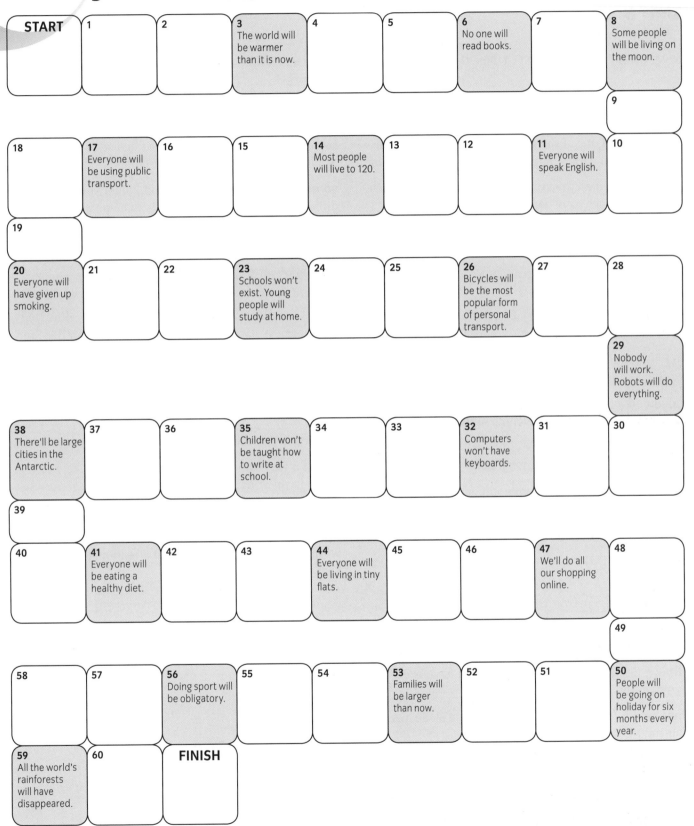

START

1

2

3 The world will be warmer than it is now.

4

5

6 No one will read books.

7

8 Some people will be living on the moon.

9

18

17 Everyone will be using public transport.

16

15

14 Most people will live to 120.

13

12

11 Everyone will speak English.

10

19

20 Everyone will have given up smoking.

21

22

23 Schools won't exist. Young people will study at home.

24

25

26 Bicycles will be the most popular form of personal transport.

27

28

29 Nobody will work. Robots will do everything.

38 There'll be large cities in the Antarctic.

37

36

35 Children won't be taught how to write at school.

34

33

32 Computers won't have keyboards.

31

30

39

40

41 Everyone will be eating a healthy diet.

42

43

44 Everyone will be living in tiny flats.

45

46

47 We'll do all our shopping online.

48

49

58

57

56 Doing sport will be obligatory.

55

54

53 Families will be larger than now.

52

51

50 People will be going on holiday for six months every year.

59 All the world's rainforests will have disappeared.

60

FINISH

Word list

Unit 6

Note: the numbers show which page the word or phrase first appears on in the unit.

alert *adj* (53) quick to see, understand and act in a particular situation

branch *n* (53) one of the parts of a tree that grows out from the main trunk and has leaves, flowers or fruit on it

clearing *n* (53) an area in a wood or forest from which trees and bushes have been removed

crop *n* (56) a plant such as a grain, fruit, or vegetable that is grown in large amounts by farmers

debate *n* (56) a serious discussion of a subject in which many people take part

endangered species *n* (52) a type of animal that may soon not exist because there are very few alive now

exhaust fumes *n* (52) the waste gas from a vehicle's engine

go ahead *v* (53) to go somewhere before the other people that you are walking or travelling with

ground *v* (56) If aircraft are grounded, they are prevented from flying or ordered not to fly.

habitat *n* (59) the natural environment in which an animal or plant usually lives

idly *adv* (53) without any particular purpose

in the wild *n* (53) in natural conditions, independent of humans

keeper *n* (53) a person who takes care of animals in a zoo

level *n* (59) the height of something

litter *n* (58) small pieces of rubbish that have been left lying on the ground in public places

machete *n* (52) a large knife with a wide blade, used for cutting trees and plants or as a weapon

nature reserve *n* (59) an area of land which is protected in order to keep safe the animals and plants that live there, often because they are rare

play a part *v* (56) to help to achieve something

pollution *n* (58) damage caused to water, air, etc. by harmful substances or waste

remote *adj* (53) describes an area, house or village that is a long way from any towns or cities

scramble *v* (53) to move or climb quickly but with difficulty, often using your hands to help you

slip *v* (53) to go somewhere or do something quickly, often so that you are not noticed

sneeze *v* (56) When you sneeze, air and often small drops of liquid suddenly come out of your nose and mouth in a way you cannot control.

sniff *v* (53) to smell something by taking air in through your nose

squat *v* (53) to position yourself close to the ground balancing on the front part of your feet with your legs bent under your body

surface *n* (56) the outer or top part or layer of something

threat *n* (52) someone or something that is likely to cause harm or damage

wander *v* (53) to walk around slowly in a relaxed way or without any clear purpose or direction

watchful *adj* (53) paying careful attention and ready to deal with problems

Complete First Certificate by Guy Brook-Hart © Cambridge University Press 2008 PHOTOCOPIABLE

Unit 7 My first job

Unit objectives

- **Reading Part 1:** scanning the text, training in reading the text before the multiple-choice options
- **Writing Part 1:** planning and writing a letter of application
- **Use of English Part 2:** reviewing language work done previously in the unit
- **Listening Part 3:** listening for gist, identifying main ideas in questions
- **Speaking Part 3:** talking about glamorous jobs, making suggestions, asking opinions, agreeing and disagreeing
- **Vocabulary:** confusion between *work* and *job*; *possibility*, *occasion* and *opportunity*; *fun* and *funny*
- **Grammar:** countable and uncountable nouns, definite and indefinite articles, zero article

Starting off

❶ *As a warmer* Before students open their books, either with the whole class or in groups:

- ask them what jobs students typically do to earn extra money
- ask them what jobs they do/did as students
- ask them if they have heard of any unusual jobs done by students.

Students then do the exercises in Starting off.

> **Answers**
> 1 bank cashier   2 call centre worker   3 waiter/ waitress   4 hospital porter   5 hotel receptionist   6 teacher

Extension idea Ask students in which of these jobs it would be useful to speak English.

❷, ❸ & ❹ *As a warmer* You can ask what things make a job difficult – and elicit skills, training, hard work, long hours, etc.

Extension idea Ask what students gain or learn from doing jobs like these. Is it just money, or is there something else?

Listening Part 3

❶ 🎧 Tell students you are only going to play the recording once for this task – they have to get a general idea of what each speaker says rather than understand all the details.

> **Answers**
> **Speaker 1: D** hospital porter, positive   **Speaker 2: E** hotel receptionist, positive   **Speaker 3: A** bank cashier, negative   **Speaker 4: B** call centre worker, positive   **Speaker 5: F** teacher, positive

Recording script   CD1 Track 16

Speaker 1: My first job was when I was a student. I worked part-time in a hospital and had to fetch patients and wheel them to different hospital departments for treatment. I'm not sure if you can still get jobs like that if you're a student. Anyway, it was hard physical work, you know, lifting people and helping them into wheelchairs and pushing them, but I think I'd expected that. The thing I found most fascinating was chatting to the patients I had to collect. I got to know some of them quite well and you know, we'd talk about all sorts of things. They'd done all kinds of different and unusual things in their lives, so they often had plenty of interesting stories to tell. I think I learnt a lot from them in fact.

Speaker 2: I got my first job as an assistant receptionist in a hotel when I was just eighteen. I didn't have much self-confidence to start with because I was quite shy as a teenager, but I was really happy with the job because I thought it was a great opportunity to get some work experience. Anyway they gave me lots of responsibility quite early on so I learned to do all sorts of things which you need for almost any job, really practical things like dealing with people, answering the phone correctly, maintaining the hotel database. And on some occasions I was left on my own as the only person in charge of the whole of this enormous hotel. Doing that successfully certainly built up my self-confidence, I can tell you.

Speaker 3: Well, this wasn't my first job, but it was what I'd call my first serious job, I mean not just a job for a month or two as a student. I worked behind the counter in a bank and I got the job just after leaving university. I applied for it because I thought at the time that it would be a good way to get to work in finance. Unfortunately, I soon found that that wasn't necessarily true and that's why I eventually left. Before starting, <u>I'd expected the work to be quite routine until I was given more responsibility, but in fact it was very challenging right from the beginning</u> and needed a lot of concentration, especially while I was learning the job.

Speaker 4: It wasn't a very well-paid job, but then first jobs often aren't. I worked in a call centre for a large computer company. I had to answer the phone when customers rang in with their queries or complaints or whatever. Sometimes all they wanted was some information, but they often rang in with a real problem which I had to help them sort out. You see, I already had computer skills because I'd studied computer technology at college. <u>I felt at the time that I was doing something really useful because there were all these people phoning in with urgent problems to do with their computers.</u> Usually just a few simple instructions over the phone were enough, and customers were very grateful, so it could be quite satisfying in fact.

Speaker 5: My first job? Can you believe it? I did it for nearly fifteen years. I started when I was fresh out of university and I worked at the same school until just about a year ago. I have to say though that <u>I found teaching fun and challenging.</u> It's a job where you're doing something serious but at the same time having lots of laughs. Students prefer it if you have a sense of humour and say something funny from time to time, you know, make a joke. On the other hand, <u>I always had a great deal of homework to correct in the evenings and I hated that.</u> I found it was just a chore, so the job did have a few drawbacks. Now I'm headteacher of another school just down the road, but that's another story …

❷ *Alternative treatment*
- Tell students to predict the correct answers since they have already heard the speakers once in Exercise 1.
- Ask them to listen to check if they were correct.

> **Answers**
> *Suggested phrases to underline:* **B** surprisingly hard work   **C** people I met interesting   **D** opportunity to achieve my ambitions   **E** learning useful skills
> **F** enjoyed some parts of the job more than others

❸ 🎧 In the exam, the speakers are unlikely to use the same words as occur in the question. When going through the answers, ask your students what words they heard which gave them the answer. If necessary, play the recording again asking students to focus on the words or idea that gave the answer.

> **Answers**
> 1 C   2 E   3 B   4 A   5 F

❹ *Alternative treatment* Play 'What's my job?' Students take turns to think of a job and mime one action they would have to do in this job. Other members of the group then ask questions to find out what the job is. The student who is being questioned can only answer Yes or No.

Vocabulary
Work or *job*; *possibility*, *occasion* or *opportunity*; *fun* or *funny*

❶ ⊙ *Alternative treatment* Ask students to read the explanations from the *Cambridge Advanced Learner's Dictionary* before they do this exercise. They then make their choices and listen afterwards to check.

> **Answers**
> 2 job   3 job, jobs   4 opportunity   5 occasions
> 6 fun   7 funny

❷ If you have a class set of the *Cambridge Advanced Learner's Dictionary*, you can take this opportunity to show students other features, e.g. the extra examples, collocations, and (on CD-ROM) the thesaurus and the pronunciation guide.

> **Answers**
> 2 fun   3 possibility   4 occasions
> 5 opportunity   6 job   7 work   8 jobs

Extension idea Ask students to write four sentences of their own illustrating some of these words. Ask them to leave the word itself blank. They then pass their sentences to another student who must write the correct word in the space.

Grammar
Countable and uncountable nouns

❶ *As a warmer* Write on the board:
- *He's had three jobs since he left school.*
- *I'm going to give you two advices.*

Ask which sentence is correct, and ask them to correct the other. (*Answer:* I'm going to give you some advice.) Ask which you can count: *advice* or *jobs*. Point out that all nouns in English are either countable or uncountable. Then move to the exercise in the book.

❷ Go through the notes in the Grammar reference section on page 158 (Countable and uncountable nouns) with them. If your students have the concept of countable/uncountable nouns in their own language(s), point out that nouns that are countable in their language may be uncountable in English and vice versa. You could invite them to give examples (e.g. in Spanish *muebles* and *consejos* are countable, while in English *furniture* and *advice* are uncountable).

Point out that *news* is uncountable although it ends in 's', and is therefore grammatically singular. You can also elicit ways of expressing the uncountable nouns in a countable form, e.g. *an item of news, a piece of news*.

Answers

countable	uncountable
accident	accommodation
bed	advice
bus	damage
dish	equipment
hotel	food
instrument	furniture
meal	homework
service	information
suggestion	knowledge
suitcase	luggage
task	news
tool	software
	transport

❸ Tell students that when they are speaking or writing they should look out for these mistakes and correct them.

Answers
2 ~~an advice~~ *some / a piece of / a bit of advice*
3 ~~a work~~ *work / a job* 4 correct
5 ~~accommodations~~ *accommodation* 6 correct
7 ~~furnitures~~ *furniture* 8 ~~many damages~~ *much damage*

❹
Answers
2 number 3 piece/bit 4 piece/bit 5 deal

This would be a suitable moment to do the photocopiable activity on page 64.

Reading Part 1

Background information Lucy Irvine has written several books including *Castaway*, her account of a year she spent on a desert island, also made into a film, and *Runaway*, the first part of her autobiography.

❶ ***Extension idea*** In some countries it is more usual to work for one's parents than in others. You can develop the discussion by asking some of these questions, as appropriate:

- Do you think children should go directly into the family business, or should they get experience elsewhere?
- Should they be treated the same or differently from other workers?
- Would you like to work for your parents? Would it be easier or more difficult than working for another employer?
- Do you think children have a duty to work for their parents if they are asked to?

❷ Give students three minutes to do this.

Answers
1 She was a waitress.
2 She cooked cakes and puddings.

❸ These questions are nearly the same as the stems of the multiple-choice questions in Exercise 4. The intention is to encourage students to find the part of the text which answers the questions *before* looking at the options A–D. Students are often confused by looking at the options first and then reading the text to find the correct answer. In most cases, better results are obtained by understanding the text first and then finding the option which corresponds.

Answers
Suggested phrases to underline: 1 None of us had ever worked in a hotel before 2 I worked as a waitress at breakfast and dinner. This gave me the middle of the day free for studying 3 impressive chef's hat and a terrifying ability to lose his temper and get violent 4 my cold expression used to change into a charming smile 5 The guests, staring with pleasure at the view, I enjoyed getting on well with the people at each table. In the evenings it was funny how differently people behaved; they talked with louder, less friendly voices, and did not always return my smile 6 However, that all changed when Dad created a special role for me which improved my status considerably. I started by making simple cakes for guests' picnics and soon progressed to more elaborate cakes for afternoon teas. This led to a nightly event known as Lucy's Sweet Trolley 7 Most of them were of my own invention, I had cooked them all myself, and some were undeniably strange

❹ Point out that these are the same questions as in Exercise 3 (with the exception of question 8 which is a general question). Tell students to read what they have underlined for Exercise 3, then look at the options to find which one coincides.

> **Answers**
> 1 C   2 A   3 B   4 D   5 B   6 C   7 D   8 B

Extension idea Ask students to work in small groups.

- Tell them to underline unfamiliar vocabulary in the text and then ask each other in their groups if they can explain any of the vocabulary they have underlined.
- Tell them to choose a maximum of three items of vocabulary they would like to have explained (this will encourage them to discriminate between working on more or less useful vocabulary – if they are not sure how to choose, tell them to choose vocabulary which prevents them understanding part of the text).
- Write the words each group has chosen on the board. Then ask each group to guess the meanings from the context.
- If you wish to make it competitive, tell them that the group which guesses the most correct meanings is the winner.
- As a follow-up, students can check by using their dictionaries.

❺ You can also ask students if it is easy for teenagers to find holiday jobs in their country, or whether it is better to travel abroad.

Grammar
Articles

❶ Extension idea Ask students to find other examples for each rule in the text.

> **Answers**
> 2 c   3 f   4 d   5 e   6 a

❷ Go through the notes in the Grammar reference section on page 158 (Articles) with the students before doing the exercise. Ask them to suggest other examples for each rule as you go through them.

> **Answers**
> 2 an   3 the   4 –   5 a   6 a   7 –   8 the   9 the
> 10 –   11 the   12 a

❸ ⊙ Tell students to pay careful attention to articles when they are writing and speaking, and to correct mistakes when they notice them.

> **Answers**
> 2 ~~my age~~ the age   3 town ~~the~~ next year   4 useful information on *the* internet   5 parking in *the* city centre   6 are *the* most effective   7 ~~The money~~ Money   8 listening to ~~the~~ music; on *the* radio   9 ~~the~~ foreign cities; ~~the~~ shopping   10 having *a* wonderful time   11 ~~a~~ plenty of spare time at ~~this~~ *the* moment; have ~~a~~ dinner   12 ~~an~~ accommodation

Extension idea Collect examples of mistakes your students have made with articles in their own recent written work and ask them to correct them.

Speaking Part 3

❶ *As a warmer* With books closed, ask students to suggest glamorous jobs. Ask why the jobs they suggest are glamorous. Perhaps take a vote with a show of hands to find out which job the class in general thinks is the most glamorous.

🎧 Before they listen, ask students to work in pairs and decide which of the things 1–7 are good things to do in the Speaking paper and which they shouldn't do.

Alternative treatment 🎧 Ask them to listen to the candidates with their books closed and decide what things the candidates are doing well, e.g. listening and reacting to each other's opinions.

> **Answers**
> They do these (✓): 1, 3, 4, 6
> They don't do these (✗): 2, 5, 7

Recording script   CD1 Track 17

Teacher:	Now, I'd like you to talk about something together for about three minutes.
	I'd like you to imagine that your college has invited some people with glamorous and exciting jobs to come and talk to students. They are jobs which many people dream of having.
	First, talk to each other about why people dream of doing these jobs. Then decide which two jobs would be the most interesting to hear about. All right?
Irene:	So, why do you think people dream of being footballers, or sports stars?
Miguel:	Perhaps people think that it's a job where they'll earn lots of money and become famous.
Irene:	Yes, and it's easier than other jobs because you don't have to study.
Miguel:	No, but you do have to train a lot and be talented.

Irene:	That's true. Now, what about this next one? What do you think?
Miguel:	The TV reporter? That must be quite exciting, don't you think?
Irene:	Yes, because you're reporting the news and you're on television. I think that's quite attractive. What about you? Do you agree?
Miguel:	Sure. And this job. Being an actor …
Irene:	It's quite creative, don't you think?
Miguel:	Yes, it is. I wouldn't mind being an actor! I mean, you're in the theatre, so it's glamorous, and people come to watch you, so you can become quite famous.
Irene:	Yes. Lots of people dream of becoming famous, don't they?
Miguel:	Possibly. I'm not sure. I think that actually people want to do something which they enjoy more than do something which makes them famous.
Irene:	I think you're right. And this job teaching skiing is a good example. I think it's glamorous because you are being paid to do something which most people can only do on holiday.
Miguel:	And you can ski all winter.
Irene:	And have a good social life as well.
Miguel:	That's true. What about this one, being a photographer?
Irene:	Well, I suppose it's fun because you're doing something creative and that's always better than doing something which is just routine.
Miguel:	Maybe, but you probably travel a lot too.
Irene:	Yes, and it would be lovely to have a job where you can travel.
Miguel:	Like the pilot in this picture.
Irene:	Yes. And flying big planes around the world is probably quite exciting as well. You have lots of responsibility.
Miguel:	You're right. Shall we move on to the second question?
Irene:	OK.
Miguel:	I think all these jobs would be interesting to hear about.
Irene:	Really? I'm not sure … I wouldn't be interested in listening to a talk by a ski instructor.
Miguel:	Yes, but all jobs have something of interest.

Irene:	That's true, but I think if I had to choose, I'd be more interested in listening to a television reporter talking about her job.
Miguel:	Why's that?
Irene:	Well, TV reporters talk to people who are in the news and they witness important events.
Miguel:	Maybe, but I think footballers and actors would also be very interesting to listen to because they do things that other people find entertaining. And they earn a lot of money! What do you think?
Irene:	Well, perhaps we should have a footballer or an actor and a TV reporter and that way we'll have a balance.
Miguel:	I think that's a good idea. Perhaps an actor, then, don't you think? That would be more interesting for everyone.
Irene:	I think you're right, because football usually interests boys more than girls, doesn't it?
Miguel:	Yes. So the TV reporter and the actor, then?
Irene:	Fine.
Teacher:	Thank you.

❷ *Alternative treatment* Ask students to note down the opinions the candidates express. They can then discuss which opinions they agree or disagree with.

Answers	
suggesting ideas	Perhaps people think that if they do this job, they'll … People may/might think a job like this is …
asking your partner's opinion	What about you? Do you agree? What do you think? … don't you think? Why's that?
agreeing	Yes, and … I think you're right. Sure. That's true.
disagreeing	I'm not sure. I think … No, but … Maybe … Possibly …

Extension idea Ask students to add other phrases of their own to each column.

❸ *Alternative treatment* You can give students an alternative task, which you can read to them:

- The pictures show some glamorous jobs people dream of having. Talk to each other about why each of these jobs is glamorous.
- Decide which two jobs should be paid the most money.

Extension idea You can follow up with questions in the style of Speaking Part 4.

- Do you think footballers and pop musicians are paid too much for what they do?
- Do you think young people should dream of doing glamorous jobs?
- How well do schools prepare students for finding a job?
- Which is more important: an enjoyable job or a well-paid job?
- Is it difficult for young people in your country to find work? Why (not)?

Use of English Part 2

❶ *As a warmer* You can ask these questions.

- Why do people volunteer?
- What sorts of jobs can volunteers do? What organisations in your country employ volunteers?
- How can you become a volunteer?
- What advantages are there especially for young people without work experience of volunteering?

If any of your students have personal experience of volunteering, draw on it and ask them to tell the class about what they do/did.

> **Answers**
> It gives young people experience they need; the jobs are all rewarding and interesting; volunteers learn organisation and communication skills; they gain experience working in a team environment; they gain self-confidence and this helps when applying for jobs; they become responsible for themselves; it gets young people ready for life

> **Answers**
> 1 the 2 spend 3 there 4 do 5 well 6 a
> 7 deal 8 for 9 or 10 what 11 other 12 such

❹ Ask students to look at the words in the box. Point out the sort of words they need for this task, i.e. grammar words such as articles, prepositions, pronouns, possessive adjectives, adverbs, etc. and verbs which form collocations, e.g. *do, make, spend*, etc.

❺ Elicit jobs people can do as volunteers and write them on the board. Then put students in groups to do the task.

Writing Part 1

❶ *As a warmer* Ask your students if they have ever written a letter of application. Ask them if they think it's better to send a letter or an email.

❷ Elicit what a letter of application should contain – students should look at the handwritten notes.

When students have written their plans, ask them to compare them with other students' plans.

❸ Elicit what each paragraph is about.

❹ You can point out that in formal letters:

- when the recipient is addressed by name (*Dear Mrs Mcfane*), the letter ends with *Yours sincerely*
- when the recipient is not addressed by name (*Dear Sir or Madam*), the letter ends with *Yours faithfully*.

> **Answers**
> *Suggested phrases to underline:* I have seen your advertisement, I am writing to apply for, I am interested in doing this job because, This will give me the opportunity to, Could you please tell me, I look forward to hearing from you, Yours sincerely

❺ If your students do this for homework, tell them they should spend approximately 40 minutes doing it.

For more on writing letters, you can refer students to page 169 (Writing reference – Part 1).

> **Sample answer**
> Dear Mr Reid,
>
> I am writing to apply for a job as a sports supervisor at the International Camp, which I have seen advertised on the internet.
>
> I am a 17-year-old student from Estonia, where I am in my final year at secondary school. I am a keen sportsman. I am a member of my school's basketball team and local junior tennis champion. I enjoy organising sports for children and I hope to work as a physical education teacher in the future.
>
> I am interested in doing this job because I would like to gain some work experience as a sports supervisor. I would also like to have the opportunity to travel around Scotland afterwards.
>
> Could you please tell me how much time off I would have if I was given the job?
>
> I look forward to hearing from you.
>
> Yours sincerely,

Unit 7 photocopiable activity: Countable and uncountable quiz

Time: 30 mins (with extension idea)

Objectives
- To recognise whether countable and uncountable nouns are being used correctly
- To correct sentences which have a mistake with a countable or uncountable noun

Before class

You will need to photocopy the activity page and cut it up so you have one set of cards for each group of three students.

In class

❶ Ask students to work in groups of three and deal out the cards face down to each player until no cards are left.

❷ Students take turns to read out one of their cards, being careful not to show it to the others. The student reads the card out as naturally and convincingly as possible, choosing whether to say the sentence correctly or incorrectly.

❸ The other students must compete to be the first to say whether the sentence was correct or incorrect.

- If he/she gives the wrong answer (i.e. he/she says a correct sentence is incorrect or vice versa), he/she must give one of his/her cards to the reader.
- If he/she gives the right answer and the word was used correctly in the sentence, the reader must give the card to the student who answered.
- If he/she gives the right answer and the word was used incorrectly in that sentence, he/she must first say what the correct form of the word is in order to get the reader's card.
- If he/she gives another incorrect form, he/she must give a card from his/her pile to the reader.

❹ Listeners can ask the reader to repeat the sentence once only.

❺ Students can still compete to win new cards even if they have lost all of theirs.

❻ Students play to a set time limit, e.g. 15 minutes.

❼ The winner is the student who finishes with the most cards.

Extension idea When the game has finished, ask the groups to place all the cards face up on the table in front of them and say which of the words in the <u>correct</u> sentences are countable and which are uncountable. You can ask them to sort the sentences into two groups.

Countable and uncountable quiz

✂ Cut out along the dotted lines to divide these into cards.

It's dangerous to climb mountains in	bad weather ✓ / a bad weather ✗
She's an attractive girl with	a long fair hair ✗ / long fair hair ✓ / long fair hairs ✗
Although he's over 50 he doesn't have	a single grey hair ✓ / grey hairs ✗ / a grey hair ✗
He's spent most of his life doing	scientific research ✓ / scientific researches ✗ / a scientific research ✗
Please contact our office if you need	another information ✗ / more informations ✗ / more information ✓
I'm not carrying much – just	a suitcase ✓ / suitcase ✗
We haven't got room in the car for four passengers and all	their luggages ✗ / their luggage ✓
I prefer living in the country – in the city there's	too many noises ✗ / too much noises ✗ / too much noise ✓
Do you think the washing machine is working properly? It's making	a strange noise ✓ / strange noise ✗
Most of the questions in the quiz were questions of	general knowledges ✗ / general knowledge ✓
They are only offering the job to people with the right qualifications and	experience ✓ / experiences ✗
When she wants to relax, she listens to	a music ✗ / music ✓ / musics ✗
There's a lot of traffic, so you'd better leave in plenty of	time ✓ / times ✗
I know Paris well because I've been there	much time ✗ / many times ✓

I went to the optician to buy	a glass ✗ / some glass ✗ / some glasses ✓
Be careful with the vase – it's made of	a glass ✗ / glass ✓ / glasses ✗
I've warmed up some milk for you. You can have it in	a cup or in a glass ✓ / cup or glass ✗
There are plenty of hotels in the city, so you shouldn't have difficulty finding	a room ✓ / room ✗
We really can't buy any more furniture. We haven't got	a room ✗ / room ✓ / rooms ✗
We need to find a good restaurant for	an evening meal ✓ / evening meal ✗
You should go to Mario's restaurant. They do	a delicious food ✗ / delicious food ✓
I don't know what clothes to take with me on holiday. Can you give me	an advice ✗ / some advice ✓
Your idea of giving Jan a surprise party is	a very good suggestion ✓ / very good suggestion ✗
So Carla's coming to dinner? That's	great news ✓ / a great news ✗
Barry has been looking at job advertisements because he's trying to find	a work ✗ / work ✓
Antonio is tired of the place where he works so he's looking for	a new job ✓ / new job ✗
There was a really big storm last night which did	a lot of damage ✓ / a lot of damages ✗
We haven't got room in the house for more	furniture ✓ / furnitures ✗
She went to the bank to take out	some monies ✗ / some money ✓
We stayed indoors all afternoon because there was	terrible storm ✗ / a terrible storm ✓

Word list

Unit 7

Note: the numbers show which page the word or phrase first appears on in the unit.

blow down v (64) If the wind blows something down, it makes it fall to the ground by blowing on it.

call centre n (62) a large office in which a company's employees provide information to its customers, or sell or advertise its goods or services by telephone

cashier n (62) a person whose job is to receive and pay out money in a shop, bank, restaurant, etc.

database n (66) a large amount of information stored in a computer system in such a way that it can be easily looked at or changed

daunting adj (65) making you feel slightly frightened or worried about your ability to achieve something

elaborate adj (65) containing a lot of careful detail or many detailed parts

equip v (65) to provide a person or a place with objects that are necessary for a particular purpose

equipment n (64) the set of necessary tools, clothing, etc. for a particular purpose

grab v (65) to take hold of something or someone suddenly and roughly

have something in common v (65) to share interests, experiences, or other characteristics with someone or something

improvise v (65) to invent or make something, such as a speech or a device, at the time when it is needed without already having planned it

key in v (66) to put information into a computer or a machine using a keyboard

live up to expectations v (65) to be very good, as good as you were expecting or hoping

luggage n (64) the bags, cases, etc. which contain your possessions and that you take with you when you are travelling

neat adj (65) tidy, with everything in its place

nightly adv (65) happening every night

punctual adj (66) arriving, doing something or happening at the expected, correct time; not late

put effort into something v (64) to work hard in order to achieve something, using a lot of time and energy

stare v (65) to look for a long time with the eyes wide open, especially when surprised, frightened or thinking

status n (65) the amount of respect, admiration or importance given to a person, organisation or object

task n (64) a piece of work to be done, especially one done regularly, unwillingly or with difficulty

terrifying adj (65) very frightening

trolley n (65) a table on four small wheels with one or more shelves under it which is used for serving food or drinks

undeniably adv (65) certainly

vision n (65) an idea or mental image of something

volunteer v (68) to offer to do something that you do not have to do, often without having been asked to do it and without expecting payment
n (68) a person who does something, especially helping other people, willingly and without being forced or paid to do it

Unit 8 High Adventure

Unit objectives

- **Reading Part 2:** skimming for general ideas, using cohesive features and reference devices

- **Writing Part 2:** report writing; identifying the target reader, analysing the question, brainstorming and organising ideas, deciding when to use a formal or informal style, features of formal and informal styles

- **Use of English Part 4:** how to approach the task, avoiding common problems

- **Listening Part 4:** identifying the main idea, listening for gist and detail

- **Speaking Part 4:** introducing an opinion, adding an explanation, introducing examples

- **Vocabulary:** sports and adventure sports

- **Grammar:** infinitive and verb + -ing forms

Starting off

❶ *As a warmer* Before they open their books, ask students: Can you name any adventure sports, for example, parachuting? (*Some possible answers:* skiing, hiking, mountaineering, snowboarding, abseiling, bungee jumping, hot-air ballooning, heli-skiing + those in the book)

They then do the exercise in the book.

> **Answers**
> 2 cross-country running   3 canoeing/kayaking
> 4 karate   5 athletics   6 windsurfing
> 7 paragliding

❷

> **Answers**
> mountain biking, canoeing/kayaking, paragliding, windsurfing

❸

> **Suggested answers**
> See the list in Exercise 1 above.

❹ Ask students to tell the rest of the class about their experiences. Encourage the class to ask questions.

Reading Part 2

❶ *As a warmer* Tell students they will read and hear about a very hard type of race. Ask them to brainstorm types of races which are very hard, long or dangerous (e.g. marathons, round-the-world yacht races, Tour de France cycle race) and ask why they think people do these races.

Ask students to open their books and answer the question.

Background information Adventure racing is a combination of two or more disciplines, including orienteering, cross-country running, mountain biking, canoeing and climbing. An event can last from 24 hours to ten days or more. Adventure racing teams are traditionally made up of both men and women.

> **Suggested answers**
> mountain biking, cross-country running, canoeing/kayaking

❷ 🎧 This gives background information as a lead-in to the reading text.

> **Answers**
> 1 C   2 A   3 B   4 C

Extension idea Ask students to work in pairs and take turns to talk about a sport they do or know about.

Recording script   CD1 Track 18

Interviewer: So, Gary, just for our listeners who may not be familiar with adventure racing, what is it?

Gary: Adventure racing is a sport which has been around since the early 1990s and it's one of the toughest races you can imagine. Unlike marathons, where the winner is the individual

Q1 runner who crosses the finishing line first, <u>in adventure races the winners are the first team to get over the finishing line all together</u> at the same time. <u>Teams are made up of four to six people</u>, depending on the race, and they must all finish.

Interviewer: In what other ways is adventure racing different?

Gary: Well, these races combine a mixture of different activities or sports – running, kayaking or canoeing, climbing and cycling to name just some of them. They take place over courses which need all these skills. Occasionally, they're organised in cities – there's a famous one which takes place in

Q2	Chicago – but <u>the majority are held in the mountains or desert areas, places where there aren't too many roads or inhabitants</u>, so competitors are really isolated and on their own.
Interviewer:	And how long do they last?
Gary:	A long time – from 24 hours up to ten days, or even more. Competitors have to carry everything they need with them, all their food and drink, and if they run out they'll go hungry
Q3	or thirsty. And <u>on long races often the greatest difficulty is staying awake</u>, because there are no fixed times for breaks and teams tend to race for as many hours as possible.
Interviewer:	I hear that professional athletes are getting interested in the sport too.
Gary:	That's right. Many top sports people find adventure racing makes an interesting change because, rather than competing as individuals
Q4	as they've done all their lives, <u>they have to work in a team and help each other and they often find this very exciting and motivating</u>.
Interviewer:	Gary Peters, thank you.
Gary:	Thank you.

❸ To help them, you can ask: What do you think happens when one member of the team is much slower or faster than the others? How can teams help team members who are having problems? Do you think teams do better if all the members have the same skills or different skills?

❹ Give students three minutes to do this.

> **Answer**
> No, they had to abandon the race before the finish.

❺

> **Answers**
> 2 H   3 D   4 E   5 G   6 C   7 A   8 B

❻ You can also ask students if there is a sport they would really like to try.

Grammar
Infinitive and verb + -ing

❶

> **Answers**
> 2 f   3 g   4 b and i   5 b and i   6 i   7 d   8 a
> 9 c   10 h   11 a

Extension idea Ask students to work in pairs and write one more example for each rule.

❷ Before doing this exercise, go through the notes in the Grammar reference section on page 159 (Infinitive and verb + -*ing* forms) with them. When checking the answers, ask students to say which rule each sentence is an example of.

> **Answers**
> 2 to go   3 to hold   4 Training   5 to get
> 6 injuring   7 running   8 pushing

❸

> **Answers**
> 2 to learn   3 doing   4 taking part in

Extension idea Ask students to add two or three more questions of their own.

❹ Tell students that mistakes using the infinitive and the verb + -*ing* form are very common in First Certificate. Encourage them to check which is correct using the notes in the Grammar reference section and in their dictionaries.

> **Answers**
> 2 ~~to learn~~ learning   3 ~~to wear~~ wearing
> 4 correct   5 ~~introduce~~ to introduce   6 ~~meeting~~ to meet   7 correct   8 ~~to get~~ getting

This would be a suitable moment to do the photocopiable activity on page 72.

Listening Part 4

❶ Paragliding is a sport where you jump from a high place such as the top of a mountain or an aircraft with a special parachute that allows you to fly a long distance before you land.

As a warmer Ask the class:
- Have any of you ever done anything risky? A risky sport? If so, what?
- Why do you think people take risks, for example, parachuting or climbing?

❷ To replicate the exam, give students 45 seconds to do this.

❸ 🎧 Answers

| 1 A | 2 C | 3 B | 4 A | 5 B | 6 A | 7 C |

Recording script CD1 Track 19

Interviewer: So, Andrew, what made you want to go on a paragliding course? It sounds like an extremely risky thing to want to do, even for a journalist like yourself.

Andrew: Well, I thought it was risky too. I mean, as a sports journalist, I spend my time watching people doing different sports and I've done a fair number of them myself. It's one of the qualifications for the job I suppose. Anyway, a few years ago I was actually on holiday in Switzerland and I was playing golf with a

Q1 couple of friends when I looked up and saw these people floating in the air above me. I thought to myself, I'd like to have a go at that. It looks fun.

Interviewer: So you went on a course in France, I believe.

Andrew: That's right. I'd actually tried to go on a paragliding course in England a few years ago. I'd even paid the course fee – about £350 – but every time I went down to do the course it was either too windy or it was raining. You can't fly when your paraglider is wet, you see. So I found that I could go to this rather wonderful place, called the Dune du Pyla on the coast in south-west France. It's actually the highest sand dune in Europe – and they run courses there. I had to pay a bit more than it would have cost in Britain, especially with the extra cost of getting there, but it was

Q2 a really nice place and since sunshine was almost guaranteed I went for it.

Interviewer: Great! And can you tell me, are there any advantages to jumping off a sand dune? I imagine it's rather less dangerous than jumping off a mountain, isn't it?

Andrew: Well, it isn't so high – only about 150 metres, in fact – but of course it's quite dangerous to fall even from 20 metres, so whether you're paragliding from a mountain or from a sand dune doesn't necessarily make much difference. And of course you're strongly advised not to land in the sea. They say that if you do, it'll be almost impossible to rescue you. On the other hand, especially for a beginner,

Q3 landing on a beach or the side of a sand dune is relatively soft and comfortable.

Interviewer: And what's the main difficulty for a beginner? I imagine it's taking off and landing.

Andrew: The major problem for a complete beginner like myself is actually learning to hold your

Q4 paraglider up into the air correctly – you know, so that both sides open correctly without even beginning to fly. They only allow you to run off the edge and fly when you've mastered that technique. In fact I spent my first morning just practising how to do it and it's quite tricky, I can tell you. It makes you feel a bit silly when you see other people happily flying around below you – or above you!

Interviewer: And when you actually start flying, how does your instructor give you instructions? Does he fly along beside you?

Andrew: No, it sounds a nice idea, and I'd have loved to have someone up there beside me to make me feel safer. My instructor, Chantalle, stayed on the ground in fact and she talked to me

Q5 through a microphone. I had a radio and an earphone, so I could listen to her instructions and do what she said. All very quiet and calm. No shouting at all.

Interviewer: And is landing a problem?

Andrew: Surprisingly not. I was expecting something rather violent, you know like falling off a horse, but it was an amazingly soft landing – the sand

Q6 cushions you a bit – and it didn't really feel any more violent than hopping off a two-foot-high wall. I'd say it's much safer than horse riding altogether.

Interviewer: But is it safe, in fact?

Andrew:	They say it is. I mean there are a couple of serious accidents every year. But then that's probably true of most sports, including apparently quiet and earthbound sports like
Q7	golf. <u>What I really like about it though is the silence.</u> I mean even animals don't notice you till your shadow passes over them. It's wonderful. <u>You get a tremendous sense of freedom, beautiful views, sensations you've never had before.</u>
Interviewer:	Andrew, thank you.
Andrew:	Thank you.

❹ Encourage groups to discuss and reach agreement.

> **Suggested answers**
> According to insurance companies the most dangerous sport on the list is motorcycle racing. Less dangerous are paragliding and climbing. The least dangerous are snowboarding and scuba diving, though they are still dangerous.

Use of English Part 4

These questions practise use of the infinitive and verb + -ing. In the exam a much wider range of grammar and vocabulary items are tested.

❶ These questions highlight common pitfalls which you can point out to students, i.e. using more than five words, changing the word given, not using the word given.

> **Answers**
> 1 B 2 A

❷ These questions show a step-by-step process to reach the correct answer.

> **Answers**
> 1 (in order / so as) to get ready 2 are not allowed to touch

❸ & ❹ Students should try to do these questions without using the clues in Exercise 4, and then use the clues to help them check whether their answers are correct.

> **Answers**
> 1 taking part in 2 more expensive to hire
> 3 to give her a ring/call 4 is not so/as safe
> 5 to lose his temper

Speaking Part 4

❶ *As a warmer* Ask students if they remember what happens in Speaking Part 4. (*Answer:* This part develops the theme or topic of Part 3 into a more general discussion where the examiner asks both candidates questions.)

🎧 Students can note down answers after they have listened.

> **Suggested answers**
> **Antonia:** No, because not keen on sports – should be allowed – adults to supervise; normal sports equally beneficial **Magda:** Young people yes, old people more – to keep fitter – but often too busy

❷ 🎧

> **Answers**
>
> | introducing an opinion | adding an explanation | introducing an example |
> | --- | --- | --- |
> | I believe …
 I'm not sure. I think …
 No, I don't think so because … | I mean …
 You see … | for instance …
 such as … |

Extension idea Ask students to suggest other ways of introducing their opinions and note them down.

Recording script CD1 Track 20

Teacher:	Antonia, do you think young people should be encouraged to do adventure sports?
Antonia:	Encouraged? No, I don't think so because I'm not very keen on sports, especially ones which might be dangerous. I think young people should be allowed to do them if they really want to, of course, but with experts to supervise them to make sure they're safe. Adventure sports are OK for people who enjoy excitement and danger, but people like me can benefit just as much from taking exercise in the normal way, for instance playing tennis or running.
Teacher:	Thank you. Magda, do you think that people generally do enough sport nowadays?
Magda:	I'm not sure. I think young people in my country do quite a lot of sport, but perhaps older people should do more sport to keep fitter. I mean, older people are often too busy

to do much sport because they're busy with other things such as their jobs and looking after their families and so on, but I believe doing sport keeps you feeling younger and healthier, so they should be encouraged to do so.

3 *Alternative treatment* Before they speak, ask students to add one extra question to their lists to ask their partners.

Writing Part 2 A report

1 *As a warmer* With books closed, ask students if they would write in the same style to a friend as they would write to someone working in an office. Ask them why not. Elicit what things decide the style you will use when you write. (*Answer:* who you are writing to and the type of writing.)

Ask students to open their books and do the exercise.

> **Suggested answers**
> 2 I   3 I   4 F   5 I   6 F

2 The tasks listed are all possible First Certificate tasks. Point out to your students that the style of each task may be different, depending on who will read it, e.g. a review for an international magazine may have a more formal style than a review for a college magazine, because you don't know the readers.

> **Suggested answers**
> 2 I   3 F   4 F   5 F   6 F   7 I

3 These are generalisations, rather than firm rules.

> **Answers**
> 2a F   2b I   3a I   3b F   4a I   4b F   5a F   5b I
> 6a I   6b F

4

> **Answers**
> *Suggested phrases to underline:* types of sporting activities, how doing these activities would benefit young people

5

> **Answers**
> 1 The town council   2 formal – because the report is for the town council   3 and 4 *Students' own answers*

6 You can get feedback on these ideas from the class and put them on the board. This will supply less imaginative students with ideas for the writing task.

7 When going through the answers, you can ask students to link them to the differences between formal and informal styles highlighted in Exercise 3.

> **Answers**
> 2 a number of   3 young people   4 outline   5 the benefits of   6 activities   7 is situated   8 enjoy
> 9 Activities on the coast could include   10 organise
> 11 Similarly   12 a local mountaineering club could be employed   13 benefit   14 encouraging   15 they would become   16 I recommend   17 enjoyable
> 18 develop

8 Students can answer these questions in pairs.

> **Answers**
> 1 yes   2 four – from the headings   3 to introduce the subject   4 five   5 four   6 to summarise and recommend   7 formal

9 If you ask students to do this task for homework, tell them that in the exam they would have approximately 40 minutes to complete it.

For more on writing reports, you can refer students to page 173 (Writing reference – Reports).

Sample answer

Adventure Sports at Caxton Sports Club

Introduction

The purpose of this report is to suggest what adventure sports young people in the area would enjoy doing and to outline the benefits of doing these sports.

Which adventure sports?

I asked my friends and a number of other young people living in this area which sports they would like to try if the sports club gave them the opportunity. The most popular suggestions were skiing in the winter, and windsurfing and climbing in the summer. A number of people suggested doing other sports such as paragliding and sailing, but in general these were not so popular.

Benefits

The main benefits of these sports for young people are that they will have adventures and new experiences, as well as enjoying themselves. At the same time they will make new friends and learn responsibility and independence.

Conclusion

I recommend that the sports club should provide skiing, windsurfing and climbing activities at weekends and during holiday periods, depending on the season. I am certain that providing these sports will attract large numbers of young people to the club.

Vocabulary and grammar review Unit 7

Vocabulary

1 2 work 3 job 4 occasion 5 fun 6 opportunity
7 funny 8 possibility

Grammar

2 2 there were no rooms 3 luggage 4 equipment
5 advice 6 transport 7 facts 8 knowledge
9 information 10 food 11 meals she cooks are
12 work 13 jobs 14 furniture 15 It is

3 2 bit/piece 3 bit/piece 4 bit/piece 5 number

4 2 a 3 the 4 a 5 – 6 a 7 – 8 a 9 the
10 a 11 a 12 – 13 a 14 an 15 the 16 the
17 the 18 the 19 an 20 –

Vocabulary and grammar review Unit 8

Word formation

1 2 patience 3 Unfortunately
4 training 5 simply 6 actually
7 tired 8 uncomfortable
9 realistic 10 valuable

Grammar

2 2 to get 3 to invite 4 changing
5 to have 6 stealing 7 to finish
8 to become 9 working
10 asking 11 working 12 spending

3 2 aren't allowed to go 3 to avoid getting
4 can't bear windsurfing 5 you mind turning
6 invited Ana to play 7 you risk having
8 no point (in) going

Unit 8 photocopiable activity: The brainstorming game   Time: 25 mins

> ### Objectives
> - To quickly revise ideas and vocabulary covered in the first eight units of the course
> - To stimulate brainstorming skills

Before class

You will need one photocopy of the activity page, and perhaps the Rules below as well, for each group.

In class

1 Go through the Rules with your students.

2 If necessary, get the class as a whole to brainstorm names of adventure sports in square 2.

Rules

This is a game for six to nine players. The aim of the game is to develop your brainstorming abilities. Brainstorming is when a group of people suggest a lot of ideas very quickly before considering them more carefully. It's useful as preparation for doing writing tasks and answering interview questions.

1 Divide into three teams of two to three players each.

2 You need a dice, one counter for each team and a watch.

3 Teams take turns to throw the dice and move their counter round the board.

4 When your team lands on a BRAINSTORM square, the other teams should look at the watch, say 'Start NOW!' and give your team one minute to brainstorm as many things as you can.

5 Each BRAINSTORM square gives an example. Start by saying the example.

6 The other teams should note down the things you say while you are brainstorming.

7 The other teams should shout 'Stop!' before the minute has finished:
- if you repeat an idea when you're brainstorming
- if you say an idea which is not connected with the subject.

8 You get 1 point for each relevant thing you have brainstormed, including the example.

9 If a team lands on a square that has already been brainstormed, they should move to the next square and not repeat the brainstorm.

10 The winner is the team with the most points at the end of the game.

The brainstorming game

START	1	2 BRAINSTORM names of adventure sports, e.g. climbing	3	4 BRAINSTORM typical student jobs, e.g. waiter
9	8 BRAINSTORM different environmental problems, e.g. acid rain	7	6 BRAINSTORM sports facilities in the area where you live, e.g. tennis courts	5
10 BRAINSTORM names of subjects you can study at school, e.g. history	11	12 BRAINSTORM enjoyable things to do during a rainy weekend, e.g. watch TV	13	14 BRAINSTORM places of entertainment in the area where you live, e.g. cinema
19	18 BRAINSTORM types of holiday accommodation, e.g. hotel	17	16 BRAINSTORM types of relative, e.g. uncle	15
20 BRAINSTORM ways of communicating with friends in another country, e.g. email	21	22 BRAINSTORM different types of family home, e.g. a flat	23	24 BRAINSTORM different clothes people wear, e.g. a shirt
29	28 BRAINSTORM different means of transport, e.g. trains	27	26 BRAINSTORM different geographical features, e.g. mountains	25
30 BRAINSTORM different types of holiday, e.g. a cruise	31	32 BRAINSTORM different household tasks, e.g. making the beds	33	34 BRAINSTORM different types of fast food, e.g. pizza
39	38 BRAINSTORM names of indoor sports, e.g. squash	37	36 BRAINSTORM hobbies which are not sports, e.g. photography	35
40 BRAINSTORM different places for tourists to visit, or things for tourists to do in your area, e.g. the archaeological museum	41	42 BRAINSTORM things you can do to stay healthy, e.g. take regular exercise	43	44 BRAINSTORM nouns in English which are uncountable, e.g. sugar
49	48 BRAINSTORM the benefits of taking exercise, e.g. to keep fit	47	46 BRAINSTORM types of educational institution, e.g. college	45
50 BRAINSTORM the advantages of studying abroad, e.g. to learn a foreign language	51	52 BRAINSTORM the advantages of living at home with your parents, e.g. it's cheaper	53	54 BRAINSTORM the advantages of learning English, e.g. travelling is easier
59	58 BRAINSTORM the advantages of living in a big city, e.g. the schools and universities are better	57	56 BRAINSTORM the disadvantages of living in a city, e.g. the pollution	55
60 BRAINSTORM ways you personally can protect the environment, e.g. by recycling paper	FINISH			

Word list

Unit 8

Note: the numbers show which page the word or phrase first appears on in the unit.

blister *n* (71) a painful red swelling on the skin that contains liquid, caused usually by continuous rubbing, especially on your foot, or by burning

can't help *v* (72) If you can't help doing something, you cannot stop yourself doing it.

career *n* (71) the job or series of jobs that you do during your working life, especially if you continue to get better jobs and earn more money

carry on *v* (72) to continue doing something, or to cause something to continue

casual *adj* (73) describes clothes that are not formal or not suitable for special occasions

disappointment *n* (71) the feeling of being unhappy because something or someone was not as good as you had hoped or because something did not happen

disqualify *v* (72) to stop someone from being in a competition or doing something because they are unsuitable or they have done something wrong

drop out *v* (71) to not do something that you were going to do, or to stop doing something before you have completely finished

eternity *n* (71) time which never ends or which has no limits

flexible *adj* (71) able to change or be changed easily according to the situation

furious *adj* (71) using a lot of effort or strength

hallucination *n* (71) when you see, hear, feel or smell something which does not exist, usually because you are ill or have taken a drug

hire *v* (74) to pay to use something for a short period

individually *adv* (70) separately

it's no good *adj* (72) used to say that trying to do something has no effect

it's not worth *adj* (72) used to say that something is not useful or enjoyable enough to use time, effort or money doing

keep up with *v* (71) to move at the same speed as someone or something that is moving forward so that you stay level with them

methodical *adj* (71) describes people who do things in a very ordered, careful way

outline *v* (77) to give the main facts about something

pace *n* (71) the speed at which someone or something moves, or with which something happens or changes

peaceful *adj* (73) quiet and calm

severe *adj* (71) causing very great pain, difficulty, anxiety, damage, etc.; very serious

strategy *n* (71) a detailed plan for achieving success in situations such as war, politics, business, industry or sport, or the skill of planning for such situations

take up *v* (73) to start doing a particular job or activity

to cut a long story short *v* (71) something that you say before you describe, very briefly, something that happened, without saying all the details

train *adv* (71) to prepare or be prepared for a job, activity or sport, by learning skills and/or by mental or physical exercise

❶ Read the text below and for Questions 1 – 10 choose the correct alternative in *italics*.

I (0) *taught* / *learned* / *found out* myself how to play the guitar two years ago and I'm quite good at it. I decided that I wanted to go back to college and (1) *find out* / *study* / *know* the theory of music and maybe in the future become a guitar teacher. I went on the internet to (2) *find out* / *get to know* / *learn* what (3) *subjects* / *assignments* / *courses* were being run in my area and I discovered that there was one at a college not too far from where I live which lasted for a year. It was a great (4) *possibility* / *occasion* / *opportunity* for me, so I gave up my (5) *job* / *work* / *activity* and became a student again. The classes were (6) *amused* / *funny* / *fun* at first and it was a pleasure to (7) *hear* / *listen to* / *listen* the lecturers, but then it all became much more serious. We were given written work to do and we received (8) *degrees* / *notes* / *marks* for it. I surprised myself by doing quite well. At the end, the students (9) *joined* / *assisted* / *took part in* a concert, which was a really memorable (10) *opportunity* / *action* / *occasion* for all of us.

❷ Choose the two possible alternatives (A, B, C or D) which could complete the sentences below.

0 Paul ....A, C......... losing his job because of his frequent absences.
   A risked   B decided   C admitted   D managed

1 I never .... to work in a bank.
   A wanted   B advised   C expected   D imagined

2 The boss .... her to be back on time after the lunch break.
   A said   B demanded   C told   D reminded

3 Which computer do you .... me to buy?
   A expect   B suggest   C imagine   D want

4 I'm looking forward .... the sales team.
   A to joining   B to be in   C to being in   D to join

5 One day Cristina .... to run her own company.
   A would love   B enjoys   C likes   D plans

❸ Each of the sentences below contains one mistake with *a*, *an*, or *the*. Find and correct the mistake.

0 Jane has ~~an~~ experience working with a number of different environmental charities.

1 Sam is doing a research into alternative energy sources.

2 I hope we'll have found a solution to the problem of the global warming soon.

3 There's a huge variety of the different species in the jungle.

4 Do you know how many different kinds of birds there are in a world?

5 I read recently that Brazilian government is trying to stop the destruction of their rainforest.

6 There's the fantastic nature programme on TV tonight.

7 The cars are responsible for most of the pollution in cities.

8 I remember seeing a whale for first time – it was a fantastic experience.

9 The explorers survived on a food they found in the jungle.

10 Jo studied environmental science at the university before getting a job in Canada.

❹ Read the letter below and for Questions 1 – 10 choose the correct alternative in *italics*.

Dear Granny,

Thank you for the CD you sent me. (0) *I'm going to listen* / *I listen* / *I'm listening* to it properly tonight when I have more time. As you know, I'm working really hard at the moment. Our exams start on May 24th and I'm a bit worried about them. And then after that (1) *I'll probably go* / *I probably go* / *I'll probably have gone* on holiday with some of my friends. So in a few weeks' time (2) *I'll lie* / *I'm going to lie* / *I'll be lying* on a beach somewhere. I can't believe (3) *I'll have finished* / *I'll be finishing* / *I finish* school for ever by the end of next month.

I've just heard that I've been accepted at Edinburgh University to study engineering – great news, isn't it? I think (4) *it's* / *it's going to be* / *it's being* hard, but I know (5) *I'll enjoy* / *I'll be enjoying* / *I'm enjoying* it. So in September (6) *I'll be leaving* / *I leave* / *I left* home for the first time to start a new life. (7) *Do you come* / *Will you come* / *Will you have come* to see me when I'm there? I think (8) *I'm* / *I'll be* / *I'm being* a bit lonely to start with.

Anyway, thanks again for the CD. I'd better stop now as (9) *I'll meet* / *I'm meeting* / *I meet* my friend, Susie, in half an hour. (10) *We're going to help* / *We'll be helping* / *We'll have helped* each other with our revision. Well, that's our plan, at least!

Lots of love,

Annie

❺ Read the text and think of the word which best fits each gap. Use only one word in each gap.

An uncertain future

Are you a keen skier or snowboarder? Then you probably can't wait for winter to arrive. (0) ....*If*.......... you're lucky enough to live near the mountains, you can be on the snow every weekend. But for others, it requires a great (1) .... of planning. And recently, climate change has meant that even with careful planning, you might be disappointed. In the past, you could say 'We'll (2) .... skiing in January because there's bound to be lots of snow.' Now, you can't be sure. And there's nothing worse than arriving (3) .... your ski resort and seeing so (4) .... snow that it hardly makes the ground white. So most winter sports enthusiasts in the UK spend hours on the internet finding (5) .... when and where the snow is expected (6) .... fall and then making a last-minute reservation. In the last (7) .... years, the snow has been better later in the season and maybe this will be the trend for the future. However, there must be many low-altitude winter sports resorts in Europe that are worried about their future. If they get (8) .... snow at all, then visitors will go elsewhere. So there has been a huge investment in snow-making machines in (9) .... attempt to avoid economic disaster. (10) .... winter weather patterns miraculously go back to what they used to be, winter sports enthusiasts are going to find it harder to satisfy their passion.

❻ Complete the second sentence so that it has a similar meaning to the first sentence, using the word given. Do not change the word given. You must use between two and five words, including the word given.

0   You can't afford holidays because you spend so much money.

    TO

    If you didn't spend so much money, you ....*would be able to*............. afford holidays.

1   I might earn a lot of money, and then I'd travel the world.

    IF

    I'd travel the world .... a lot of money.

2   You'll need to do plenty of reading to pass the exam.

    READ

    You won't pass the exam .... a lot.

3   I don't think you should travel on your own.

    YOU

    If I .... travel on my own.

4   Simon can't get a job in Italy because his Italian is not good enough.

    BETTER

    If Simon .... get a job in Italy.

5   It's a good thing we have a map with us, otherwise we'd be lost.

    HAVE

    We'd be lost .... a map with us.

Unit 9 Star performances

Unit objectives

- **Reading Part 3:** including practice in identifying key ideas in questions
- **Writing Part 2:** writing an article, structuring the article, using linking words and phrases
- **Use of English Part 1:** reading the article quickly before answering the questions, advice on how to approach each question, paying attention to grammar as well as meaning
- **Listening Part 2:** including practice in predicting type of word, type of information
- **Speaking Part 1:** expressing likes, dislikes, preferences and indifference, answering questions about tastes in television and cinema
- **Grammar:** tense, pronoun and adverb changes for reported speech; expressing likes, dislikes and preferences; *although*, *however* and *despite*
- **Vocabulary:** confusion between *play*, *performance* and *acting*; *audience*, *public* and *spectators*; *scene* and *stage*

Starting off

Alternative treatment Before they open their books, put students in groups of three to brainstorm a list of different types of TV programme.

- If your students are all from the same country, ask them to give an example of each type of programme.
- When they have finished, ask students to open their books and compare their list with the list in the box. Ask them to add other types of programme they thought of to the list.

Round up the activity by discussing the final two questions with the whole class and comparing experiences and ambitions.

Listening Part 2

❶ *As a warmer* Ask students: What different quiz shows are there on TV? Which is your favourite? Which would you like to take part in?

You can elicit possible answers for the first three questions, e.g. 1 Who do you think the producer invited? – get suggestions (a relative, member of the family, friend, etc.); 2 What sort of feeling might someone have if they didn't want to go? (embarrassed, nervous, uncomfortable, self-conscious, etc.); 3 What could this be? A means of transport? A piece of clothing? etc.

> **Suggested answers**
> **1** a relation, a person, noun   **2** a feeling, adjective   **3** piece of clothing or means of transport, noun   **4** noun   **5** verb phrase – studying?   **6** a place, noun   **7** personal noun describing an occupation   **8** number/type   **9** adjective   **10** noun

❷ 🎧 Before you play the recording, remind students they will usually need between one and three words for each space.

> **Answers**
> **1** aunt   **2** too nervous   **3** hired car   **4** tie
> **5** watching quiz shows   **6** the green room
> **7** university teacher   **8** general knowledge
> **9** charming/friendly   **10** (big) television/TV

Recording script   CD1 Track 21

Dan: So Julie, have you ever been on TV?

Julie: No, but my dad was years ago. What happened was that a TV producer walked in to my grandmother's shop and asked her if
Q1 she'd let my <u>aunt</u> take part in this quiz show called The Big Question. He'd seen her working in the shop and I suppose he thought she'd look good on TV. Anyway, when she was asked, she said no. She said she was afraid
Q2 she'd get <u>too nervous</u> and be unable to speak when they asked her questions! My elder sister, who was only eleven at the time, told her she should go because it was the chance of a lifetime, but she wouldn't change her mind.

Dan: So then what happened?

Julie: Well, at that moment my dad walked in, overheard the argument and said that if she didn't want to go, he'd be happy to go himself. Anyway, the producer agreed and a couple of
Q3 weeks later my father took a <u>hired car</u> – ours was very old and he didn't trust it – and drove to the TV studios. I don't think he trusted the trains to arrive on time either.

Dan: So he risked getting caught in the traffic instead!

Julie: That's right. Anyway, when he got there, he'd got his suit but he realised that he hadn't
Q4 remembered to bring a <u>tie</u>, so he asked the producer if he could borrow one.

Star performances   (77)

Dan:	And did he study at all for the show, you know by reading encyclopedias and so on?
Julie:	Not at all! I don't think we even had an encyclopedia in the house. He told me later that the only thing he'd done was spend a
Q5	few evenings <u>watching quiz shows</u> on TV so he'd know what to expect. My dad is not one of those people who's in the habit of studying really.
Dan:	And who were the other competitors? Were they people like him?
Julie:	Well, what he told me was that before the show he waited with the other participants
Q6	in a place called '<u>The Green Room</u>', where they chatted to each other and were given something to eat and drink. Anyway, he said he was quite impressed because the other two competitors were both quite smartly dressed and looked very academic. In fact one of them
Q7	was a <u>university teacher</u>. The other wasn't though; he turned out to be a bus driver.
Dan:	And what sort of questions did they have to answer?
Julie:	As far as I remember all the questions they
Q8	had to answer were on <u>general knowledge</u>. Nothing specialist if you see what I mean, but I still think my dad felt quite lucky to be able to answer his, because he managed to beat both the other contestants.
Dan:	Fantastic! And what was the presenter like? Was he, you know, aggressive or anything?
Julie:	No, he wasn't – at least during the programme he wasn't. My dad said that he was really
Q9	<u>charming</u>. But, as soon as the show had ended, he stopped being <u>friendly</u> and left without talking to any of the contestants again. Sounds a bit strange, doesn't it?
Dan:	It does. Anyway, did your father win a lot of money and become a millionaire or something?
Julie:	No! He didn't become a millionaire, but he did
Q10	win a few prizes – there was a <u>big television</u>, I remember, and a big fluffy elephant, which he gave to me. They were pretty impressive prizes for us then, so we were all very happy. I kept the elephant for years, till I was at least 16, but then it went to a jumble sale.
Dan:	And would you like to take part in a quiz show?

Julie:	I'd love to. I'm hooked on them and I'm always phoning in to try and win some of the prize money! No luck so far though.
Dan:	Well, keep trying!

❸ *Extension idea* You can practise the second conditional. Students work in groups. Ask them to discuss: If you won a holiday at a place you could choose, where would you go? If you won a house in a place you could choose, where would you choose to have your house?

Grammar
Reported speech 1

❶ *As a warmer* Ask students to work in small groups and think of times when they have used reported speech in their own language. Ask them to think about why they used reported speech rather than reporting things using direct speech. (*Suggested answer:* Reported speech summarises the main points of a conversation and is therefore more efficient and less time-consuming; it allows speakers to report the meaning when they can't remember the exact words.)

Extension idea Ask them to work in pairs and briefly report in English a conversation they had in their own language recently.

Answers
1 a   2 b

❷ Before students do this exercise, go through the notes in the Grammar reference section on page 160 (Reported speech 1) with them. They can then use the information to complete the notes in the exercise.

Answers
2 had missed   3 would book   4 you   5 today
6 before   7 last   8 following   9 tomorrow   10 there

❸

Answers
2 she would get/come back   3 would arrive on/in
4 wasn't allowed to borrow   5 (had) made several
mistakes   6 had found the play

Extension idea Ask students to work in pairs and write five sentences in direct speech on a piece of paper. Tell them not to write questions. They then pass the paper to another pair of students who put them into reported speech.

Reading Part 3

❶ *Extension idea* Ask students to work in groups and compare their favourite actors and their favourite films, and explain why they are favourites.

❷ Point out that in the exam the questions are printed before the text. It's important to study the questions carefully before reading the text.

Alternative treatment

- Ask students to read the article but not the questions (they cover the questions).
- They then work in pairs and must write one question for each actor on a piece of paper. The correct answer to each question must be only one actor.
- They then pass the questions to another pair to answer.
- When they have finished, ask students to look at the questions in the book and compare them with their questions. Which were similar and which were different?

> **Answers**
> *Suggested phrases to underline:* **2** learnt a lot from people already working   **3** other people's suggestions improves their acting   **4** underline the whole question   **5** planned to enter a different profession   **6** underline the whole question   **7** prefers, theatre   **8** underline the whole question   **9** necessary to travel to find work   **10** unnecessary to leave Scotland to find work   **11** worried about performing in front of some important people   **12** happy to work outside Scotland   **13** motivated, well known   **14** train, somewhere else   **15** underline the whole question

❸

> **Answers**
> **1** E   **2** D   **3** E   **4** B   **5** C   **6** A   **7** C   **8** A   **9** C
> **10** A   **11** A   **12** D   **13** B   **14** D   **15** B

❹ As a follow-up question, you could ask them if they prefer performing in front of people they know or people they don't know.

Vocabulary

Play, performance and *acting*; *audience, public* and *spectators*; *scene* and *stage*

❶ ⊙

> **Answers**
> **2** performance   **3** acting   **4** stage   **5** an audience

❷ Tell students they should pay special attention to these words in order to avoid making mistakes when speaking or writing.

> **Answers**
> **2** play   **3** acting   **4** performance   **5** audience
> **6** scene   **7** stage   **8** spectators

Extension idea Ask students to work in pairs and write five sentences using five of these words. When they write the sentence, they should leave a gap where the word should be. They then pass the sentences to another pair, who should write the correct word in each gap.

This would be a suitable moment to do the photocopiable activity on page 82.

Use of English Part 1

❶ *Alternative treatment* Play 'Who am I?'.

- Prepare a number of pieces of paper with names of well-known or famous people on them, some of them possibly historical figures. Pin a name on the back of each student.
- Students then walk around the class asking *yes/no* questions to each other to find out their 'name', e.g. Am I still alive? Do I live in this country? Am I a film star? etc. They can only ask two questions to each student and then they must move on.
- When they have finished, ask them to work in groups and say what they admire or dislike about the person whose name they had. Would they like to be that person?

❷

> **Answers**
> Becoming wealthy without qualifications, doing whatever you want

❸ If you wish, let students use dictionaries to help them.

> **Answers**
> **1** A   **2** D   **3** B   **4** B   **5** A   **6** C   **7** A   **8** B   **9** C
> **10** C   **11** D   **12** B

❹ *Alternative treatment* Ask students to work in pairs and role play a discussion between Daryll's parents (who want him to be more realistic about his future) and Daryll. Tell students to think and prepare for a minute or two before the discussion.

Speaking Part 1

❶ *As a warmer* Remind students that in Speaking Part 1 they are asked about themselves, their interests and activities. Ask them to suggest questions they might be asked about television and films.

① & **②**

> **Answers**
> 2 listening   3 watching   4 watch   5 going
> 6 seeing   7 watching   8 watching   9 to go
> 10 watching

③ 🎧 *Note:* The answers given above are the ones used by the candidates. However, the following alternatives would also be grammatically correct: 5 to go, 6 to see, 9 going, 10 to watch.

Recording script   CD1 Track 22

Teacher:	Antonia, do you watch much television?
Antonia:	Yes, quite a lot. I think I watch TV about two hours a day.
Teacher:	What sorts of programmes do you like most?
Antonia: *Q1*	I really enjoy <u>watching</u> quiz programmes, you know, the ones where they ask you like general knowledge questions about history, sports, things like that. I think you learn quite a lot from them.
Teacher:	And are there any TV programmes you avoid watching?
Antonia:	Sorry, could you repeat the question, please?
Teacher:	Yes. Are there any TV programmes you avoid watching?
Antonia: *Q2* *Q3 + Q4*	Well, I can't stand <u>listening</u> to the news and programmes like that because I find it so depressing, and I'm not too keen on <u>watching</u> cartoons. I'd rather <u>watch</u> real actors acting, you know, especially when I'm watching films or series.
Teacher:	And Peter, what do you like doing when you go out in the evenings?
Peter: *Q5 + Q6*	I love <u>going</u> to the theatre and <u>seeing</u> plays. I like seeing alive performances, sorry live performances. I think the theatre is very exciting and I'd like to be an actor.
Teacher:	And which do you think is better: watching a film on TV or going to the cinema?
Peter: *Q7*	I prefer <u>watching</u> films in the cinema, because I think they're more entertaining when there's an audience, and there's a better atmosphere. If you watch films on TV, you don't pay so much attention and there are advertisements.
Teacher:	Thank you. Miguel, do you watch much television?
Miguel: *Q8* *Q9*	Not much. I don't mind <u>watching</u> music programmes, but I'm not too interested in television in general. I prefer <u>to go</u> out with my friends in the evening.
Teacher:	And are there any TV programmes you avoid watching?
Miguel:	Sorry?
Teacher:	Are there any TV programmes you avoid watching?
Miguel: *Q10*	Yes, I really hate <u>watching</u> series about doctors and hospitals because I think the plots and the characters are very unrealistic. But in fact I don't watch much television at all …

Extension idea Ask students to think of two more phrases they can add to each column.

> **Answers**
>
> | likes | dislikes | neither likes nor dislikes |
> |---|---|---|
> | I really enjoy
I'd rather
I love
I prefer | I can't stand
I'm not too keen on
I'm not too interested in
I really hate | I don't mind |

④ *Extension idea* Students walk around the class and compare sentences to find the person whose opinions are most similar to their own.

⑤ 🎧 Point out that students do not lose marks if they make a mistake and then correct it. Also, they should be careful to understand and answer the question they have been asked.

> **Answers**
> 1 Sorry, could you repeat the question, please?
> 2 Yes – he said sorry and corrected himself   3 Sorry?

⑥ *As a warmer* Ask students to brainstorm different types of film, e.g. thrillers, romantic films, science fiction, horror films, westerns, detective films, war films, comedies, etc.

Writing Part 2 An article

① *As a warmer* Ask students to work in small groups and discuss which they prefer: seeing films in the cinema or on TV and why.

Answers

Suggested phrases to underline: college magazine; Where do you prefer to see films: in the cinema or at home on TV or DVD?; article

❷ **Extension idea** When you get feedback from the whole class, ask students to match the arguments with the counter-arguments.

❸

Answer The writer prefers the cinema.

❹

Answers
1 paragraph 3   2 paragraph 2   3 paragraph 1

❺ Point out that it's important for students to use linking words in their writing: it gives their writing structure and helps the reader to follow the argument.

Answers
1 Despite   2 Although   3 However

❻ Before they do this exercise, go through the notes in the Grammar reference section on page 160 (Linking words for contrast) with them.

Answers
2 Despite   3 However   4 despite   5 However
6 although

❼ Give students about ten minutes to do this.

❽ For more on writing articles, you can refer students to page 176 (Writing reference – Articles).

Sample answer

Dreams of fame?

Many young people want to be famous because they think this is an easy way to be successful. They believe that their lives will have an extra meaning and that they will be making a difference in the world. In addition to this, they will have rich and exciting lifestyles.

However, I think that these ambitions may be a distraction from studying seriously and working hard, especially as only a small number of highly talented people can really become famous in the end and these people have to live with a lot of disadvantages. For example, they are under a lot of pressure because they are always being watched. If they make a mistake, this immediately appears in the media. Despite being famous, many celebrities are not happy.

I would prefer to be successful in my profession and respected by the people I work with, but not so well-known. Although this means working hard to build a solid professional career, you can then benefit from a comfortable and interesting lifestyle without the disadvantages of being famous.

Unit 9 photocopiable activity: Were you really at the theatre?

Time: 30 mins

Objectives:

- To use vocabulary connected with entertainment, e.g. performance, scene, actor, play, etc.
- To use reported speech and past tenses

Before class

You will need to photocopy the activity page and cut it into two parts, so that each group has one of the two cards.

In class

❶ Divide the class into pairs or groups of three.

❷ Tell students to imagine the following scenario.
- Yesterday evening someone broke into the school or college where they study and a large amount of money was stolen.
- Half the groups in the class are suspected of the crime. They have to invent a story to prove that they are innocent.
- The other groups are detectives investigating the crime. They have to ask questions to each of the suspects in a group in turn to find out if their stories are the same. If their stories are the same, they're probably innocent. If their stories are different, they're guilty.
- The suspects' story is that they went to the theatre together last night.

❸ Hand the 'suspects' the part headed Suspects, and ask them (in pairs or groups of three) to invent the details of what they did and what they saw. Tell them not to write anything down. Give them four or five minutes to discuss their story.

❹ Tell the 'detectives' that they must ask questions to find out if the suspects' stories are the same. Hand them the part headed Detectives and ask them to think of questions using the prompts. Give them four or five minutes

❺ Suspects and detectives should work apart.

❻ When everyone is ready, ask each group of detectives to interview each person from a group of suspects in turn. Tell the detectives that they needn't just ask the questions they have thought of – they can invent other questions as well.

❼ When they have finished, they should decide if they think the suspects are guilty or innocent, and report their verdict to the whole class.

❽ When they decide and report their verdict, encourage them to use reported speech to do so.

Were you really at the theatre?

Suspects

You are going to be interviewed by detectives about a crime which happened yesterday evening. Your story is that you spent the evening together at the theatre.

❶ Invent details about the following things.

- Name of theatre and name of play
- Type of play and some of the plot (the story of the play)
- Leading actors – names and roles
- Which actor gave the best performance
- Number of people in the audience

- Where you met
- What you did before going to the theatre
- What you talked about in the interval
- What you did after going to the theatre
- What you and the others thought of the play

❷ Invent details about other things you think the detectives might ask.

❸ Take turns to be interviewed by the detectives.

Detectives

You are going to interview each suspect in the group in turn. If the suspects' stories are the same, they're probably innocent. If their stories are different, they might be guilty.

❶ Think of questions about each of the points below and other questions you can ask.

- Name of theatre and name of play
- Type of play and plot (the story of the play)
- Leading actors – names and roles
- Which actor gave the best performance and which actor gave the worst performance
- Number of people in the audience
- Who each of the suspects sat next to and which part of the theatre they sat in
- Who was sitting in front of them
- What they did before and after the play
- What they did and what they talked about during the interval
- The last scene of the play
- What the other suspects thought of the play

❷ Interview each of the suspects in turn.*

❸ Decide if the suspects are innocent or guilty.

❹ Report your decision to the rest of the class.

  * When you interview the suspects, you can ask extra questions, e.g. *X said that you were sitting in the front row, but you say were sitting in the middle. Who is telling the truth?*

Word list

Unit 9

Note: the numbers show which page the word or phrase first appears on in the unit.

abandon *v* (84) to stop doing an activity before you have finished it

be supposed to *v* (84) to have to; to have a duty or a responsibility to

brutal *adj* (83) not considering someone's feelings

by accident *adv* (83) without intending to, or without being intended

celebrity *n* (84) someone who is famous, especially in the entertainment business

chance of a lifetime *n* (81) an opportunity which only comes once in your life

cheering *n* (84) shouts of encouragement and approval

come down to *v* (83) If a situation or decision comes down to something, that is the thing that influences it most.

contract *n* (82) a legal document that states and explains a formal agreement between two different people or groups, or the agreement itself

delighted *adj* (84) very pleased

exhilarating *adj* (83) making you feel very excited and happy

fascinating *adj* (81) very interesting

further *adj* (84) extra; additional

get involved *v* (83) to do things and be part of an activity or event

invaluable *adj* (83) extremely useful

lifestyle *n* (84) someone's way of living; the things that a person or particular group of people usually do

live *adj* (83) (of a performance) broadcast, recorded or seen while it is happening

make sense *v* (82) to be a good thing to do

miss *v* (81) to not see or hear something or someone

outlet *n* (83) a way in which emotion or energy can be expressed or made use of

reject *v* (83) to refuse to accept someone for a job, course, etc.

show off *v* (83) to behave in a way which is intended to attract attention or admiration, and which other people often find annoying

steady *adj* (84) steady career/job, etc.; work that is likely to continue for a long time and that will pay you regular amounts of money

strip away *v* (83) to gradually reduce something important or something that has existed for a long time

superb *adj* (84) of excellent quality; very great

take time out *v* (83) to spend a period of time doing something that is not your normal job or course of study

taste *n* (83) a short experience of something

turn something down *v* (83) to refuse an offer or request

wealthy *adj* (84) rich; having a lot of money

well-known *adj* (82) famous

Unit 10 Secrets of the mind

Unit objectives
- **Reading Part 1:** finding and understanding the relevant section of text before looking at the alternatives
- **Writing Part 2:** writing a story, giving background information and a setting using a variety of tenses
- **Use of English Part 4:** identifying what grammar, vocabulary, etc. is required, revision of language from previous units
- **Listening Part 1:** linking key words on the recording with correct alternatives, listening for gist and global meaning
- **Speaking Part 3:** using a range of vocabulary and grammar, using modal verbs to speculate
- **Grammar:** modal verbs to express certainty and possibility in the present and past
- **Vocabulary:** confusion between *make, cause* and *have*; *stay, spend* and *pass*; adjectives describing personality

Starting off

❶ *As a warmer* With books closed, ask students in small groups to brainstorm things which make them happy or would make them happy. They then do the exercise.

> **Answers**
> 2 a 3 b 4 g 5 d 6 e 7 h 8 f 9 j 10 i

❷ *Alternative treatment* Ask students to choose the three most essential and the three least important.

❸ Other possible contributors to happiness: good health, personal freedom, a generally happy social environment, a happy disposition, etc.

> *Extension idea* Ask students to work in pairs and talk about the happiest time of their lives. When was it? Why were they so happy?

Reading Part 1

❶ Give students three minutes to do this. Tell them before they start that they should not try to understand every word, but to read quickly to get the general ideas which will answer the question.

> **Answers**
> The writer thinks happiness comes from: earning enough money to live comfortably; having a challenging job and/or pursuing an absorbing hobby; from concentrating hard on something

❷ Remind students how in Unit 7 in Reading Part 1 (on page 65) they read the question, then found the answer in the text and then looked at the four alternatives A–D. This activity also encourages them to follow this procedure: tell them to make sure they understand the underlined section before reading the alternatives.

> **Answers**
> 1 C 2 B 3 D

❸ Encourage students to follow the same technique as in Exercise 2, i.e. finding and understanding the relevant section of the text before looking at the alternatives, then underlining the words in the text which gave them the answer.

> **Answers**
> 4 D 5 A 6 A 7 B 8 A

❹ Encourage students to back up their ideas with examples from their personal experience.

Vocabulary
Stay, spend and *pass; make, cause* and *have*

❶ ⊙ Ask students to look at the example in question 1 and the dictionary extracts. Elicit why *have* is the correct answer. (*Answer:* have an effect / have an impact) Ask them to do the other questions in pairs.

> **Answers**
> 2 caused 3 spent 4 spent 5 stay

❷ Tell students to check when they use these words in their writing and speaking so as to avoid mistakes.

> **Answers**
> 2 pass 3 stay 4 have 5 spend 6 spent
> 7 causing 8 makes/made 9 have
> 10 make/made

> *Extension idea* Ask students to write their own example for each of the six words.

Listening Part 1

❶ To get students started, ask them to look at the first statement and elicit what other things we could base first opinions (or impressions) on, e.g. looks, facial expressions, clothes, body language, etc. Ask students to discuss how important each of them is. For all discussion points, ask students to give examples and talk from personal experience.

❷ You can point out to students that predicting possible vocabulary before they listen will improve their performance in this type of task.

❸ 🎧

Recording script   CD2 Track 2

Presenter: One. You hear an expert on a television programme giving advice about meeting people for the first time. What has the most impact?

A how you speak
B how you look
C what you say

Interviewer: In the studio tonight we have Dr Richard Bazey, a psychologist. Doctor Bazey, we all know just how important it is to make a good impression on someone we're meeting for the first time. What can we do to make sure the meeting goes really well?

Dr Bazey: Well, this is interesting. People generally think that it's words that count and they may spend quite a lot of time thinking about how they're going to start the conversation. However, that's

Q1   not the case at all; the fact is that <u>before we've even opened our mouths people have already decided what they think of us just from our appearance alone</u>. Then after that they don't listen to what we're saying so much as how we're saying it – you know, our intonation, the

tone of our voice. Only seven per cent of first impressions are based on the actual words we hear. So, dressing carefully is probably time well spent!

Presenter: Two. You hear a man and a woman talking about successful marriages. What does the man think is the most important factor in a successful marriage?

A similar personalities
B similar interests
C the same friends

Mandy: So, Rob, congratulations! Still happily married after 25 years! What's the secret?

Rob: No secret, really. A bit of give and take and consideration for each other. I mean even if we don't like all of each other's friends at least we put up with them and don't show it. We don't

Q2   take each other for granted, and <u>we have lots of things in common – I'd say that's vital – things we like doing together</u>. Not that we're too alike character-wise. I mean, I'm rather outgoing and dominating and I tend to go to extremes, while Liz is more sensitive and cautious. But that probably helps because I think we complement each other quite well.

❹ 🎧 Remind students to listen to the whole of each extract before they choose an answer. Sometimes the answer will depend on a global meaning.

Recording script   CD2 Track 3

Presenter: Three. You hear a radio programme in which a psychologist is talking about intelligence. What does she say is improving?

A our ability to do certain tests
B our intelligence
C our performance in exams

Psychologist: Psychology is quite a young science, which means psychologists aren't too sure how our minds are changing, or whether in fact we're becoming more intelligent. It's quite difficult to show that our intelligence is actually

Q3   increasing even if <u>we tend to get higher marks on intelligence tests than our fathers and grandfathers did</u>. This could be caused by the fact that we eat really well and have lots of educational opportunities. Surprising, perhaps, because school results don't really seem to be improving – in fact there have been quite a few complaints in the newspapers just recently about educational standards …

Presenter: Four. You overhear a student telling a friend about a project on what makes people happy. What does he say makes people happiest?

    A becoming rich
    B getting married
    C having children

Jess: Hi, Mike. How's your project going? Have you learnt anything interesting from it?

Mike: It's going pretty well actually – and I've come across one or two facts which will probably surprise you.

Jess: Really? Such as?

Mike: Well, for example, lottery winners are often no happier a year later than they were before they won …

Jess: So all that great excitement is really temporary then.

Mike: So it seems.

Jess: And what else have you come up with?

Mike: Well, you know how we're always hearing jokes and things with husbands and wives complaining about each other? Well, in fact it turns out that married people are generally a lot happier than before they got married.

Q4

Jess: Really?

Mike: Yes, and another thing …

Jess: What's that?

Mike: Well, you know how delighted everyone gets when they have kids?

Jess: Yes.

Mike: Well, it just doesn't seem to last. I found that generally people with children are no happier than people who haven't got any kids at all.

Jess: That's sad, isn't it?

Mike: It is.

Presenter: Five. You overhear a man talking about things which frighten people. What frightens him?

    A flying
    B heights
    C lifts

Man: Oh yeah, you know, I'll do anything to avoid them.

Woman: Including walking up seven or eight flights of stairs?

Man: **Q5** Oh, yes. Or more. I mean, however high the building is, I won't go in them. It does mean that I sometimes arrive at places a bit breathless, but then the exercise isn't a bad thing either.

Woman: Do you know how you got this phobia, this thing which frightens you so much?

Man: I think it must be because I got trapped in one when I was a child and there was a power cut. I can't have been alone in it for more than ten minutes, but it seemed like an hour. It may sound silly to you because I know they're really safe. It's quite irrational, but there you are. I suppose I should get treatment for it – hypnosis or something – but I really can't face that either.

Woman: Well, see you up there in about ten minutes then … breathless!

Presenter: Six. You hear a girl talking to a friend about her dreams. What does she dream?

    A She's flying.
    B She's falling.
    C She's running.

Friend: Do you have recurring dreams – you know, one of those dreams which repeats itself from time to time?

Girl: **Q6** Occasionally, yes, I'm with my mum or my brother and I suddenly take off and go floating above them and I always think, 'This is dangerous, you're going to fall, you're going to fall!' But I never do – and the scenery is fantastic – it's very exhilarating.

Friend: And do you think dreams have any meaning?

Girl: Well, I've heard that when you fall in your dreams it's because you may feel you've failed in some way, or you might just be afraid of failure. And the ones where you're running to get away from someone are because something or someone could be threatening you in your real life.

Friend: And what about flying dreams?

Girl: I don't know. Do you have any ideas about that?

Friend: You must have a secret ambition to become a pilot!

Presenter:	Seven. You overhear two students talking about a friend. Why do they think she is stressed?
	A She hasn't been sleeping well.
	B She's been working too hard.
	C She's been having problems with a relationship.
Rob:	Cathy's been behaving a bit strangely lately, hasn't she? I mean she's been very quiet and not talking much.
Ellie:	Yes, she looks pretty stressed out and I guess it's been giving her bad nights.
Rob:	She certainly looks as if she needs a bit more sleep. What's the problem, do you know? Is it to do with her exams or something?
Ellie:	Well, she had a maths exam last week, so she must have studied hard for it. But she's always been pretty hard-working, so she can't have got stressed by it. Anyway, she finds maths easy.
Rob: Q7	Lucky her! <u>I suppose she may have had a row with her boyfriend</u> – he can be a bit difficult sometimes, don't you think?
Ellie:	<u>Yeah, it must be something like that. Now you come to mention it, I haven't seen him around recently. Perhaps we'd better ask her about him.</u>
Rob:	And try and cheer her up.
Presenter:	Eight. You hear a man and a woman talking about the man's free-time activities. What do they show about his personality?
	A He's friendly and sociable.
	B He's shy and prefers being alone.
	C He's creative and adventurous.
Man:	I was reading an article in a newspaper the other day about how important it is to do sports and hobbies.
Woman:	Why's that?
Man:	Because they say so much about you; more, according to the writer, than what you've studied at university or what you've done in your job.
Woman:	Really?
Man:	Yes. For example, if you play a team sport, it shows that you're probably quite an outgoing sort of person, someone who likes to be with
Q8	other people. On the other hand <u>if, like me, you do something solitary, for instance reading or painting, it probably shows the opposite, you</u>

	<u>know, that you're not too comfortable with other people.</u>
Woman:	Or you're happy with your own company.
Man:	That's right. Then again, people who travel a lot are likely to enjoy taking risks and be quite inventive if you see what I mean.
Woman:	But <u>you're the stay-at-home type</u>.
Man:	Yes. <u>That's me</u>!

5 *Alternative treatment* Ask students to choose one of the two questions and prepare a short one-minute talk on it. Give them two or three minutes to think of ideas and make a few notes. They then take turns to give their talks in pairs or small groups.

This would be a suitable moment to do the photocopiable activity on page 91.

Grammar
Modal verbs to express certainty and possibility

1 You can ask students to look at the first extract and ask these questions.

- Does *must* here express an obligation – something it's necessary to do – or does it express something the speaker is certain about? (*Answer:* Something he's certain about)
- Does *can't* express something the speaker isn't able to do, or something he's sure is not true? (*Answer:* Something he's sure is not true)

Go through the notes in the Grammar reference section on page 161 (Modal verbs to express certainty and possibility) with the students.

Answers
1 2 can't 3, 4 and 5 may, might, could
2 The underlined verbs refer to the present.
---

2 *Alternative treatment* You can say clearly absurd things about the photograph and provoke students to correct you, e.g. She must be a politician, She may be about 60 years old, etc.

Possible answers
2 She can't be going shopping. 3 She might be French. 4 She could be famous. 5 She must be at the opening of a new film. 6 She may be about 30.
---

3 If your students all speak the same first language, discuss what are typical mistakes they make with modal verbs, e.g. following them all with infinitive + *to*.

Answers
2 ~~mustn't be tired~~ can't be tired 3 ~~can have~~ may/might/could have 4 correct 5 ~~can't~~ must
---

Point out that modals expressing certainty and possibility are all followed by *have* + past participle.

Answers
1 must have   2 can't have   3 may have

Extension idea Ask students to write their own example sentences for each modal verb here.

❺

Answers
2 must be   3 must have had/must have been having   4 may/might/could have had to, may/might/could have stopped   5 can't be   6 may/might/could rain   7 may/might/could have left   8 may/might/could go/be going

Use of English Part 4

❶ The grammar and vocabulary in this exercise come from items covered in Units 9 and 10. Tell students that the questions test different aspects of grammar and vocabulary: they must identify what is being tested.

To remind them of problems to avoid when doing this task, you can ask them these questions.

- How many words can you write in the space? (*Answer:* between two and five)
- Is it necessary to use the word given? (*Answer:* Yes)
- Can you change the word given, e.g. make it past or make it plural? (*Answer:* No)

Answers
2 had spoken to Maria the   3 reminded him to lock   4 did not feel well / was not feeling well   5 despite the loud music   6 can't have been   7 may have found   8 did you spend writing

Speaking Part 3

❶ *As a warmer*

- Ask students to work in pairs and say what free-time activities they most enjoy and why they chose them.
- Then ask them to look at the list of adjectives in Exercise 2 and say which three adjectives best describe them.
- Ask them to say if there is a connection between their choice of free-time activities and the adjectives which describe their personality.

Alternative treatment Ask students to look at the pictures, but not at the vocabulary list and ask them to suggest adjectives to describe the people's personalities. They then compare their adjectives with those in the book and do the exercise. If you do this, you will have to omit Exercise 2.

Suggested answers
painter: creative, hard-working, solitary, thoughtful   **climber**: adventurous, good at working with other people, well-organised   **referee**: responsible, good at working with other people, interested in other people, well-organised   **choir-singer**: creative, sociable, good at working with other people, friendly   **reader**: solitary, thoughtful   **visitor to old people's home**: caring, friendly, responsible, interested in other people, sociable, unselfish, thoughtful   **person chatting in café**: friendly, interested in other people, sociable, easy-going

❸ You can ask them to look at the list of adjectives in Unit 1 on page 10 in the Student's Book.

❹ 🎧 Elicit from students that they should discuss together and preferably deal with each picture in turn. Elicit also why it's important to use a range of vocabulary and grammar (to maximise their marks).

Answers
2 yes   3 no   4 yes   5 yes

Recording script   CD2 Track 4

Teacher: I want you to imagine that a social club for young people in your town is looking for someone to organise activities in the evenings and at weekends.

The pictures show some of the people who have applied for the job doing their favourite free-time activity. First, talk together about what sort of personality you think each of these people has. Then decide which two might be best for the job.

All right?

Irene: Well, I think the woman in this picture must be quite creative because she's painting a picture …

Miguel: Yes, but it's quite a solitary activity, so she can't be very sociable, although she may be more sociable when she's doing other things and probably quite hard-working. What about the person in this picture?

5 🎧 Tell students they will have three minutes to do this. When you monitor this activity, if you're not satisfied with their performance, give feedback, then ask students to change partners and do the activity again.

Writing Part 2 A story

1 Perhaps, to stimulate students, you could tell them about a happy day in your life. If you do so, try to begin the story with the words *I will always remember that day as one of the happiest days of my life.*

2 Give students five to ten minutes to do this. Point out to students that their story should be reasonably interesting, and if they can base it on personal experience rather than inventing the story, they will find it easier to do.

3 In the exam, American spellings are accepted as correct as long as the candidate uses American spellings consistently throughout the exam. Similarly, British spellings should be used consistently throughout.

> **Spelling errors**
> ~~marvelous~~ marvellous, ~~experence~~ experience, ~~The~~ They, ~~confortable~~ comfortable, ~~fell~~ felt, airplane (American spelling) aeroplane (British spelling), ~~trough~~ through, ~~waitting~~ waiting, ~~exiting~~ exciting, ~~especial~~ special

4 *Alternative treatment* Instead of going to page 155, elicit from students when to use the past perfect and past continuous tenses.

5 Tell students to make a few notes while they are thinking.

6 Give students a minute or two to prepare before they speak. Ask them to listen to their partner and ask a question at the end.

7 If you decide to give this task for homework, tell students that in the exam they would have about 40 minutes for it.

For more on writing stories, you can refer students to page 174 (Writing reference – Stories).

> **Sample answer**
> I will always remember my sixteenth birthday as something special and I still feel excited when I think how I met Leila again after so many years.
>
> My parents had arranged for us all to go to a restaurant for dinner to celebrate. At the next table there were two grown-ups and a beautiful girl with dark hair and wide brown eyes. My mother looked at them and immediately recognised them as friends of hers from years ago. Then I recognised Leila. She had been my best friend at primary school but when she was ten she and her family had moved to another town. Now they were back!
>
> My parents quickly suggested that we should all sit together at the same table and have dinner together. Leila and I sat next to each other and talked and talked. It was as if we had never been separated. She told me that they had come back to my town to live.
>
> It was a wonderful, surprising reunion and that one meeting made it a day I'll never forget.

Vocabulary and grammar review Unit 9

Vocabulary

1 1 C   2 B   3 A   4 C   5 A   6 D

2 2 despite / in spite of   3 While/Whereas
4 Despite / In spite of   5 However   6 while/whereas
7 although / even though   8 while/whereas

Grammar

3 2 the tickets were expensive   3 despite not feeling
4 even though her salary is   5 she had spent all/the afternoon   6 would call at/after the

Vocabulary and grammar review
Unit 10

Vocabulary

❶ **2** well-organised **3** adventurous **4** thoughtful
5 responsible **6** creative **7** easy-going **8** sociable

❷ **2** have **3** causes **4** pass **5** had **6** made
7 spent **8** caused

Grammar

❸ **2** can't have turned **3** may not have heard
4 could have left **5** might answer **6** might have
forgotten **7** can't have forgotten **8** might see

Unit 10 photocopiable activity:
Left brain – right brain Time: 40 mins

Objectives
- To talk about personality, behaviour, likes and dislikes
- To speak fluently

Before class

You will need one photocopy of the text here and the activity page for each student.

In class

❶ *As a warmer* Ask students if they know about left-brain and right-brain thinking. Elicit from them what they think are right-brain qualities and what are left-brain qualities.

❷ Ask them to read the text and decide which part of the brain they use more. They should discuss their answers in pairs.

❸ Give students the questionnaire and ask them to work through it discussing their answers in pairs. Encourage them to extend their answers where possible by giving reasons and examples. Tell them that if none of the alternative answers to a question suits them, they should write their own answer down but choose the answer on the page which is closest.

❹ When they have finished, ask students to add up their scores.

❺ As a whole-class activity, ask students these questions.
- How accurate or useful are psychological tests like these?
- Are you surprised by your result?
- Does / Did your school education develop your right brain or your left brain more? Why?
- Which type of thinking is more enjoyable?

❻ *Extension idea* Ask students to work in pairs and look at question 13. Ask them to note down other hobbies and interests they have and decide if they reflect right-brain or left-brain thinking.

Left brain – right brain

Read the text. Which do you think you use more: your left brain or your right brain?

The two halves of your brain – the right side and the left side – are responsible for different functions. The left hemisphere controls the right side of the body, as well as dealing with logic, lists and patterns. The right hemisphere deals with the left side of the body, plus your imagination, rhythm, emotions and appreciation of colour and music.

If you spot a spelling mistake in your work, for example, it's the 'right brain' that tells you it looks or 'feels' wrong. However, it will be your 'left brain' that actually tells you to pick up a dictionary to look for the correct version.

Most people have a preferred or dominant side. Some disciplines – for instance, sport, painting and acting – attract right-sided (and therefore more creative) thinkers. Accountants, chemists and engineers tend to be left-brain dominant, and therefore more analytical.

If you learn to use both sides, you will think more efficiently. The first step is to discover whether you are predominantly left- or right-brained.

Complete First Certificate by Guy Brook-Hart
© Cambridge University Press 2008 PHOTOCOPIABLE

Left brain – right brain

Work in pairs and do the questionnaire below to find out which your partner uses more: his/her left brain or right brain.

Tick (✓) the answer which is most true for your partner in questions 1–12. Then tick (✓) the answers to question 13 for your partner.

1 When you have a problem, do you:
   a go for a walk to think about solutions?
   b make a list of possible solutions and choose the best?
   c remember how you solved problems like this before, and do the same?
   d do nothing and wait to see if things get better?

2 Day-dreaming …
   a is a waste of time.
   b is amusing and relaxing.
   c helps to solve problems.
   d is a good way to plan the future.

3 How do you feel about your intuitions?
   a I have strong intuitions and I pay attention to them.
   b I have strong intuitions, but I don't take much notice of them.
   c I sometimes have intuitions, but I don't depend on them.

4 How do you plan your day?
   a I make a list of what I need to do and who I need to see.
   b I picture all the places I'll go to, the people I'll see, the things I'll do.
   c I don't plan it – it just happens.
   d I make a schedule and arrange a time for each activity.

5 Do you frequently change your furniture or the pictures in your room?
   a Yes
   b No

6 Do you learn athletics and dancing by:
   a imitating, getting the feel of the game or the music?
   b learning the theory and repeating the steps mentally?

7 In sports or public performances do you tend to do better when people are watching you?
   a Yes
   b No

8 When you want to remember things do you …
   a visualise the information?
   b write notes?
   c repeat it to yourself?
   d connect it with other information?

9 Do you remember faces easily?
   a Yes
   b No

10 When are you more comfortable?
   a When talking
   b When listening

11 How would you prefer to work?
   a Alone
   b In a group

12 Do you enjoy taking risks?
   a Yes
   b No

13 Which of the following do you most enjoy doing? Tick (✓) your ten favourites.

☐ swimming ☐ travelling ☐ acting ☐ walking
☐ tennis ☐ bicycling ☐ dancing ☐ running ☐ golf
☐ collecting ☐ camping/hiking ☐ sewing ☐ skiing
☐ writing ☐ reading ☐ fishing ☐ chess
☐ arts/crafts ☐ chatting ☐ singing ☐ card games
☐ cooking ☐ debating ☐ gardening ☐ photography
☐ playing a musical instrument ☐ doing nothing

SCORING *Now add up your partner's score for questions 1–12.*

1 a) 7 b) I c) 3 d) 9	**3** a) 9 b) 3 c) I	**5** a) 9 b) I	**7** a) 9 b) I	**9** a) 7 b) I	**11** a) I b) 9
2 a) I b) 5 c) 7 d) 9	**4** a) I b) 7 c) 9 d) 3	**6** a) 9 b) I	**8** a) 9 b) I c) 3 d) 5	**10** a) 3 b) 6	**12** a) I b) 9

Add up your partner's score for question 13. Then divide it by 10. Add the result to the score for questions 1–12.

13 • swimming 9 • travelling 5 • acting 5 • walking 8 • tennis 4 • bicycling 8 • dancing 7 • running 8 • golf 4 • collecting 1 • camping/hiking 7 • sewing 3 • skiing 7 • writing 2 • reading 3 • fishing 8 • chess 2 • arts/crafts 5 • chatting 4 • singing 3 • card games 2 • cooking 5 • debating 2 • gardening 5 • photography 3 • playing a musical instrument 4 • doing nothing 9

RESULT **More than 50:** You use your right brain more than your left brain   **Less than 50:** You use your left brain more than your right brain

Word list

Unit 10

Note: the numbers show which page the word or phrase first appears on in the unit.

appropriate *adj* (89) suitable or right for a particular situation or occasion

be to do with *v* (89) to be caused by or connected with something

devote something to something *v* (88) to use time, energy, etc. for a particular purpose

divide *v* (89) to (cause to) separate into parts or groups

earn *v* (89) to receive money as payment for work that you do

fascinated *adj* (88) very interested

feel like *v* (88) to want to do something

financial *adj* (88) relating to money or how money is managed

give out *v* (88) to make a sound

immeasurably *adv* (89) in an extreme way

impact *n* (90) a powerful effect that something, especially something new, has on a situation or person

income *n* (89) money that is earned from doing work or received from investments

intense *adj* (89) very strong

lead *v* (89) lead a busy/happy/normal, etc. life; to live in a particular way

match *v* (88) to choose someone or something that is suitable for a particular person, activity, or purpose

neighbourhood *n* (88) the area of a town that surrounds someone's home, or the people who live in this area

objective *n* (89) something which you plan to do or achieve

observation *n* (89) a remark about something that you have noticed

original *adj* (88) existing since the beginning, or being the earliest form of something

poverty *n* (89) the condition of being extremely poor

prove *v* (88) to show that something is true

reward *n* (88) something good that you get or experience because you have worked hard, behaved well, etc.

sample *n* (88) a small amount of something that shows you what the rest is or should be like

slightly *adv* (89) a little

start out *v* (88) to begin your work or a task in a particular way

turn out *v* (89) to be known or discovered finally and surprisingly

Unit 11 Spend, spend, spend!

Unit objectives

- **Reading Part 1:** including practice in skimming and exam technique
- **Writing Part 2:** writing a report on improvements to a school and a neighbourhood, making suggestions and recommendations, structure and format of a report
- **Use of English Part 2:** skimming the text, identifying the type of word needed
- **Listening Part 4:** listening for gist and detail, focusing on the stems of the questions
- **Speaking Part 2:** ways of comparing, expressing impressions using *look, seem* and *appear*
- **Grammar:** modal verbs and other phrases to express ability; *as* and *like*; language patterns following *look, seem* and *appear*
- **Vocabulary:** types of shop, phrasal verbs, words to do with money

Starting off

❶ *As a warmer* Before students open their books ask them to brainstorm a list of different types of shop and then choose their three favourites.

> **Answers**
> 2 fashion boutique   3 delicatessen
> 4 supermarket   5 market stall   6 bookshop

❷ *Extension idea* Ask students if they ever have to entertain foreign visitors. What sorts of shops do visitors to their countries most enjoy? What sorts of things do they buy to take home?

❸ *Alternative treatment* Ask students to walk around the class and ask questions to find people who have similar shopping tastes to themselves.

Listening Part 4

❶ *As a warmer* Ask students: Do you ever go to shopping centres? Which is your favourite? Why?

To get students started you can elicit some of the advantages and disadvantages listed below from the whole class.

> **Suggested answers**
> Advantages: many shops in one place, easy parking, places to relax, protected from the heat, cold rain, etc., safe   Disadvantages: crowded, noisy, may be expensive, may need a car to reach them

❷ 🎧 You can tell students to take notes while they listen and then compare their notes with their lists.

> **Answers**
> Advantages Will Payne mentions: access (underground station and motorway), good shops, good quality, caters for every taste including people who don't want to shop, family fun, safe and crime free, luxurious surroundings, reduce family conflicts

❸ Ask students to work in pairs and discuss what they think are the answers to each question.

❹ 🎧 Play the recording again for students to check their answers.

❸ & ❹

> **Answers**
> 1 B   2 C   3 B   4 A   5 A   6 B   7 C

Recording script   CD2 Track 6

Interviewer: Where would you expect to find a shopping centre? We used to think the most convenient place was in the city centre. Then they started building them among green fields where everyone could go by car and park easily. But a
Q1   new one, Redsands Park, <u>has taken over some abandoned industrial land on the edge of the city</u> and is pulling in eager shoppers from all over town. Will Payne, you're the chief architect of Redsands Park, why here?

Will Payne: Principally for the access. We could have put the shopping centre out in the country and we did give it serious consideration, but <u>the area</u>
Q2   <u>we've chosen has got its own underground station and it's also close to the motorway, so it's not hard to get here either by car or public transport</u>. What surprised us though were the protests from local people. We'd expected to be able to get permission easily because we'd be bringing jobs and business to the area. In fact, people worried that there'd be more traffic noise, fumes, more crime and that sort of thing, so getting permission took quite a long time. We were able to get it in the end though, as you can see.

Interviewer: Sure. And judging by the milling crowds of people, I can see the place is a great success. What's drawing them all in, do you think?

Will Payne: Well, surveys of our customers show that people aren't just coming to shop, they're coming to spend the day. Lots of the best stores have branches here, so it's not particularly cheap, but people know they can **Q3** get quality and there's something here for everyone. It caters for every taste including people who'd rather not shop at all but would prefer to see a film or go to the gym instead. Families can have fun in the same place without having to hang around with each other.

Interviewer: The interior really is astonishing. From where I'm standing I can see trees, plants and fountains in the malls. There are cafés, relaxing music and even a free fashion show in one of the halls. Where did the inspiration for all this come from, Will?

Will Payne: A visit to the United States. I went there a number of years ago and visited a couple of malls in San Francisco and Seattle. I was really taken by their appearance. Of course these places offer safe, crime-free shopping, but the **Q4** truth is they're a bit like palaces. People can spend the day there surrounded by expensive things without having to pay a penny. People treat you well and you only have to pay for what you buy.

Interviewer: So, Will, can you explain to me, why is the combination of shopping and other activities so successful?

Will Payne: Well, when we started planning Redsands, we discovered that around half of normal family shopping expeditions end with a family argument, and we wanted to avoid that. We want people to have a seriously good time.

Interviewer: Why is it that families argue so much when they're shopping?

Will Payne: Because they're spending the day together **Q5** and probably not all of them enjoy shopping, or at least they don't enjoy shopping for the same things. When they're at home they can each go off on their own and do what they really enjoy doing separately.

Interviewer: And how does Redsands cater for this?

Will Payne: By organising shops, cafés and other establishments into groups. This means that families can still be fairly close to each other even though they're doing different things. So **Q6** mum can wander into the clothes shop if that's what she wants to do, while dad can pop into the computer shop next door and the kids can go to a game shop or a music shop. They're all nearby and they can find each other easily. We've found this cuts down on a lot of family rows and makes Redsands a great day out for everyone.

Interviewer: And what of the future, Will?

Will Payne: Well, we're now looking at ways of making shopping less tiring. You know, a day at the shops wears people out and we considered a number of ideas. Carrying shopping around is very tiring and we looked at ways to avoid that. We thought of hiring out small electrically-driven cars to shoppers, but we came up against problems of space – there just isn't enough room. We also thought about those moving walkways like the ones you see at airports where people have to walk long distances. We decided against them however, because they'd involve a major redesign of the whole centre. What we've actually come up with is a new technology where you buy what you want and then just leave it in the shop. That way you don't need to carry your heavy shopping around with you all day. When **Q7** you want to go home, our computer system automatically sends everything you've bought to your exit point, and you pick it up there.

Interviewer: Remarkable. Will Payne, thank you.

Will Payne: My pleasure.

5 *Extension idea* Ask students to work alone and make a short shopping list of different things they'd like to buy (maximum five items). Then ask them to work in small groups and plan a shopping trip together in their own town. Tell them they should decide:

- how much time they need
- which shops to visit
- when and where to meet.

Vocabulary
Phrasal verbs

❶ *Alternative treatment* Ask students to guess approximate meanings from the context before doing the matching exercise in the book. In this case, you will have to play the recording again and pause it after each sentence containing one of the phrasal verbs.

> **Answers**
> 2 a   3 g   4 h   5 d   6 c   7 f   8 e   9 i   10 b

❷ *Extension idea* When they have completed the sentences, ask students to work in pairs and write five more sentences with blank spaces where the phrasal verbs should be. They then pass their sentences to another pair to answer.

> **Answers**
> 2 cut down on   3 pop into   4 caters for
> 5 hanging around   6 wore us out   7 pulling in
> 8 taken over   9 come up against   10 pick up

Grammar
Modals expressing ability

❶ The main confusion is with *could* and *was/were able to* in the affirmative. You may wish to highlight that:

- *could* expresses a general ability in the past; it does not say whether the thing was actually done or happened on a particular occasion
- *was/were able to* expresses the idea that someone actually did the thing on a particular occasion.

> **Answers**
> 2 c   3 a   4 b

❷ Before doing the exercise, go through the notes in the Grammar reference section on page 162 (Expressing ability) with the students.

When they have finished the exercise, ask them to write four of their own sentences using *can, could, was able to* and *could have*.

> **Answers**
> 2 couldn't sleep   3 could   4 Can you
> 5 could have been   6 were able to do

❸ ⊙ Elicit why *can't* is wrong in sentence 1. (*Answer:* The sentence talks about the past and therefore needs *could*. Note: *wasn't able to* is also correct.)

When going through the exercise with students, elicit why each sentence is wrong. Remind them that they should look out for mistakes with *can, could* and *be able to* when they do writing tasks.

> **Answers**
> 2 ~~could~~ was able to / ~~that I could~~ to be able to
> 3 ~~can~~ could   4 ~~could~~ can   5 ~~can~~ could   6 ~~could~~
> were able to   7 correct   8 ~~could~~ can

This would be a suitable moment to do the photocopiable activity on page 99.

Use of English Part 2

❶ *Alternative treatment* Ask students to work in pairs and predict the answers that another pair will give to the questions. They then work in groups of four and compare their predictions with the truth.

❷ When they finish, ask them to work in pairs and summarise their answers.

> **Answers**
> Women: take time to search for the right item at the right price, shopping is a leisure activity, they enjoy looking at things   Men: know what they want and go directly to buy it, they don't compare prices and they spend 10% more than women   Reasons: our origins as hunters and gatherers

❸ Remind students to decide what type of word they need for each space. Also, they should read their completed text to make sure it all makes sense.

> **Answers**
> 1 when   2 like   3 until   4 as   5 hand   6 what
> 7 it   8 result/consequence   9 on
> 10 according   11 not   12 that/which

❹ You can also ask them: What type of shopper are you?

Grammar
As and like

❶ *As* and *like* are often confused: in many languages they are translated by the same word. When students have answered the two questions, go through the notes in the Grammar reference section on page 162 (*As* and *like*) with them.

> **Answers**
> 1 a   2 b

❷ Ask students to find other examples of *as* in the text in Use of English Part 2 and to say what use of *as* from the Grammar reference section each has.

Remind students to pay special attention when writing or speaking to avoid mistakes with *as* and *like*.

Extension idea After students have done the exercise, they work in pairs and write five other similar sentences but leaving a gap for *as* or *like*. They then read their sentences to another pair who have to say whether *as* or *like* should go in the gaps.

Reading Part 1

❶ *As a warmer* Ask students:

- how much pocket money they received when they were 12 or 13
- what they spent it on
- if they had problems with their parents over pocket money.

This exercise pre-teaches vocabulary which will appear in the reading text.

❷ If your students are all the same nationality, they can discuss the first question talking about their own currency.

❸ Give students three minutes to do this. Tell them they should read quite quickly to get a general idea, but not pause over things they find difficult to understand.

❹ *Note:* **iTunes** is a website run by Apple where people can pay for music using their debit or credit card number and download it to their computer or iPod. **Virgin Mobile** is a mobile phone company. A mobile phone **top-up** is money you pay in advance to be able to use your mobile phone.

❺ *Extension idea* Ask students what they think of the attitudes and behaviour of the parents and teenagers mentioned in the article.

Speaking Part 2

❶ *As a warmer* Ask students to work in pairs and list feelings different members of their families have when they go shopping, e.g. happy, impatient, etc.

🎧 Elicit why *look*, *seem* and *appear* are useful language for talking about photos. (*Answer:* Because you can't *know*; you can only go on appearances)

Alternative treatment Before playing the recording, elicit from students how the people in the photos may be feeling. Remind them of modals to express certainty and possibility (see Unit 10).

Recording script CD2 Track 7

Teacher: In this part of the test, I'm going to give each of you two photographs.
I'd like you to talk about your photographs on your own for about a minute, and also to answer a short question about your partner's photographs.

Magda, it's your turn first. Here are your photographs. They show people shopping. I'd like you to compare the photographs, and say what you think the people are feeling.

Magda: Well, both photos show people shopping. In the first photo there are two girls, they're teenagers and they look as if they're shopping for music; I mean, they're buying CDs. They seem to be having a good time and they both look quite happy. In the other photo there's a couple, a man and a woman, who are looking, I mean, they're doing the shopping in a supermarket. In contrast with the young people, they don't appear to be so happy. The man looks rather tired and he's concentrating quite hard, looking for something. On the other hand the two girls seem quite relaxed and they look as if they're having fun.

Teacher: Thank you.

Magda: I imagine that the man and the woman are doing the shopping as a weekly chore, but not for pleasure, not for fun.

Teacher: Thank you. Peter, what sort of shopping do you like doing?

Peter: Oh, I quite enjoy shopping for clothes. I'm not too keen on going to supermarkets though and doing the routine shopping.

Teacher: Thank you.

2 🎧 Remind students that in Speaking Part 2 they will have to compare two photos. Tell them that these are useful phrases to introduce their comparisons. Point out that *whereas* joins two sentences; *in contrast* and *on the other hand* introduce new sentences.

You can write on the board: *The teenagers look as if they're enjoying themselves, whereas the husband and wife look bored. The teenagers look as if they're enjoying themselves. In contrast / On the other hand, the husband and wife look bored.*

Ask students to make other comparisons between the photos in these ways.

> **Answers**
> in contrast, on the other hand

3

> **Suggested answers**
> He looks quite tired. He seems to be searching for something. He doesn't appear to be enjoying himself.

4 *Alternative treatment* Ask students to work in pairs and prepare what they can say about one of the photos, including language previously presented. They then change partners and take turns to talk about their photos.

Writing Part 2 A report

1 *As a warmer* Say to your students: *Imagine this school was given a large sum of money (say 100,000 euros) by the government. How do you think this money should be spent?* Get suggestions and invite discussion.

> **Answers**
> *Suggested phrases to underline:* improving the classrooms, students' social activities, director of your college, report describing the benefits of both ideas, which one you think should be chosen and why

2 Elicit why it's important to identify the target reader, i.e. so you use the right style, content, etc.

> **Answers**
> 1 the director of your college   2 formal   3 benefits of both ideas, which should be chosen and why

3

> **Answers**
> 2 spent   3 make   4 contains   5 find   6 benefit
> 7 improve   8 participate   9 reduce   10 recommend

Extension idea Ask students: How important is it to be comfortable in class? Are there more important things? How important is a social programme for students? Why?

4

> **Answers**
> 1 The writer recommends new furniture and an air-conditioning system   2 He/She can look at the section headings and find what he/she needs
> 3 Yes   4 *The Introduction* states the purpose of the report, *The classrooms* talks about the need for improvements, *Social activities* about the effect of the money on these, *Recommendation* makes a recommendation for spending the money and gives a reason   5 The present tense to talk about the present situation and the conditional to talk about the effects if the money were spent in the ways suggested
> 6 No – it uses a formal style, as appropriate in a report

5

> **Answers**
> 2 spending   3 buy   4 to equip

6 Ask students to suggest ideas for spending money on the school or college before they write the sentences.

7 If your students don't live in the same neighbourhood, they can talk about the district where the school or college is situated. Get feedback from the whole class and write ideas on the board. Ask students to select which ideas they think are most suitable to include in the writing task.

8 If you give the task for homework, tell students that in the exam they would have 40 minutes for it.

For more on writing reports, you can refer students to page 173 (Writing reference – Reports).

> **Answers**
> *Suggested phrases to underline:* large amount of money available to spend on improving the neighbourhood where you live, town council, making recommendations

Sample answer

Improvements to the Palmar District

Introduction

The aim of this report is to suggest how the town council can spend the money which it has available for improving this district.

The streets

The Palmar District is an old part of the city with narrow streets and pavements. Because the pavements are so narrow, it is difficult for pedestrians to walk together or pass each other without stepping into the road, which can be dangerous. Also, many of the streets are badly lit at night, which means that it can be quite frightening to walk there.

The traffic

Unfortunately, the district has a lot of traffic, which makes it very noisy and polluted. Also there is very little space available for residents to park their cars.

Recommendations

It would be a good idea to make some of the main streets for pedestrians only, with wider pavements. I also suggest that the council should provide good street lights and build a car park for residents. Finally, I recommend that the council should build a ring road so that traffic does not have to enter the neighbourhood.

Unit 11 photocopiable activity: Redsands 2 Time 30–40 mins

Objectives

- To discuss and reach a decision about where to locate a shopping centre
- To justify decisions
- To write a report explaining decisions (optional)

Before class

You will need one photocopy of the activity page for each group. Cut out the cards labelled **For groups who choose Option …** on this page and keep them separate.

In class

❶ *As a warmer* Before giving students the activity page, ask them to work in pairs or small groups and brainstorm reasons why people welcome shopping centres in their areas (*Suggested answers:* lower prices, convenient shopping, more variety, more jobs) and reasons why people sometimes don't want a shopping centre to be built in the area (*Suggested answers:* increased traffic and traffic noise, possible damage to the environment).

❷ Tell students that they work for a company which is thinking of building a shopping centre near a town. Give them the activity page and ask them to discuss the advantages and disadvantages of each location (1–5) for the shopping centre. They should then decide which is most suitable.

Note: Though some options may be better than others, there is no correct option that students should choose.

❸ When each group reaches a decision, they should tell you what they have decided and you then give them the corresponding card from the ones labelled **For groups who choose Option …** on this page. Students then discuss the options with the extra information you have given them and:

- decide what they want to do
- suggest how to deal with any problems which might arise.

❹ Ask students to form new groups with one student from each of the old groups. They then take turns to report and justify their decisions.

❺ *Extension idea* Ask students to write a report explaining the different options and recommending what should be done. This writing task can be done for homework.

For Groups who choose Option 1: The town council won't give permission for the shopping centre unless you build a large underground car park as well (cost: €2 million).

For Groups who choose Option 2: The newspapers have heard about your plans to build a shopping centre here and are already protesting about the damage to the environment. The regional government will give you €2 million if you choose Option 3 instead.

For Groups who choose Option 3: The regional government has offered you €2 million to help you build a car park near this site. However, your market research shows that customers will not be happy to come here as the area is very ugly.

For Groups who choose Option 4: The regional government will only give you permission to build here if you build the access road round the edge of the woods. Extra cost: €1 million. The villagers of Warmley are organising protests against having a shopping centre near their village.

For Groups who choose Option 5: The regional government will help you by lending you the money you need to pay for the access road.

Complete First Certificate by Guy Brook-Hart © Cambridge University Press 2008 `PHOTOCOPIABLE`

Redsands 2

❶ Work in groups of three or four. You work for a large company called Redsands. Redsands has sent you to Newton in Ireland because the company wants to build a new shopping centre there. They are looking at five possible sites in or near the town. You have been asked to look at the five options and decide which one you think would be most suitable.

Look at the fact sheet and map below. Discuss and decide which option you think would be the best.

Fact sheet

Redsands has €10 million to spend on the new shopping centre. Building it will cost at least €5 million apart from the price of buying the land. It wants to attract customers not just from Newton but also from other towns in the area. It expects most of its customers to come by car.

Redsands has a 'green' policy and wants to do as much as possible to protect the environment.

Option 1: Situated in the city centre just near the station. Price of the land: €5 million. The centre of Newton has narrow streets and frequent traffic jams. The car parks are usually full. This option would be convenient for local people.

Option 2: Situated near the motorway in an area with beautiful scenery. Price of the land: €2.5 million. A car park could be provided by cutting down the woods to the north of the shopping centre. This option would be convenient for people coming down the motorway to the shopping centre.

Option 3: On the edge of Newton in an old industrial area with ugly factories which are no longer being used. Price of the land €3.5 million. Access to the area from the motorway is by road through the town centre.

Option 4: Situated next to the beautiful village of Warmley. Price of the land: €2.5 million. An access road would have to be built through the woods costing another €2 million.

Option 5: Situated in an area of farmland about 5 km southeast of Newton. Price of the land: €2 million, but access roads would be needed costing another €4 million.

---

❷ When you have decided, tell your teacher what you have decided and he/she will give you a card with extra information. Read the extra information and decide if you want to change your decision and what you want to do.

❸ When you have finished, change groups and report what you decided to your new group.

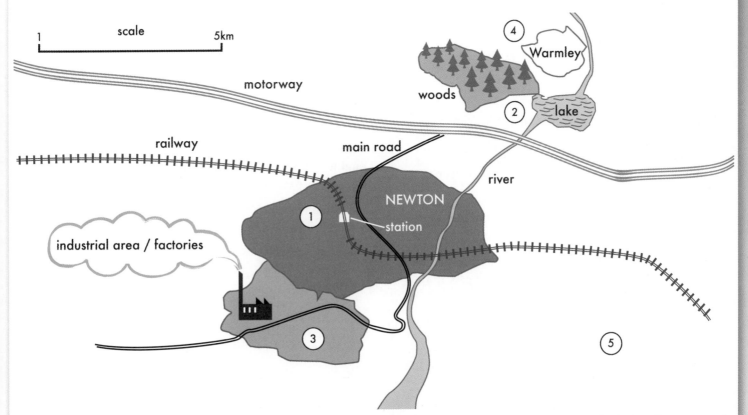

Word list

Unit 11

Note: the numbers show which page the word or phrase first appears on in the unit.

abuse *n* (102) rude and offensive words said to another person

accessory *n* (102) something added to a machine or to clothing, which has a useful or decorative purpose

brilliant *adj* (101)
1 very good
2 extremely clever or skilled

concern *n* (102) when you feel worried or nervous about something, or something that makes you feel worried

convenient *adj* (99) near or easy to get to or use

delivery *n* (99) when goods, letters, parcels, etc. are taken to people's houses or places of work

deny *v* (102) to not admit that you have knowledge, responsibility, feelings, etc.

ensure *v* (103) to make something certain to happen

get by *v* (102) to be able to live with difficulty, having just enough money

glance *v* (102) to give a quick, short look

grateful *adj* (100) showing or expressing thanks, especially to another person

harm *v* (99) to hurt someone or damage something

high-quality *adj* (99) very good and well made

hoover *v* (102) to clean a floor by using an electric machine which sucks up the dirt

hunter *n* (100) a person or an animal that hunts animals for food or for sport

interactive *adj* (105) describes a system or computer program which is designed to involve the user in the exchange of information

item *n* (102) something which is part of a list or group of things

permission *n* (99) If someone is given permission to do something, they are allowed to do it.

rate *v* (100) to judge the value or character of someone or something

regard *v* (100) to consider or have an opinion about something or someone

rental *n* (102) an arrangement to rent something, or the amount of money that you pay to rent something

replace *v* (105) to take the place of something, or to put something or someone in the place of something or someone else

reputation *n* (101) the opinion that people in general have about someone or something, or how much respect or admiration someone or something receives, based on past behaviour or character

reveal *v* (100) to make known or show something that is surprising or that was previously secret

security *n* (99) protection of a person, building, organisation or country against threats such as crime or attacks by foreign countries

slam *v* (102) to close violently and noisily

tackle *v* (102) to try to deal with something or someone

toiletries *n* (102) things such as soap, toothpaste, etc. that you use for keeping yourself clean

vehicle *n* (99) a machine usually with wheels and an engine, which is used for transporting people or goods on land, especially on roads

underwear *n* (102) clothes worn next to the skin, under other clothes

Unit 12 Staying healthy

Unit objectives

- **Reading Part 2:** focusing on information before and after the gaps, identifying and using cohesive features
- **Writing Part 2:** writing an essay, finding ideas, structuring the essay, including examples, using relative clauses
- **Use of English Part 3:** negative prefixes, spelling problems
- **Listening Part 3:** listening for global meaning and gist
- **Speaking Part 4:** thinking of a range of ideas to answer questions, giving extended answers
- **Grammar:** defining and non-defining relative clauses, relative pronouns
- **Vocabulary:** words connected with health, e.g. *treatment, infection, prescription* and *diagnose,* parts of the body

Starting off

❶ At this stage, don't check the answers with your students as this will be done when they listen to the speakers.

Alternative treatment With books closed, follow these steps.

- Ask students to work in groups and come up with a definition of what it means to be healthy. Ask them to write their ideas down.
- They then compare their different definitions with the rest of the class.
- They open their books and read the speech bubbles in the book to see which is closest to their definition.

❶ & **❷**

Answers
2 workout **3** infection **4** get over **5** check-up
6 treatment **7** illness **8** intake **9** putting on

Recording script CD2 Track 8

Speaker 1: I think I'm pretty healthy. I mean I have a lovely life. I've been retired now for nearly 20 years, no financial problems and here I am, in my 80s,
Q1 still quite <u>active</u> – I mean I go shopping, visit my friends and go to the cinema when I want to. What more can you ask for?

Speaker 2: I really do believe in a healthy mind in a healthy body, so I get up pretty early, about 6.30. I do
Q2 an hour's <u>workout</u> in the morning before going to college, and in the evening I usually have time for a couple of hours' sport, so I really think I'm very fit.

Speaker 3: Me healthy? I should think so. Of course, I
Q3 do get the occasional cold or other <u>infection</u>. You really can't avoid them in my job being a
Q4 doctor, but I <u>get over</u> them pretty quickly and they don't usually stop me going to work. I've never been stopped from doing anything I want to do because of an illness.

Speaker 4: I take my health pretty seriously. I think you have to. I go to the doctor regularly once a
Q5 year for a <u>check-up</u>. Once or twice I've needed
Q6 <u>treatment</u> for something she's found, but I think I can expect to live for quite a long time.

Speaker 5: I'm just a naturally happy, relaxed person and I think that's a large part of the secret of good health. I never go to the doctor and in fact I don't even know my doctor's name. I'm lucky,
Q7 I've never had a day's <u>illness</u> in my life.

Speaker 6: I'm healthy, but then I take care of myself. I'm very careful about what I eat – very little meat,
Q8 a high daily <u>intake</u> of fresh fruit and vegetables
Q9 – and I'm careful about not <u>putting on</u> weight, so I take a moderate amount of exercise as well. You know what they say: everything in moderation!

❸ *Extension idea* Ask students to work in small groups and:

- brainstorm a list of things people can do to stay healthy
- decide which three are the most important
- they then change groups and compare ideas.

Reading Part 2

❶ *As a warmer* Ask students: What things do students do at school which make teachers angry? You can give an example such as talking in class. Ask students to work in small groups and tell each other about a time they behaved badly at school.

When they have finished, ask them to open their books and discuss the causes of bad behaviour. If appropriate, ask them to discuss the causes of bad behaviour at the school where they study now or where they studied.

❷ *Alternative treatment* Ask students to predict what they think the article will say about how a healthy diet affects students' behaviour.

Tell students to read the article in three minutes to find the answers.

> **Answers**
> Students no longer misbehave, fight, drop litter, attack teachers; there's no longer any vandalism; instead of getting final marks 11% below the national average, their marks are 5% above

❸ Tell students this is an important step in doing Reading Part 2: if they read the text carefully, when they come to the missing sentences they should immediately recognise where some of them go.

❹ Remind students that there are also words and phrases in the main text which connect with the missing sentences. You can elicit some of these. For example:

- what phrase after gap 2 connects with something in the missing sentence? (*Answer:* As a result)
- what phrase before gap 4 connects with the missing sentence? (*Answer:* The first change – because this implies that there will be other changes)

Students can then look for other words and phrases in the text before looking at the sentences.

> **Answers**
> *Suggested phrases to underline:* **B** It is certainly true (that our eating habits have dramatically changed)   **C** exactly this relationship   **D** The next step was   **E** It soon became evident, in this school   **F** They, some of them   **G** Today he   **H** While he was there

❺

> **Answers**
> 1 F   2 H   3 G   4 D   5 A   6 B   7 C

❻ These questions should give rise to lively discussion. You can add extra questions if you like, such as these.

- Do you think good discipline is important in schools and education? Why (not)?
- Should students treat teachers with respect?
- How much do you think students' behaviour depends on their parents rather than their school and their teachers?
- Can you imagine a situation where there's a police officer patrolling the school in your country?

Vocabulary
Parts of the body

❶ *Extension idea* You can play the following game.

- Students stand up. Ask them to touch parts of their body, e.g. you say, 'Touch your hip!'
- Students who touch the wrong part of their body, or are the last to do so, must sit down.
- The winner is the last student left standing.
- You can make the body parts progressively more difficult.

> **Answers**
> 2 chin   3 neck   4 shoulder   5 back   6 chest   7 elbow   8 wrist   9 hip   10 thigh   11 knee   12 heel

❷ *Extension idea* Ask students to do this exercise with five internal parts of the body, e.g. heart, brain, etc.

Grammar
Relative pronouns and relative clauses

❶ In sentences 2 and 3 *that* would also be a correct answer. Tell students that it is a little less formal than *who* or *which*.

> **Answers**
> 2 who/that   3 which/that   4 whose   5 where

❷ Before doing this exercise, go through the notes in the Grammar reference section on page 163 (Relative pronouns and relative clauses) with your students. When doing the exercise, don't let students just rely on whether there are commas or no commas to decide whether the clauses are defining or non-defining. Ask them if it is essential information and, if so, why; if it is extra information, and if so why. For example, in sentence 1 unless we say *where I go for my holidays* we don't know which village is being talked about. In sentence 2, we already know who we are talking about because her name is given, so *who you met on the train* is extra information.

> **Answers**
> 2 non-defining   3 defining   4 defining   5 non-defining   6 defining

❸ Remind students of the rule *that* that can be used instead of *who* or *which* in defining relative clauses, but not in non-defining relative clauses.

> **Answers**
> 3, 4 and 6

❹

> **Answers**
> 3 and 4

Extension idea Ask students to write five sentences of their own as examples of different rules for relative clauses. They should refer to the Grammar reference section on page 163 (Relative pronouns and relative clauses) to do this.

❺ Tell students that it's important to avoid these mistakes when writing or speaking and that they should pay attention when checking their written work. Tell them also that using relative clauses correctly and appropriately in the Writing paper will gain them marks as it shows their range of grammar.

> **Answers**
> **2** Frank has a brother ~~his~~ *whose* wife is in hospital with a broken leg.   **3** She's a student of yoga, ~~that~~ *which* is done by thousands of people in this country.   **4** Can I read that essay which you wrote ~~it~~ last week?   **5** Mandy supports the football team which ~~it~~ won the league last year.   **6** I'm afraid I can't understand ~~that~~ *what* you are saying.
> **7** Aziz lives in a large house which ~~it~~ has a view of the sea.   **8** Gaby's friends, who you met ~~them~~ this morning, are going to the beach this afternoon if you want to come.

❻

> **Answers**
> **2** He studied hard for his maths exam, which he found quite easy.   **3** The man (who/that) they sold the car to is a taxi driver.   **4** Could you give me the newspaper (which/that) you were reading earlier?   **5** That white house over there is the house where he was born.   **6** Where's the envelope (which/that) I put the money in?   **7** Every morning I go running in the park with Patricia, whose brother you know.   **8** Karen and Teresa, whose dog we're looking after, are on holiday in the Caribbean at the moment.

This would be a suitable moment to do the photocopiable activity on page 108.

Listening Part 3

❶ ***As a warmer*** With books closed, tell students they will hear five people talking about visits they made to the doctor. Put them in small groups and ask them to brainstorm vocabulary connected with doctors and health that they might expect to hear when they listen. Then ask them to do the exercise in the book.

> **Answers**
> **2** f   **3** h   **4** a   **5** e   **6** d   **7** g   **8** b

❷

> **Answers**
> diagnose, infection, prescribe, examination, sick note, check-up

❸ ***Alternative treatment*** Ask students to take notes on each speaker with their books closed. Let them listen twice. Then ask them to open their books and answer the questions. If necessary, play the recording again.

> **Answers**
> **1** F   **2** D   **3** C   **4** A   **5** B

Recording script   CD2 Track 9

Speaker 1: Well, I arrived at the surgery at a quarter past eight for an appointment at eight-thirty but in fact I had to wait till nearly half past nine to see him. I felt pretty frustrated because there were only two other patients ahead of me. My problem wasn't too important – I had a sore throat – so I was only in there for five minutes. Anyway my doctor diagnosed that it was only a slight infection. I was expecting him to say that – I mean, I was pretty sure myself that it wasn't very serious. Anyway, he prescribed me some antibiotics, which was fine. But I did find having to wait so long was a bit annoying, especially as he only had to see me so briefly.

Speaker 2: I haven't been feeling very well for some time now and I've been to the doctor several times to find out what's wrong. Anyway, the last time I went my regular doctor was away on holiday and there was a new doctor there. What a difference! My usual doctor doesn't say very much though I suppose he does try to help. But this new doctor was so sympathetic. She asked me all sorts of questions about my medical history and my family background and she took lots of notes. She spent a really long time and sounded so interested that I left her feeling a lot better already. She couldn't diagnose my problem straightaway though, but she did send me off for tests, so I'm hoping we'll find a solution soon.

Speaker 3: I went along to see my doctor the other day because I wasn't feeling very well. I thought I'd got the flu and I needed to stay at home for a few days and not go to work. Anyway, I went to the doctor who gave me a very thorough examination. <u>She then told me I wasn't very ill and refused to give me a sick note. Frankly, I was amazed because I'd been coughing and sneezing all week and feeling quite ill.</u> Anyway, I couldn't change her mind so I had to go back to work the same morning, worst luck!

Speaker 4: <u>My doctor hardly looked at me when I went in.</u> She just asked me a few questions without looking up from her notes. <u>She didn't even examine me.</u> She then wrote me a prescription and said that if the symptoms continued, I should come back the following week. I told her I wanted a proper examination straightaway and I stayed there sitting in my chair. I must say she looked a bit surprised, but then she got up from her desk and came and gave me a good check-up. In the end she apologised and said she'd been on duty all night in the local hospital.

Speaker 5: I went to my doctor complaining of neck pains and I was there for what seemed like hours. She took a long time over it and gave me a very complete check-up. She looked at my neck, asked about my medical history and my daily routine. <u>Then she told me that the problem was probably caused by stress. She said that what I needed was a good rest</u> and my neck would heal itself. She suggested that I was probably suffering from overwork and that with a bit of time off the pain would disappear.

Use of English Part 3

❶ *As a warmer*

- Write *misuse* on the board and ask students to work in pairs and brainstorm other words beginning with the prefix *mis-*.
- If you want to make it a game, the winning pair is the one with the most correct words.
- Write the correct words they suggest on the board.
- Follow up by asking them to suggest the meaning of *mis-*.

> **Answers**
> 1 a   2 b   3 a   4 *mis-*: it means *to do something wrongly*

❷ Point out that these are isolated sentences, whereas in the exam there will be a paragraph with spaces to complete.

Draw students' attention to spelling, e.g. of *disappoint* – a common spelling mistake is **dissapoint** – and *misspell* – remind them that the base word is *spell* and by adding the prefix *mis-* the word then has a double 's'.

Remind students that in this part of the exam, words must be spelled correctly.

> **Answers**
> 2 disappoint   3 misuse   4 untie   5 misspell
> 6 disappeared   7 undress   8 misinformed

❸ *Extension idea* Ask students to write five sentences, each using one of these words in its negative form. They should leave the space for the word blank. They then pass their sentences to another student who should write the correct word in the space.

> **Answers**
> misunderstood   unsatisfied/dissatisfied
> disrespect   mispronounce   displeased   disobey
> unlikely   misinterpret   unhealthy   unhappy
> impossible   incapable   incorrect   unaware
> disappoint   disagree   incomplete   unable
> (*disable* is a verb)   impatient

❹ Point out that they do not just need negative forms in this exercise.

> **Answers**
> 1 announcement   2 stressful   3 security
> 4 occasionally   5 unexpected   6 height   7 flights
> 8 agreement   9 assistance   10 unnecessary

Speaking Part 4

❶ To get students started, for the first question suggest they answer by starting: *It's very important because* and then elicit ideas from the whole class. (*Suggested answers:* It's important because you feel better, keep slim, don't put on weight, it prevents diseases, you live longer, people behave better – see the text in Reading Part 2)

❷ 🎧

> **Answers**
> 1 e   2 f   3 b   4 c

❸ 🎧 You will probably need to play the recording twice for students to complete their notes.

Answers
Candidate 1: not important if health good, perhaps young people and people over 50 **Candidate 2:** more time to relax by taking more exercise, doing sport **Candidate 3:** exercise, right food, not smoke **Candidate 4:** in some lessons – social problems, smoking, what to eat – but not a formal programme

Recording script CD2 Track 10

Candidate 1: It depends on the circumstances. I think that if you feel your health is good generally, I don't think it's too important. Perhaps young children should go regularly and older people, say, over the age of 50, but I don't think it's really necessary for people my age.

Candidate 2: I'd like to have more time to relax. I think being relaxed and not stressed is important for health. And I think the best way to be more relaxed is by taking more exercise, perhaps by doing more sport. I think if I did that I'd have a healthier lifestyle.

Candidate 3: Well, I think it's important to take plenty of exercise and to eat the right food. I mean, you should eat plenty of vegetables and fruit. Also, you shouldn't smoke because all the doctors say that's bad for your health.

Candidate 4: I'm not sure. I think perhaps they do in some lessons, perhaps those lessons where students discuss social problems and how to deal with them, things like smoking and what to eat, but I don't think they do usually, I mean, as part of a formal programme.

❹ *Extension idea* Ask students while they are listening to their partners' answers to evaluate how well they are answering the questions and to think of suggestions they can give to improve their partners' performances.

Writing Part 2 An essay

❶ To help start the discussion, you can ask students: How does the environment affect our health? Do you think the environment we live in is better or worse than in the past?

❷ *Alternative treatment* Ask students to read the essay and say which things they agree or disagree with.

Answers
1 lots/plenty 2 what 3 which 4 able 5 they
6 it 7 more 8 at 9 there 10 so

Answers
1 paragraph 2 2 paragraph 1 3 to summarise the essential argument of the essay 4 For instance, we know that smoking is dangerous, which is something our grandparents didn't realise. For example, at work most people spend long hours sitting in front of computers, and in their free time they watch television or play computer games
5 Relative clauses: what is necessary for a healthy lifestyle, which is something our grandparents didn't realise, who live in rich countries, which allow them to take all the exercise they need (two relative clauses), which keep us fit

❺ Give students about five minutes to do this.

❻ *Alternative treatment* Ask students: Which of these statements would be true for you? Tell your partner.

Answers
Marina **B**   Saleem **F**   Claire **E**   Paul **C**   Vicky **A**

Recording script CD2 Track 11

Presenter: Marina

Marina: I know it's supposed to be bad for you, although I feel fine and I don't notice it affecting my health in any way. I mean it doesn't prevent me from doing lots of sports, so I'm not really interested in stopping. But I guess I'll have to around 30 when I start thinking about having a family of my own. But that's a long way off still, after all I'm only 17.

Presenter: Saleem

Saleem: My girlfriend was pretty keen for me to give it up. She went on and on at me about how my health would improve, even if, as she said, I wouldn't notice any changes straightaway. She insisted that in a month or so I'd feel much fitter. I haven't given up meat as a question of conscience. I mean I might start eating it again if I change my mind, but I reckon I'll give it six months.

Presenter: Claire

Claire:	I hate team games. All that 'Well done, Claire, nice shot' just irritates me. Besides, I've just got so much to do what with my university entrance exams and my part-time job at the hospital. I just think athletics and football and all that are such a bore and a total waste of time! Still, I enjoy a nice long walk in the country when I have the time.
Presenter:	Paul
Paul:	I like clubbing, discos, going out with my friends and coming home late at night. I also enjoy smoking, eating fast food, riding my motorbike really fast and generally having a good time. So whatever my mum and dad say, I want to carry on. I expect I'll think differently and start taking care of myself when I'm old and responsible, say when I'm 30, but I don't want to be responsible now. Life is far too good!
Presenter:	Vicky
Vicky:	I reckon I've been putting on weight since I left school, probably because at school we had compulsory sport three afternoons a week and now I'm at university I don't do that, so I guess I should join a sports club – there are plenty going here – and it would probably make me feel good too. So I'll probably do that next term.

8 If you give the task for homework, tell students that in the exam they would have 40 minutes for it.

⟶ For more on writing essays, you can refer students to page 177 (Writing reference – Essays).

Sample answer

Young people generally don't pay enough attention to their health and fitness

In my country there is a lot of discussion in the media about the health problems young people have as a result of eating fast food and not taking enough exercise.

There are a number of reasons given why young people are not so careful about their health and fitness. Firstly, computers and television mean people have increasingly sedentary lifestyles. Secondly, young people are so busy these days that they often do not have so much time for sports.

On the other hand, fewer people smoke than in the past, and I know a lot of young people who are very careful to have a balanced healthy diet. Also, a lot of young people have access to plenty of health information and know what they should do to have a healthy lifestyle.

On balance, therefore, I believe that young people generally pay plenty of attention to their health and fitness, although of course we could always pay more.

Vocabulary and grammar review Unit 11

Vocabulary

1 **Down:** 1 bargain 2 pocket money 5 saving 6 afford
Across: 3 credit card 4 get by 6 allowance 7 fare

Grammar

2 2 were able to / could 3 managed to / was able to 4 can/could 5 be able to 6 not been able to 7 was able to / managed to 8 could

3 2 as 3 as 4 as 5 like 6 as 7 as 8 Like 9 like 10 like

Vocabulary and grammar review
Unit 12

Vocabulary

1 2 heal 3 treatment 4 infection 5 put on
6 fit 7 prescription 8 cure 9 check-up
10 get over

Word formation

2 2 disobey 3 dissatisfied 4 incorrect
5 disappointing 6 unlikely 7 incapable
8 misbehave 9 undo 10 unable

Grammar

3 3 when/that 4 where 5 which/that/–
6 whose 7 which/that/– 8 who 9 where
10 why

4 2 ~~his~~ whose 3 correct 4 ~~anyone liked~~ anyone who
liked 5 ~~that~~ who 6 correct 7 ~~that~~ what
8 ~~her~~ whose

Unit 12 photocopiable activity: Are you sure it's correct?

Time: 30 mins

Objectives

- To focus on common mistakes made by First Certificate candidates with relative pronouns

Before class

You will need one photocopy of the activity page for each pair of students.

In class

1 Give each pair of students the activity page and go through the rules with them. Use the examples to clarify the rules.

2 Tell them first to concentrate on deciding if a sentence is correct or not, and if it is not correct, they should write the correct sentence in the second column.

3 When they are ready, ask them to place their bets in the third column, depending on how confident they feel about their answer.

4 When they have finished, elicit the correct answers from the class.

Answers

3 correct 4 I use the internet to talk to my friends **who** live in other countries. 5 I was late last night because I received a phone call from a friend **who** was in trouble. 6 correct 7 I like reading books with happy endings, not ones **which/that** end sadly. 8 I'd like to visit you in August, **which** is a perfect time for me. 9 I'm sorry to tell you that the only time **when** I'll be available is Wednesday morning. 10 I've got two sisters who are younger than me **and** they will meet you at the airport. I've got two sisters who are younger than me, **who** will meet you at the airport. 11 My brother, **who** is a museum guide, will take you to the best parts of the museum. 12 My home town has two excellent museums (**which/that**) you can visit. 13 correct 14 The reason (**why**) I'm writing to you is to invite you to my home town next summer. 15 We can stay in central London, **which** is perfect because we will be near all the best tourist sights. 16 We visited the village **where** I went on holidays / **which** I went **to** on holidays when I was a child. 17 You should have called the police because **what** happened last night was terrifying. 18 You'll be here at the time of our annual festival, **which** is held at the beginning of September.

Are you sure it's correct?

❶ ⊙ Work in pairs. Most of the sentences below contain a mistake often made by First Certificate candidates. However, some are correct. Decide what the mistake is in each sentence and write the correction in the second column. If you think a sentence is correct, write *correct*. Sometimes the mistake is a wrong word, sometimes there are one or two words missing.

❷ You have 100 points which you can bet on the answers

you have given in the second column. You must bet at least 1 point on each answer. You can bet a maximum of 15 points on an answer. If you are sure your answer is correct, bet 15 points. If you are not sure, bet between 1 and 14 points.

❸ If your answer is correct, you double the points. If your answer is wrong, you lose the points.

❹ The winners are the pair who win the most points.

		Correction	Your bet	Your total
1	Alan gave me a book to read during the journey what I found really entertaining.	*Alan gave me a book to read during the journey* <u>*which*</u> *I found really entertaining.*	–	–
2	Although I spend the week studying, I take plenty of exercise at weekends, which keeps me fit.	*Correct*	–	–
3	He works in a hospital where they carry out important medical research.			
4	I use the internet to talk to my friends that live in other countries.			
5	I was late last night because I received a phone call from a friend which was in trouble.			
6	I'd like to invite you to a restaurant I know whose speciality is fresh seafood.			
7	I like reading books with happy endings, not ones they end sadly.			
8	I'd like to visit you in August, that is a perfect time for me.			
9	I'm sorry to tell you that the only time in which I'll be available is Wednesday morning.			
10	I've got two sisters younger than me they will meet you at the airport.			
11	My brother, that is a museum guide, will take you to the best parts of the museum.			
12	My home town has two excellent museums where you can visit.			
13	The man the police arrested was wearing a long dark raincoat and carrying a gun.			
14	The reason which I'm writing to you is to invite you to my home town next summer.			
15	We can stay in central London, it is perfect because we will be near all the best tourist sights.			
16	We visited the village which I went on holidays when I was a child.			
17	You should have called the police because which happened last night was terrifying.			
18	You'll be here at the time of our annual festival, it is held at the beginning of September.			

Word list

Unit 12

Note: the numbers show which page the word or phrase first appears on in the unit.

arise *v* (111) to happen

at first glance *n* (107) when first looking

canned food *n* (107) food which is sold in cans (= closed metal containers)

change your mind *v* (107) to change your decision or opinion

check-up *n* (106) a general medical examination to see if you are healthy

counsellor *n* (107) someone who is trained to listen to people and give them advice about their problems

crew *n* (111) the people who work together on a ship, aircraft, or plane

discreetly *adv* (111) in a way that will not cause embarrassment or attract too much attention

dramatically *adv* (107) suddenly or obviously

drastic *adj* (107) (especially of actions) severe and sudden or having very noticeable effects

fasten *v* (110) to (cause something to) become firmly fixed together, or in position, or closed

get over *v* (106) to get better after an illness, or feel better after something or someone has made you unhappy

get rid of *v* (107) to remove or throw away something unwanted

in mid-air *n* (111) in the air or sky

instance *n* (107)
1 a particular situation, event or fact, especially an example of something that happens generally
2 **for instance** said before you give something as an example

intake *n* (106) the amount of a particular substance which is eaten or drunk during a particular time

IQ *n* (107) intelligence quotient: a measure of someone's intelligence found from special tests

on board *n* (111) on a boat, train or aircraft

patrol *v* (107) (especially of soldiers or the police) to go around an area or a building to see if there is any trouble or danger

profoundly *adv* (107) deeply or extremely

put on *v* (106) If people or animals put weight on, they become heavier.

queue *n* (111) to wait in a line of people, often to buy something

treatment *n* (106) the use of drugs, exercises, etc. to cure a person of an illness or injury

troublemaker *n* (108) someone who intentionally causes trouble

vandalism *n* (107) the crime of intentionally damaging property belonging to other people

workout *n* (106) when you do a series of exercises to make your body strong and healthy

Vocabulary

❶ Read each sentence and decide which word or phrase (A, B or C) best fits each gap.

0 I watch TV for entertainment, so good ....B........... help me escape from reality.

    A documentaries   **B** dramas   **C** the news

1 My neighbours are so proud of their garden that they've opened it to ....

    A spectators   **B** an audience   **C** the public

2 The .... that Robin Hughes gave in *Hamlet* was absolutely fantastic.

    A play   **B** acting   **C** performance

3 Children now .... more time on computers than watching TV.

    A spend   **B** pass   **C** stay

4 Many actors find it hard to .... on the money that they earn.

    A get over   **B** get along   **C** get by

5 The doctor recommended acupuncture as .... for the dancer's injury.

    A treatment   **B** prescription   **C** workout

6 During the shooting of the film, stuntman Gary Hart hurt himself by falling through a window. The cuts to his face took two weeks to ....

    A cure   **B** heal   **C** treat

7 Emma's extraordinary behaviour on stage .... a big effect on the audience.

    A made   **B** had   **C** caused

8 Kate is really .... in her private life, but when she's working on a film she's very organised and disciplined.

    A easy-going   **B** sociable   **C** unselfish

9 The director .... an original interpretation of *A Midsummer Night's Dream* that proved to be a great success with both critics and audiences.

    A came across   **B** came up against   **C** came up with

10 The star's attitude has .... a problem with the other actors on the film set.

    A had   **B** caused   **C** made

❷ Use the word given in CAPITALS at the end of each sentence to form a word that fits in the gap.

0 I don't understand why anyone wants to live there because it's such an ...*unattractive*... place.   ATTRACT

1 Jane and her boyfriend had a .... about money and haven't talked to each other for three days.   AGREE

2 The cost of living is high in the UK but clothes are surprisingly .... so I can afford to buy plenty of them.   EXPENSE

3 Adam's phone bill is still .... and it looks likely that the telephone company are going to cut him off.   PAY

4 There was a .... between my parents and I didn't get any pocket money last week.   UNDERSTAND

5 Jo waited .... in the queue at the bank. She needed to get back to the office before her boss realised she'd gone out.   PATIENT

❸ Match the beginning of each sentence with the most suitable ending.

0	You can't be tired	**a** their engagement.
1	You could have passed your exams	**b** if the car is repaired in time.
2	You might not agree with the decision	**c** if you'd worked harder.
3	You can't have played very well	**d** but that's what everyone else wants.
4	We might go away this weekend	**e** because you've just had a holiday.
5	You must be pleased about	**f** because the team lost.

0 ...e.... 1 .... 2 .... 3 .... 4 .... 5 ....

❹ Choose the correct alternative in *italics* to complete each of these sentences.

0 The jacket was expensive but I (was able to)/ *could* get a discount because there was a small mark on the sleeve.

1 Ian locked himself out of his flat yesterday but fortunately he *could / managed to* get in through an open window.

2 *Can / Could* you hear someone crying, or is it just the TV?

3 When I was about ten years old I *was able to / could* swim much better than nowadays.

4 When you've finished your training, you *can / will be able to* cook fantastic meals.

5 Look! I *am able to / can* see someone standing on top of that mountain.

❺ Complete the sentences below by writing one word in each gap.

0 My sister was ten years older than me so she was ......*like*........ a second mother to me.

1 .... the cold weather, we decided to go for a walk.

2 Did you .... till the end of the party or did you leave early?

3 Phil is going to .... over the job of shop manager from his current boss when she leaves.

4 Edinburgh is regarded .... one of the liveliest cities in the UK.

5 The town .... I live is next to the sea.

❻ Complete the second sentence so that it has the same meaning as the first.

0 'Someone has stolen my money, so I can't buy a ticket,' said Liz.
Liz explained ....*that someone had stolen her money, so she couldn't buy a ticket.*....

1 'Can you lend me some money, Mike?' asked John.
John asked Mike ....

2 'I'll go to the beach with you at the weekend,' Lena said to me.
Lena told me ....

3 'You'll have to work overtime this weekend,' my boss told me.
My boss told me ....

4 'What time does the film start?' Dan asked.
Dan wanted to know ....

5 'The coat's here and ready to be collected,' the shop told me.
The shop told me ....

❼ **Complete the email below by writing one word in each gap.**

Hi Roger,

I've got a new regime! I'm determined to (0) ....*get*........ fit. After work, I'm going to go straight to the gym. No more popping (1) .... the coffee shop which is (2) .... I would normally do. I've really got to cut (3) .... on the junk I eat and drink.

Anyway, a colleague at work told (4) .... about a gym near our office so I went there last night to have a look. (5) .... it was a bit expensive, I joined. It seems to cater (6) .... all sorts of people from kids to grannies. I've got the first session with my personal trainer this week! That sounds good, doesn't it? Her name's Debbie and she (7) .... be about the same age (8) .... me because I discovered we were both in the same class in primary school. She's (9) .... enthusiastic I'm sure it'll encourage me to work hard. So I'll be (10) .... on Friday after work! I'll let you know how it goes.

Love,

Mel

❽ **Complete this conversation. Write one word (*who, which*, etc.) in each space. In one sentence, no word is necessary.**

Maria: I finished studying, (0) ....*which*......... is great because it means I've got the whole weekend free to have fun. Let's go clubbing on Saturday night.

Sarah: OK. To Farrago's?

Maria: No, that place (1) .... they've got the brilliant DJ.

Sarah: You mean the DJ (2) .... tells jokes all the time?

Maria: Yeah. I think that's (3) .... I like about the place, because it has its disadvantages. Do you remember we met a girl there (4) .... boyfriend had just left her and she was really upset?

Sarah: How could I forget!

Maria: I thought we could invite my friend Dennis, (5) .... has got a car, to come with us – then we'd have transport as well.

Sarah: Good thinking!

Unit 13 Animal kingdom

Unit objectives

- **Reading Part 3:** studying the questions before reading, attention to tenses and time adverbs
- **Writing Part 2:** a letter of advice, ways of giving advice, dealing with content points
- **Use of English Part 1:** including revision of words often confused by First Certificate candidates covered in previous units
- **Listening Part 1:** identifying the main idea in the question, listening for the global meaning
- **Speaking Part 1:** including ways of adding reasons, extra information, opinions
- **Grammar:** third conditional, *wish*, *if only* and *hope*
- **Vocabulary:** confusion between *named* and *called*

Starting off

❶ *Alternative treatment* With books closed, ask students to brainstorm different roles that animals play in our lives and to give examples of animals which play these roles. Start them off by suggesting that animals provide food, e.g. chickens. When they have produced a number of ideas, ask them to open their books, but cover over the text. They should look at the photos and say which photo corresponds with which idea they suggested.

> **Answers**
> wild animals: **6**; working animals: **1, 2, 3, 4**; pets: **1, 2, 5**

❷

> **Answers**
> provide us with company: **2** and **5**;   entertain us: **1, 5, 6**;   provide us with food: **3** and perhaps **4**; participate in sport: **1**;   are used for transport: **4**; help us in other ways: **2**

❸ Elicit ideas for the first photo as an example.

Listening Part 1

Alternative treatment Ask students to work in pairs. With books closed ask them what they know about Listening Part 1. Then with books open, they do the Exam round-up exercise.

❶

> **Answers**
> **1** eight   **2** different subjects   **3** twice   **4** read and hear

❷

> **Answers**
> **1** C   **2** B   **3** C   **4** C   **5** B   **6** B   **7** A   **8** A

Extension idea After doing the listening task, ask students: Do you think children should have a pet to look after? Why (not)? Should people who live in cities keep pets? Why (not)?

Recording script   CD2 Track 12

Presenter:	One. You overhear a woman talking about different animals. Which animal would she let her family have?
	A a cat
	B a dog
	C a horse
1st woman:	Aren't you a good boy? Good boy! Lovely dog.
2nd woman:	Yes, isn't he?
1st woman:	Very well behaved. What's he called?
2nd woman:	He's called Bandy. Good boy!
1st woman:	Good boy, Bandy! My husband is always saying he wishes he had a dog to go for walks with. He says it would keep burglars away as well, as we live in the country.
2nd woman:	So do you think you'll get one?
1st woman:	I don't know. It's a bit of a commitment. I mean, you've got to feed them and take them with you when you go on holiday, that sort of thing. Then my daughter, Patsy, would like a horse. She says we could keep it in the field behind us.
2nd woman:	But that's a commitment too.
1st woman:	I know, which is why I hesitate, but it would give Patsy something to do, an interest, you know, and get her out in the fresh air …
2nd woman:	What about a cat?
1st woman: **Q1**	They don't do anything for me really. I think if <u>we had an animal, I'd go for the horse</u>, but I'm not wildly enthusiastic, quite honestly. You've got to think of the expense, as well.
2nd woman:	Yes, I can see that.

Presenter:	Two. You hear part of a television programme about zebras. What does the presenter say about their appearance?
	A All members of a family of zebras have the same stripes.
	B Zebras can recognise each other by their stripes.
	C Male and female zebras have similar stripes.
Man:	Of course, seen as a vast herd, every zebra looks alike. During their migration, all the stripes moving in the bright African sun form a confusing pattern which helps to protect the zebras from lions and other predators. But while they look exactly the same to you and me, each individual zebra in fact has a unique pattern of stripes and these different stripes help other members of their family to know who they are. Not only that, male zebras have wider, darker, more shiny stripes than their females, although at a distance and in a mass they may all look the same. It's also worth remembering that different species of zebra have different types of stripe.

(Q2 appears beside the Man's paragraph.)

Presenter:	Three. You overhear a woman talking about the birds which come to her garden. How does she feel about them?
	A She enjoys watching them.
	B She finds them annoying.
	C She worries about them.
Man:	Lovely here in the park, isn't it?
Woman:	Yes. Do you know what I saw in the garden this morning?
Man:	What?
Woman:	A flock of long-tailed tits. They came to the plum tree and seemed to be eating insects off the tree, greenfly probably.
Man:	That's good.
Woman:	Yes. We get quite a variety of birds at this time of year. I always hope the cats don't get them. There are an awful lot of cats in our neighbourhood and I hate the idea of them catching birds.

(Q3 appears beside the Woman's paragraph.)

Man:	Yes.
Presenter:	Four. You overhear part of a conversation in which two men are talking about dogs. What do they say about them?
	A They are good company.
	B They are good at protecting property.
	C They shouldn't live in cities.

1st man:	Have you still got your dog?
2nd man:	Yes, yes, but he's a bit of a nuisance frankly.
1st man:	Really, why's that?
2nd man:	He's just pretty useless, quite honestly. You think your dog is going to warn you about burglars, but mine only seems to bark when there are other dogs around. I suppose people imagine they'll be safer with a dog in the house, but I doubt if they really are. Mine just barks all night, which annoys the neighbours.
1st man:	And keeps you awake I suppose.
2nd man:	That's right. I certainly don't enjoy having him in the house. I think I'd be happier having a dog if I lived in the country where I could take it for long walks, but living here in the city centre it's just not very practical.

(Q4 appears beside the 2nd man's paragraph.)

1st man:	Yes, I know what you mean. I think it's a mistake to have them here too, especially big ones like yours.
Presenter:	Five. You hear a woman giving part of a lecture about animal rights. What does she say about zoos?
	A They are no longer necessary in modern times.
	B They should be closely supervised.
	C They should only be for endangered species.
Woman:	It would I think be ignorant to suggest that zoos no longer serve a useful purpose. The fact is that many of them do quite valuable work conserving rare species. What I do think, and I'm sure you'd agree with me here, is that those old-fashioned zoos which were designed and built in the nineteenth-century just don't give animals enough space. There's no feeling that animals are in a natural habitat. Those zoos should all be closed and banned, while the more modern zoos need to be strictly inspected to make sure that the animals are kept in the best conditions possible.

(Q5 appears beside the Woman's paragraph.)

Presenter:	Six. You hear a young woman talking about some animals she worked with. How did she feel when she was with them?
	A frightened
	B relaxed
	C strange

Girl:	Last summer, you see, I went to help on a wildlife conservation project in Africa and I was asked to look after these young lions which had lost their mother. It's curious, because I'd expected to feel quite nervous – I mean, they're dangerous animals, aren't they? In fact, after I'd spent a few days feeding them and playing with them <u>we had a very easy, comfortable relationship</u>. I had to be a bit careful, because they could be quite rough when playing with each other, but I never felt they were going to attack me. You wouldn't expect that with young lions, would you?
Q6	
Presenter:	Seven. You hear part of a radio programme in which a man talks about how he was attacked by a hippopotamus. What does he say about hippos? A They are one of the most dangerous animals in Africa. B They often attack people for no reason. C They're usually very timid animals.
Man:	You'd think that hippos are quite easy to run away from with their big barrel-like bodies and shortish legs, but they can move surprisingly fast. I was on holiday in South Africa and walking along a river bank when suddenly there was a crashing noise in the grass beside me and a hippo rushed at me. Fortunately, I was able to leap to one side and run. If I hadn't reacted quickly, the hippo would have killed me, for sure! Later, at the hotel, I was told how they get nervous if someone walks between them and the river, which is their natural habitat. <u>Apparently more people are killed by hippos in Africa every year than by any other animal</u>. And for that reason: they get between them and the water.
Q7	
Presenter:	Eight. You hear a woman talking to her husband. Why is she talking to him? A to make a suggestion B to make a complaint C to remind him of something
Woman:	Brian ...
Man:	Yes?
Woman:	You remember you were asking me what we should do with the children over the holidays?
Man:	Yes?

Woman: *Q8*	Well, I've been looking in the paper and it's given me an idea. <u>Why don't we take them to the circus? That's something we haven't done for a few years and there's one coming to this area next week</u>.
Man:	Well, it's an idea. Do you think they'll enjoy it? I mean the last time we went to a circus a couple of years ago, it wasn't exactly fun, was it?
Woman:	I think that's because they had all those acts with tired-looking animals and things, you remember. I think if they'd had more acrobats, we'd have enjoyed the circus more. Anyway, this one's different. It might be much better.
Man:	OK, well let's ask the children if they'd be interested in going. What's the circus called by the way?
Woman:	Let's see … here it is. It's called Giffords Circus.
Man:	Oh yes, I've read about them. Apparently they're pretty good according to what I read.

Vocabulary
Named and *called*

❶ ⦿ If necessary, play extract 8 again. Tell students that they should take care to correct mistakes with these words when speaking or writing.

> **Answers**
> called, called

❷
> **Answers**
> 1 both *call* and *name*   2 *call*   3 *call*

❸ ⦿
> **Answers**
> 2 ~~named~~ called   3 correct   4 ~~named~~ called

Extension idea Ask students to follow up by writing their own examples for *call* and *name*.

Grammar
Third conditional

❶ If students are unfamiliar with the third conditional, you need to use these questions and the questions in Exercise 2 to focus on the form (*If* + past perfect, *would have* + past participle) and the meaning (refers to the past, talks about something which did not occur).

❷ When students have done this exercise, go through the notes in the Grammar reference section on page 163 (Third conditional) with them.

> **Answers**
> 1 b   2 a   3 b   4 a   5 b   6 a   7 a

❸ This exercise concentrates on the form of third conditionals, but if you wish to reinforce the concept you can ask questions such as, for question 1: Did Martin concentrate on his work? With what consequence? For question 2: Did I have a pet dog as a child? Why not? etc.

> **Answers**
> 2 would have had   3 would have bitten   4 had been   5 hadn't been   6 had paid / had been paying   7 wouldn't have made   8 wouldn't have heard

❹ *Extension idea* Tell students to work in pairs and write three more similar questions. They then change partners and take turns to ask their questions and answer their partner's questions. If you do this activity, you will need to monitor carefully that they have the correct form of the questions, i.e. *What would you have done if* + past perfect.

This would be a suitable moment to do the photocopiable activity on page 119.

Reading Part 3

❶ *As a warmer* With books closed, ask students to make a list of the five most dangerous animals to humans. They then open their books to do the task.

> **Answers**
> Photos: elephant, shark, scorpion, polar bear, pelican   *Most dangerous:* any of the first four
> *Least dangerous:* pelican

❷ Students will have to read the questions carefully, concentrating on tenses and time adverbials.

> **Answers**
> 1 b / c   2 b   3 a / b / c   4 c   5 b   6 a / b / c
> 7 b   8 c   9 b / c   10 a / b   11 a   12 b
> 13 b   14 b   15 c

❸ *Alternative treatment*

- Ask students to work in pairs and read one of the extracts only.

- They then match the questions which correspond to that extract and make sure that they both understand the extract.
- Ask them to form groups of five with students who have read other extracts.
- Students then take turns to tell the story of their extract and explain which questions correspond with their extract and why.
- If their answers overlap in any cases, they can then discuss and solve the questions together.

> **Answers**
> 1 C   2 E   3 D   4 B   5 A   6 A   7 C   8 C   9 E
> 10 D   11 E   12 A   13 B   14 B   15 C

❹ Ask students to say which incident was the most dangerous, most frightening, least dangerous, etc.

Alternative treatment

- Ask students to write a short paragraph describing a dangerous situation they have been in. The situation can be real or fictional.
- Students then work in groups of four or five. Ask them to read (and if necessary correct) each other's stories.
- Ask them to write two questions for each story on a separate piece of paper and in random order (like the questions before the reading texts).
- They then pass their questions to the rest of the class (you may have to photocopy them so that everyone has a copy).
- They then read their stories aloud to the class and students from other groups have to say which questions match the stories.
- As a follow-up, they can discuss which story was the most frightening, incredible, etc.

Use of English Part 1

❶ *As a warmer* Ask students what animals they would expect to see in circuses. What do the animals do? Do they enjoy seeing animals in circuses?

❷

> **Answers**
> 1 12   2 15   3 the text quickly   4 after   5 the alternatives   6 you have finished   7 all the questions

❸

> **Answer**   horses

❹ *As a warmer* Ask students to look at question 0 and say why C is the correct answer. Elicit that for A we say 'The circus *belongs to* them', and B and D have the wrong meanings.

Note: Although *own* in the example (0) and *own* in question 5 are different parts of speech, in the actual exam it is unlikely that the same word would be tested twice in the same task.

5 *Alternative treatment* Tell students they will debate these questions. Divide the class into two groups and ask one group to brainstorm reasons why using or keeping animals in circuses and zoos is cruel. Ask the other group to brainstorm reasons why it's OK. Then divide them into groups of approximately six (with three for and three against) to debate the question.

Grammar
Wish, if only and *hope*

1 Point out that *if only* is an emphatic way of saying *I wish* but that its grammar is the same.

Answers
1 a, b and d 2 a and d 3 b 4 past tense and *would* + infinitive 5 c 6 past perfect 7 e and f
8 present simple

2 Before doing this exercise, go through the notes in the Grammar reference section on page 164 (*Wish, if only* and *hope*) with your students. When they do the exercise, remind them to correct their own mistakes with *wish* and *hope* when speaking or writing.

Answers
2 ~~wish~~ hope 3 correct 4 ~~wish~~ hope 5 correct
6 ~~wish~~ hope 7 correct 8 ~~wish~~ hope

Extension idea Ask students to write five sentences which are true for themselves using *wish, if only* and *hope*. Encourage them to use different tenses to show they know how to use the patterns. They should then work in small groups and read out their sentences to their group.

3 Ask students to look at the example in sentence 1 and say what the difference is between cook in the question and the answer (in the question it's a verb, in the answer it's a noun) and why the past tense is correct here (the speaker wants the present situation to be different).

Elicit the answer to the second question by asking: does it refer to the present or the past? What tense do we use with *if only* when talking about the past? Then let them work on the other questions in pairs.

Answers
2 I had studied harder 3 would make less / would not make so much 4 hadn't cancelled 5 wish you had met

Speaking Part 1

1 *As a warmer* Elicit from students what happens in Speaking Part 1. Then ask them to do the Exam round-up.

Answers
1 yourself, your life and your interests
2 answer giving reasons and examples if possible
3 about three minutes

2 Encourage students to give answers of two or three sentences.

3 You can make the point of this exercise explicit by saying that the candidates are going a little beyond the basic question and are offering extra information or opinions. This actually helps the examiner, who can concentrate on assessing the candidate's level of English.

Suggested answers
Student 1 a, b   Student 2 b, c   Student 3 a, c

Recording script   CD2 Track 13

Teacher:	Do you have any pets or animals at home?
Student 1:	No, but my aunt has a white cat and I wish I had one too, but my mother is not too keen on animals.
Teacher:	Do you enjoy visiting zoos?
Student 2:	Yes, occasionally. We have a very large modern zoo in my city where I go about once a year when we have visitors. I don't like those small old zoos with animals in cages.
Teacher:	Do you enjoy watching programmes about animals on television?
Student 3:	Yes, I find it relaxing and also it educates you about wildlife, so I think we become more careful about protecting the environment.

4 Tell students these are typical Part 1 questions. Encourage them to give each other feedback on how well they answered the questions and how they could improve their answers.

Writing Part 2 A letter

❶ *Note:* Candidates can answer a question about one of the two set texts in question 5. These set texts are optional. The writing tasks will be the same as the ones listed in the answer to question 3 below. Information about the set texts in any given year can be obtained from http://www.cambridgeesol.org/exams/settexts.htm. If your students have not read one of the set texts, they will have a choice of three tasks, not four.

> **Answers**
> **1** four   **2** 120–180 words   **3** a letter, a review, a report, a story, an essay or an article   **4** about 40 minutes for this part

❷ *As a warmer* Ask students to discuss: if you were visiting Britain for the first time, what advice would you ask for from a British friend before going? You can suggest areas such as accommodation, driving on the left, food, etc.

When students look at the task in the book, point out the difference in spelling between *advice* and *advise* (*advise* – verb; *advice* – noun).

> **Answers**
> **1** where to go, what to see and the best way of getting around to see countryside, scenery and wildlife   **2** *Students' own answers*   **3** informal style – it's a letter to a friend – she has written to you in an informal style

❸

> **Answers**
> **1** I'm very glad to hear that you're thinking of visiting my country this summer   **2** yes – advice about visiting Asturias, what to see while there, and hiring a car   **3** yes – he adds information   **4** quite informal

❹

> **Answers**
> **1** I'd advise you to go to Asturias   **2** You should visit the 'Picos de Europa'   **3** If I were you, I'd hire a car to get around   **4** The best idea would be to hire it online   **5** Make sure that you take warm clothes and a raincoat

❺ *Alternative treatment* As a light-hearted activity, ask students to think of 'wrong' advice which they could give foreign visitors which might get them into trouble, e.g. 'Public buildings are kept very clean, so make sure you always take your shoes off before entering them.'

❻ If you decide to give this task for homework, tell students that in the exam they would have about 40 minutes for it.

→ For more on writing letters, you can refer students to page 172 (Writing reference – Letters).

Sample answer: See the model letter in Exercise 3.

Unit 13 photocopiable activity: Third conditional pelmanism

Time: 20 mins

> **Objectives**
> To form third conditional sentences when speaking

Before class

You will need to photocopy the activity page and cut up the cards so that you have one set for each group of three or four students.

In class

❶ Hand one set of cards to each group and ask them to mix the cards and then spread them out face down on the table.

❷ Tell students they will have to take turns to pick up two cards. When they pick up the cards they should try to make a sentence using a third conditional.

❸ Write these two sentences on the board: *I put my wallet in the back pocket of my trousers. I lost my money and my identity card.* Elicit a sentence using the third conditional and write it on the board: *If I hadn't put my wallet in the back pocket of my trousers, I wouldn't have lost my money and my identity card.*

❹ Tell students that they have to find two cards which go logically together and then make a third conditional sentence using the ideas on the two cards. If they can do this, they keep the cards.

❺ If they can't make a logical third conditional sentence, they must place the cards face down where they found them. In case students can't agree if a sentence is logical or accurate, you will have to act as referee.

❻ Give students 15 minutes to play the game.

❼ The winner in each group is the student who has the most cards at the end of the 15 minutes.

❽ If you or your students wish, they can change groups and play the game again.

Third conditional pelmanism

I put my wallet in the back pocket of my trousers.	I lost my money and my identity card.
I was late for class today.	All my friends were envious of me.
I didn't do any homework last week.	I bought a new car.
I went swimming with a friend.	I caught a cold.
I went to a party.	I failed an exam.
I missed the bus.	I fell in love.
I felt really tired.	I had a slight accident.
I found a lot of money lying on the ground.	I had a two-week holiday in London.
I didn't feel like walking to class.	I invited all my friends to a party at my house.
I needed some exercise.	I met a famous pop star.
I felt really stressed.	I met someone really interesting.
I cleaned the house from top to bottom.	I put on some really old clothes.
My family went on holiday without me.	I relaxed with my favourite DVD.
I went to stay with an English friend.	I spent all afternoon walking round town.
I was in a hurry.	I spent the summer travelling.
I was trapped in a lift.	I spoke English all day.
I met some tourists who were lost.	I stayed at home all weekend.
I won first prize in a competition.	I stayed in bed till lunchtime.
I appeared on television.	I took a taxi.
My parents gave me a lot of money.	I was rescued by firemen.
I got a really good job this summer.	I went for a meal in an expensive restaurant.
I went dancing.	I went running.
I went to a concert.	My friends went to the cinema without me.
The weather was bad.	The teacher got angry with me.

Word list

Unit 13

Note: the numbers show which page the word or phrase first appears on in the unit.

ashore *adv* (119) towards or onto land from an area of water

backpack *n* (119) a bag that you carry on your back

bark *v* (118) (of a dog) to make a loud rough noise

charge *v* (119) to move forward quickly and violently, especially towards something which has caused difficulty or anger

crash *v* (119) to hit something, often making a loud noise or causing damage

crunch *v* (119) to crush hard food loudly between the teeth, or to make a sound as if something is being crushed or broken

enraged *adj* (119) extremely angry

flat out *adj* (119) as fast or as hard as possible

intimate *adj* (120) If a place or event is intimate, it is small in a way that feels comfortable and private.

numb *adj* (119) If a part of your body is numb, you are unable to feel it, usually for a short time.

pan *n* (119) a metal container that is round and often has a long handle and a lid, used for cooking things on top of a cooker

pay attention *v* (118) to watch, listen to, or think about something carefully or with interest

penultimate *adj* (119) second from the last

pet *n* (116) an animal which is kept in the home as a companion and treated kindly

pierce *v* (119) (of a light, sound, etc.) to suddenly be seen or heard, despite darkness, noise, etc.

pot *n* (119) any of various types of container, usually round, especially one used for cooking food

prick *n* (119) the quick feeling of pain that you get when something sharp makes a very small hole in your skin

root *n* (119) the part of a plant which grows down into the earth to get water and food and which holds the plant firm in the ground

rural *adj* (120) relating to the countryside and not to towns

scratch *n* (119) a slight cut or a long, thin mark made with a sharp object

scream *v* (119) to cry or say something loudly and usually on a high note, especially because of strong emotions such as fear, excitement or anger

smash *v* (119) to cause something to move with great force against something hard, usually causing damage or injury

snorkelling *n* (119) the activity of swimming while using a snorkel (= a tube that you breathe through when your face is under the water)

supervise *v* (117) to watch a person or activity to make certain that everything is done correctly, safely, etc.

survive *v* (119) to continue to live or exist, especially after coming close to dying or being destroyed or after being in a difficult or threatening situation

tangle *v* (119) to become twisted together, or to make something become twisted together

thick *adj* (118) made of strong, heavy material

timid *adj* (117) shy and nervous; without much confidence; easily frightened

wave *v* (119) to raise your hand and move it from side to side as a way of greeting someone, telling them to do something or adding emphasis to an expression

zip *n* (119) a fastener consisting of two rows of metal or plastic teeth-like parts which are brought together by pulling a small sliding piece over them, and which is used for closing openings, especially in clothes or bags

Unit 14 House space

Unit objectives

- **Reading Part 1:** including practice in skimming, work on references and inferencing
- **Writing Part 2:** an article describing your ideal home, analysing the task
- **Use of English Part 2:** including thinking about the type of word needed
- **Listening Part 2:** including predicting the type of information and types of words needed
- **Speaking Part 2:** comparing places to live, speculating about what it would be like, how people feel
- **Grammar:** causative *have*, expressing obligation and permission
- **Vocabulary:** types of unusual home, confusion between *space, place, room, area, location* and *square*, vocabulary for house maintenance

Starting off

❶ *Alternative treatment*

- Before students open their books, ask them to work in small groups and make a list of unusual places where people live, e.g. a castle.
- Ask them to discuss, if they could choose anywhere in the world to live, where they would live and in what type of house.
- Ask them what the most important things are when deciding where to live, e.g. a safe neighbourhood, being near the place where they work or study, etc.
- Students then open their books and do the exercises.

> **Answers**
> 1 e – a housing estate   2 f – a houseboat
> 3 c – a block of flats with several storeys
> 4 b – a country cottage   5 a – a castle
> 6 d – a townhouse

❷ Encourage students to give reasons for their opinions.

❸ Other possibilities: near friends, near other members of family, the size and quality of the house itself, close to good roads, e.g. if you have to travel regularly by car, not far from work, near or in a major city, etc.

❹ You can get them started by eliciting: Why might someone choose to live in a castle? What would you think of a friend who lived in a castle? Would you be interested in visiting them? What advantages might there be for living there? Could you use the castle as a business? A hotel, for example? Do you know anyone who lives in a castle? Encourage students to look at the photos from different points of view.

❺ Groups of three or four would be ideal. Tell them that they should discuss each of the options and try to reach agreement. This activity is similar to Speaking Part 3.

Reading Part 1

❶ *As a warmer* Ask students what they know about Venice. Ask them if they think it would be a good place to live. You can ask about getting about by canal (perhaps not having a car), climate (it may be damp), numbers of tourists, etc. Students then do the exercise in the book.

❷ *As a warmer* Ask students to work in small groups and brainstorm what they already know about Reading Part 1.

> **Answers**
> 1 eight   2 20   3 the text quickly before reading the questions   4 after   5 must

❸ Give students three or four minutes to do this.

> **Suggested answers**
> It seems like a palace, it's elegant, it's conveniently situated close to the Grand Canal, the district is interesting

❹ Remind students to find and read the relevant section of the text before they study the alternatives.

> **Answers**
> 1 B   2 C   3 B   4 A   5 C   6 D   7 D   8 A

❺ Before they start, you can suggest possible places: somewhere they have spent a holiday, a friend's house, their grandparents' house, etc. Suggest things they can say, e.g. where the house is, what sort of house it is, what the neighbourhood is like, what they enjoy doing there, etc.

Vocabulary

Space, place, room, area, location and *square*

❶ ⊙

> **Answers**
> **2** square **3** location **4** area

❷ Tell students they should pay special attention when they use these words. If they notice they have made a mistake, they should correct it.

> **Answers**
> **2** room **3** space **4** location **5** area **6** space
> **7** square **8** area **9** space **10** room

Extension idea Ask students to write their own sentences with each of the words.

Listening Part 2

❶ ***As a warmer*** Ask students if any of them have lived in a really old house; ask them what it was like and what were the good things about living in a house like this. Then move to the question in the book.

❷

> **Answers**
> **1** F – it has ten questions **2** F – you will need between one and three words **3** T **4** T **5** F – you should read and try to predict the type of information and type of words you need **6** T

❸ ***Alternative treatment***

- Ask students to work in pairs and tell them they are competing with the rest of the class.
- Tell them to actually predict the answers, i.e. they write a plausible answer in each space.
- They compare and discuss their predictions with another pair.
- They do the listening exercise.
- The winning pair is the pair with the most correct predictions.

> **Suggested answers**
> **2** probably a noun **3** a person **4** name of a room
> **5** probably a verb + *-ing* **6** another type of room
> **7** another type of building **8** swimming pool, or other facility **9** a noun **10** an adverb

❹

> **Answers**
> **1** seven / 7 years **2** (very) strange experiences
> **3** mother-in-law **4** the library **5** (standing) behind **6** bedroom **7** battle **8** tennis court
> **9** blood **10** at weekends / part-time

Recording script   CD2 Track 14

Interviewer: Now I'm standing outside the rather unusual house of crime-writer Jeff Bowen. It's large and very old and has views of some of the most beautiful countryside in the west of England. Jeff, how long have you been living here?

Jeff: *Q1* We've been here for about <u>seven years</u> now. We came here from Hollywood, where I'd been working on a film script. We house-hunted for about six months and couldn't find anything we really liked. Then finally we saw this place and my wife just fell in love with it immediately, so we bought it.

Interviewer: I believe it's rather unusual, isn't it? Can you tell us about that?

Jeff: Sure. You know, I'm fairly convinced that this house is haunted by ghosts and I'm not joking.
Q2 A lot of people have had some <u>very strange experiences here</u>.

Interviewer: Such as?

Jeff: Well, a few months ago, we were having a family party in the house. We'd just had lunch and were *Q3* relaxing with coffee when my <u>mother-in-law</u> went white as a sheet and dropped her coffee cup. I asked her what the matter was, thinking she'd been taken ill or something. She said she'd just seen a group of men dressed up as medieval soldiers go past the window. We ran outside to look but there was nobody there. But she could describe their appearance in quite a lot of detail, so she wasn't just making it up.

Interviewer: Rather alarming I should think.

Jeff: And that's not all. A week or two later quite a different visitor, a friend of mine from London *Q4* was reading in <u>the library</u> when a desk began to move. Apparently it floated from one side of the room to the other and then back again. He sat watching it, too frightened to move.

Interviewer: Have you personally had any experience of supernatural phenomena?

Jeff: Nothing as direct as the things I've just mentioned. Just a feeling really; when I'm in my study working, I've occasionally felt the hair on the back of my neck stand on end as if there's *Q5* someone <u>standing behind</u> me. When I've turned round, there's been no one there, but as you can imagine it doesn't help my work concentration.

Interviewer: So what have you done about this?

Jeff:
Q6
First I decided to change my workplace. I got the builders in and I had a <u>bedroom</u> turned into a study. I hoped I'd be able to work in there without being interrupted by these uninvited visitors! Then I called in a specialist in supernatural phenomena, someone I'd met while I was working on films and I had the whole house checked.

Interviewer: What did they come up with?

Jeff:

Q7
She didn't come up with anything very firm, but she checked the local history records and discovered that the house is actually located somewhere where a <u>battle</u> took place nine hundred years ago, so there could be quite a few dead people buried here.

Interviewer: Really?

Jeff:
Q8

Q9
Yes, and interestingly, a few months ago I was having the <u>tennis court</u> built in the garden. Anyway, one of the workmen, a lad of about 19, was on his own here one morning when he felt someone was watching him. He had the sort of feeling I had when working in my study. When he turned round, he saw something which literally made his hair stand on end: there was a man in ancient clothes standing there with a white shirt covered in <u>blood</u>. The lad shouted and the man just disappeared.

Interviewer: But none of this discourages you from living here?

Jeff:

Q10
Not at all. I don't feel physically threatened. Anyway, I'm in London a lot of the week and we mostly come here <u>at weekends</u>, so I only feel haunted <u>part-time</u>!

Interviewer: Jeff, tell me about the house itself. Apart from its spirit life, what other features attracted you to it?

❺ *Extension idea* Ask students if they know the history of the house they live in, e.g. when the house was built, who built it, who lived in it before, etc. Ask them to tell their partners what they know.

Grammar
Causative *have*

❶ Students needn't answer this question using the grammar being focused on.

Answers
He had a bedroom converted into a study and a tennis court built.

❷
Answers
1 b   2 a – I did it myself; b – I asked someone else to do it for me

❸ When students have answered the question, go through the notes in the Grammar reference section on page 164 (Causative *have*) with them.

Answer   builders

❹
Answers
2 had a tooth pulled out   3 having the house painted   4 have it cut down   5 have it extended
6 has all his meals delivered

Extension idea Ask students to say or write down three things they have had done recently. They then work in pairs and their partners ask them *yes/no* questions to find out what they were.

❺ You can suggest that it's not necessary to spend the whole budget.

Extension idea Ask students if it's a good idea to try to do as much as possible yourself to save money, or whether it's better to employ people to do a professional job.

Use of English Part 2

❶ You can ask students if they think living on a houseboat is cheaper or more expensive; safer or more dangerous; more convenient or less convenient; more comfortable or less comfortable, etc.

❷ Ask students what they think is being tested in Use of English Part 2 (mainly grammar). Before doing the Exam round-up, ask them how they think they should go about doing the task.

Answer
1 12   2 grammar   3 general idea   4 before and after   5 every question   6 the completed text

❸ Students can answer this question in pairs.

❹ When students have finished, ask them to work in pairs or small groups to compare their ideas before going through the answers with them.

Answers
1 as   2 spite   3 since   4 than   5 who   6 takes
7 out   8 should/must   9 to   10 been   11 there
12 enough

⑤ You can follow up this question with questions such as:

- What do you enjoy doing when friends visit you?
- How do you entertain visitors to your home in your country? etc.

Speaking Part 2

❶ *As a warmer* With books closed you can ask students what they remember about Speaking Part 2. You can ask questions such as these.

- Do you do this part of the exam in pairs, or do you work alone?
- Do you have to talk about photographs, or just answer questions?
- How long do you have to speak for? etc.

You can then ask them to answer the questions in the Exam round-up.

Answers
1 T   **2** F – two photos   **3** T   **4** T

❷ *Extension idea*

- Ask the student who is listening to imagine he/she is the examiner in the Speaking paper.
- Tell them they have to decide how well their partner has done in this part of the test.
- Elicit a number of criteria for assessment and write them on the board, e.g. fluency, grammatical accuracy, range and appropriateness of vocabulary, pronunciation.
- Ask the 'examiner' to listen to their partner and at the end say which things they did well, and which things they could do better.
- Finally, ask the 'examiner' to answer the same question to show how he/she thinks it could be done better.

Grammar
Expressing obligation and permission

❶ *As a warmer* If appropriate, ask students if they have ever stayed with a host family, or had a student staying with them. What was the experience like?

Suggested answers
Advantages: you hear lots of real English, practise English, get to know new culture, gain confidence; Disadvantages: strange food, possible cultural misunderstandings, it may be difficult to say what you really feel, it may be difficult to fit into a strange family

❷

Answers
1 a I have to; b I can't, they won't let me; c I can, They let me   **2** b

❸ 🎧

Answers
1 Marcos: D   **2** Lidia: E   **3** Ana: C   **4** Erich: B
5 Claudia: A

Extension idea Ask students: Whose host family sounds the nicest? Would you enjoy having a student staying in your house?

Recording script   CD2 Track 15

Claudia:	So, what's your host family like, Marcos? Are they friendly?
Marcos:	They're great fun, especially the mother. She's always cracking jokes and suggesting interesting things to do. And she's got a couple of daughters my age who don't stop laughing! The house is always full of their friends too, so it's like a permanent party, and that's great for
Q1	my social life. The only drawback is that <u>I can't stay out too late because they all have to be up early the next morning.</u> I don't have to do anything around the house, or things like that – though I do help from time to time, just to fit in and make things easier for them. What about you, Lidia?
Lidia:	You sound really lucky with your family, Marcos. Mind you, I haven't got any complaints, but my family certainly isn't such fun as yours. I mean, they didn't let me invite a couple of friends to dinner the other day. They told me it just wasn't convenient and I can see that's not being unreasonable – I mean, it is their house after all. And anyway, it's not
Q2	always like that – for example, <u>the other day when I wanted to go down to the seaside for the day they actually lent me their car.</u> I thought that was really nice of them and very trusting. I mean, <u>I've only just passed my test!</u> Are you living with a nice family, Ana?
Ana:	Well, we have our ups and downs. The other day my landlady told me off because I'd got home a bit late and missed the family dinner. Apparently I was supposed to phone to say
Q3	I wasn't coming. <u>Then when I went to see if there was anything left over in the fridge, I got into trouble again. She told me I couldn't just help myself to things without asking her first.</u>

Marcos:	So, what did you do? Walk out?
Ana:	No, I apologised for being late and explained that I had to finish some project work at university. She calmed down and said 'Never mind,' and then she helped me to cook myself a really nice meal. So we were all friends again.
Erich:	Quite right. Still, all your families sound really nice to me.
Ana:	And isn't yours, Erich?
Erich:	Well, they're all right I suppose. Not very tidy, which is one thing I would complain about. I'm not the tidiest person myself, but I think they're just taking advantage of homestay students by
Q4	saying <u>that anyone staying in their home must do their share round the house.</u> You know, like clearing up a bit, doing a bit of the hoovering, a

bit of the cooking. I needn't clean the bathroom or do any shopping, fortunately, because I wouldn't have the time. But I doubt if they'd let me have my friends in for dinner or anything like that. <u>Not like you, Claudia.</u>

| Claudia: Q5 | <u>Well, I'm lucky. Ana, you've been round for dinner and so has Erich. I had to buy the food and cook it of course</u> and they don't allow me to have a real party, but a couple of friends is OK. And they join in too which makes it really interesting because we have, I don't know like a sort of international evening. It's quite good fun. And I cook traditional Sicilian food which makes a change for everyone. |
| Marcos: | It sounds as if we're all quite lucky then. Not like a friend of mine who went back to Chile last year … |

❹

> **Answers**
> **1** Marcos   **2** Claudia   **3** Claudia   **4** Ana   **5** Lidia   **6** Erich

❺ When students have completed the table, go through the notes in the Grammar reference section on page 164 (Expressing obligation and permission) with them.

Answers

	obligation	prohibition	permission	no obligation
present	I must I'm supposed to I have to	I can't I'm not allowed to They won't let me They don't allow me to	I can They let me	I don't have to I needn't
past	I had to I was supposed to	They didn't let me		

❻ Remind students that these questions are similar to Use of English Part 4.

> **Answers**
> **2** do not have to   **3** am supposed to take   **4** are not allowed (to go)
> **5** to let Celia borrow

Extension idea If your students are staying or have stayed with host families, ask them to work in groups of four or five.

- Each student should write a brief sentence about his/her experience with the host family (similar to the ones in the listening exercise) on the same piece of paper, so they appear as a list.
- They can then, as a group, add a distractor, i.e. one extra sentence which doesn't apply to any of them.
- Each student then prepares a short talk about his/her experience. They should not write it down, but they can make notes.
- You should then photocopy each group's list and give copies to the other groups.
- Students from each group then take turns to talk to the whole class, who listen and decide which sentence from the list each student has talked about.

This would be a suitable moment to do the photocopiable activity on page 128.

Writing Part 2 An article

❶

> **Answers**
> **a** 6   **b** 4   **c** 1   **d** 3   **e** 2   **f** 5   **g** 7

❷ Here you can encourage students to be as extravagant as they wish – they are not limited by money. Encourage them to recycle vocabulary from the unit.

❸ Ask students to speak for about a minute. This will help their sense of timing for Part 2 of the Speaking paper.

❹

> **Answers**
> **1** readers of the college magazine, i.e. other students, teachers, etc.   **2** informal   **3** conditional – it asks you to imagine your ideal home   **4** the type of house, its location and features of the house   **5** for example, by surprising the reader, by saying interesting things about yourself

❺

> **Answers**
> **1** *Students' own answers*   **2** Yes – location Paris or Vienna; conveniently close to theatres, art galleries, and shops; sort of house: small, stylish, modern flat; features: cosy bedroom, well-equipped kitchen, balcony, etc.

❻

> **Answers**
> **2** from   **3** where   **4** who   **5** own   **6** what   **7** of   **8** have   **9** much   **10** If

❼

> **Answers**
> **2** T   **3** F   **4** T (he/she would like to live alone and make his/her own decisions, he/she enjoys theatre, art, music and reading, he/she wants an active social life)   **5** T   **6** F – he/she lives in a small suburban house

❽ If you give the task for homework, tell students that in the exam they would have 40 minutes for it.

→ For more on writing articles, you can refer students to page 176 (Writing reference – Articles).

Sample answer: See the model answer in Exercise 5.

Vocabulary and grammar review Unit 13

Vocabulary

❶ **2** called   **3** called/named   **4** named   **5** called

Grammar

❷ **2** c – If Chris hadn't picked up the cactus, the scorpion wouldn't have stung him.   **3** d – If Zebedee hadn't provoked the pelican, it wouldn't have attacked him.   **4** a – If Craig hadn't reached the shore, he would have died.   **5** e – If no one had heard the polar bear, it might have attacked them without warning.

❸ **2** was/were   **3** would have had / could have had   **4** wouldn't make   **5** lived   **6** would have heard   **7** hasn't missed / didn't miss   **8** would speak   **9** would have been   **10** wasn't   **11** change / are going to change / will change   **12** had studied

❹ *Suggested answers:*

You should take it for walks twice a day.

Make sure that you take it to the vet for vaccinations.

The best idea would be to train it to behave properly.

I'd advise you to give it baths from time to time.

If I were you, I wouldn't let it bark at night.

Vocabulary and grammar review Unit 14

Vocabulary

❶ **2** room   **3** place   **4** location   **5** area   **6** place   **7** space   **8** square

Grammar

❷ **2** supposed   **3** let   **4** can't   **5** had   **6** needn't   **7** have   **8** Can   **9** must   **10** couldn't

❸ **2** you had your hair   **3** have a tennis court built   **4** you have the car checked   **5** had the tree cut down   **6** have to do   **7** are supposed to pay   **8** are not allowed to speak

Unit 14 photocopiable activity:
House rules   Time: 40 mins

Objectives

- To use ways of expressing obligation and permission including modal verbs to decide on a set of rules to follow
- To persuade and negotiate in a group discussion

Before class

You will need to photocopy the activity page and cut it into three parts as indicated.

In class

❶ *As a warmer* Ask students if any of them have ever shared a house or flat with other students. Ask:

- What problems did you have with the other people in the house or flat? OR What problems do you think you might have if you shared a house or flat?
- Did you have any rules to make sharing the house or flat easier? (What rules?) OR Would you make any rules so that sharing the house or flat was easier? (What rules?)
- Did you enjoy sharing the house or flat, or would you prefer to live with your family or live alone? OR Would you like to try sharing a house or flat? Why (not)?

❷ Hand out the first part of the activity page. Ask students to read the scenario in the instructions, then ask the whole class if they think Rule 1 is reasonable or unreasonable. Elicit reasons why or why not. Ask them to discuss Rules 2–8 with their partners.

❸ Divide the class into an equal number of Groups A and B and hand out the role cards.

- Ask them to do step 1 on their role cards.
- Tell Group As to think of some reasonable rules and some unreasonable rules.
- Help Group Bs to formulate correct questions.
- When all groups are ready, ask Group As and Group Bs to work together and find out or discuss the rules.
- When they have finished, get feedback from the groups for the whole class. Ask questions such as: *Were you happy with the rules which were explained to you? Would you like to live with the people in your group?*

Extension idea Ask the class: Do you think we need rules in order to live together?

Unit 14 photocopiable activity
House rules

1 Work in small groups. Imagine you are university students and you share a large house together. The house has a kitchen with a washing machine, a sitting room with a TV, one bathroom and six bedrooms.

Read the rules on the right which some friends of yours wrote for the house which they share. Decide which rules you think are reasonable and which are unreasonable.

2 You will do a role play where you are:

- a group of students who already share a house and you are looking for some more housemates to share the house with you (Group A) OR
- a group of students who are interested in moving into a house which already has some students in it (Group B).

Read the role card your teacher gives you and follow the instructions.

House rules

1 You mustn't use the shower after 10 pm at night. Other people are trying to sleep!
2 You must clean the shower after you have used it.
3 You needn't wash up after you have eaten. We do all the washing-up at the end of the day.
4 You can invite friends and have parties whenever you want.
5 Everyone is supposed to spend two hours cleaning the house on Saturday mornings.
6 You are not allowed to smoke in this house.
7 Everyone should be home by 10 pm.
8 The first person to get up in the morning has to make coffee for everyone else.

Group A

The rent is quite high in the house where you live and you need two or three more students to share it and help pay the rent. You think you have found the right students (Group B), but when you meet them, you want to tell them about the house rules.

1 Before you meet them, decide what the house rules are. Use the questions below to help you.
- Does each person cook for themselves, or do people take it in turns to cook for everyone? If so, when will each person have to cook?
- Who does the shopping, and how much must each person pay for shopping each week?

- Can your housemates invite their friends whenever they want?
- The washing machine is quite noisy. What are the rules for using it?
- Who decides what to watch on TV?
- What about cleaning? Who must clean the house and when?
- Are there any rules for using the bathroom?
- What about general rules, e.g. for smoking, having parties, etc.?

2 When you are ready, meet with the students who want to share the house. Answer their questions, explain and discuss the rules.

Group B

You are interested in sharing the house occupied by Group A. When you meet them, you want to find out the rules for living in the house.

1 Before you meet them, decide what questions you want to ask them about the rules. Here are some things you can ask about:

cooking shopping inviting friends using the
washing machine using the TV doing housework and
cleaning using the bathroom smoking parties

You can ask using phrases like: *Do we have to ...?, Can we ...?, Are we allowed to ...?, Are we supposed to ...?* *Examples: Do we have to cook for everyone in the house? Can we use the washing machine whenever we want?*

2 When you are ready, meet with the students who have the house (Group A) and ask your questions. If there are any rules you don't agree with, discuss them together and try to get them changed.

Complete First Certificate by Guy Brook-Hart © Cambridge University Press 2008 **PHOTOCOPIABLE**

Word list

Unit 14

Note: the numbers show which page the word or phrase first appears on in the unit.

anxiety *n* (125) an uncomfortable feeling of nervousness or worry about something that is happening or might happen in the future

arch *n* (125) a structure consisting of a curved top on two supports, which holds the weight of something above it

block *n* (124) a large, usually tall building divided into separate parts for use as offices or homes by several different organisations or people

cellar *n* (125) a room under the ground floor of a building, usually used for storage

consultant *n* (128) someone who advises people on a particular subject

cruel *adj* (125) causing suffering

customary *adj* (125)
1 usual
2 traditional

cut down *v* (127) to make a tree fall to the ground by cutting it near the bottom

dealer *n* (125) a person whose work is to buy and sell something

elegant *adj* (125) graceful and attractive in appearance or behaviour

fetch *v* (125) to be sold for a particular amount of money

handrails *n* (125) a long bar that you hold in order to support yourself when walking, for example at the side of stairs

haunted *adj* (126) describes a place where ghosts appear

housing estate *n* (124) an area containing a large number of houses or apartments built close together at the same time

jumbled *adj* (125) mixed together in an untidy way

print *v* (125) to produce writing or images on paper or other material with a machine

request *n* (125) when you politely or officially ask for something

rounded *adj* (125) smooth and curved

saucer *n* (128) a small curved plate which you put a cup on

sense of humour *n* (125) your ability to understand amusing things

shutter *n* (125) a wooden cover on the outside of a window which prevents light or heat from going into a room or heat from leaving it

site *n* (127) a place where something happened or was built in the past

store *v* (125) to put or keep things in a special place for use in the future

storey *n* (124) a level of a building

struggle *v* (125) to experience difficulty and make a very great effort in order to do something

suspicious *adj* (125) feeling doubt or no trust in someone or something

trade *n* (125) a particular business or industry

warehouse *n* (125) a large building for storing things before they are sold, used, or sent out to shops

Unit 15 Fiesta!

Unit objectives

- **Reading Part 2:** including using cohesive features in the text and the missing sentences
- **Writing Part 1:** email giving information and opinions, using linking words
- **Use of English Part 3:** including forming personal nouns and forming nouns from verbs, identifying the type of word needed
- **Listening Part 4:** identifying main ideas in the question, listening for gist and detail
- **Speaking Part 3:** discussing celebrations, effective turn-taking, prompting partners, suggesting ideas
- **Grammar:** the passive and patterns after passive reporting verbs, i.e. *that* + clause or infinitive, practice of this grammar with Use of English Part 4 task
- **Vocabulary:** collocations for festivals and celebrations, features of festivals

Starting off

❶ *Alternative treatment* Before they open their books, ask students to work in small groups and say what events are typical for public festivals and celebrations in their country. When are the most important festivals? Then move to the exercise in the book.

> **Answers**
> **2** dress up   **3** perform   **4** march   **5** commemorate
> **6** hold   **7** play/perform   **8** gather round
> **9** let off   **10** wearing

❷

> **Suggested answers**
> **Photos: 1** fireworks   **2** traditional costumes, traditional dances   **3** street party   **4** parade, band
> **5** disguises   **6** street performers, street theatre

Extension idea Ask students to suggest other photos which could be included with these ones.

❸ Give students about three minutes to do this.

> **Answers**
> **1** and **2** *Students' own answers*   **3** The photos were taken in: **1** Sydney, Australia   **2** Brittany, France   **3** Britain   **4** USA   **5** Venice, Italy
> **6** Britain

❹ *Alternative treatment* Ask students to work alone first and prepare a short talk to answer this question. If they wish, they can use dictionaries or the internet (if available) to prepare what they want to say. Allow them to make notes. They then give their talk to a partner, or to the rest of the class.

Listening Part 4

❶

> **Suggested answers**
> fire-eating, sword-swallowing, acrobatics, clowning and comedy, singing and dancing, etc.

A possible follow-up question: Why do you think people become street performers?

❷

> **Answers**
> **1** interview   **2** seven   **3** underline, different words
> **4** general ideas

❸ Encourage students to underline the main ideas as they read the questions.

Alternative treatment Before listening, ask students to read the questions and discuss what they think the answer to each question will be (and why).

> **Answers**
> **1** C   **2** A   **3** B   **4** A   **5** B   **6** A   **7** C

Recording script   CD2 Track 16

Interviewer: Today *South Live* visits the Winchester Hat Fair, an extravaganza of processions, fireworks and street theatre with performers from as far away as Australia and Brazil. And we're talking to a veteran performer at the Hat Fair, Mighty Max, who's come all the way from Canada once again. Max, why is the festival called the Hat Fair?

Max: Well, I've been told the fair was only started in 1976, as a way of encouraging street performers like myself. It's not like there was one of those great old English traditions like hat-making here in the eighteenth century or anything. A lot of people come to the fair wearing funny hats because it's called the Hat Fair, but that wasn't its origins. It was always supposed to be about street theatre, and typically a hat is passed around so that people like me can earn a living. That's in fact where the name comes from.

Q1

Interviewer: Now, you've been coming here for a number of years. Why do you keep coming back?

Max: I just love performing here. There are artists like myself from all over the world who come here year after year and we get to know each other and stuff. But what makes the Hat Fair unique is the people who come to watch. You know, people from this part of the country are usually a bit reserved and shy in public, but during the Hat Fair all that seems to change. They let their hair down and get involved in the acts. They really seem to love it when they're being laughed at by other members of the audience. It's amazing and great fun for the entertainers as well.

Q2

Interviewer: So, how did you get involved in street theatre in the first place?

Max: Well, as a kid I was always fascinated by the circus and dreamt of being a circus performer. I actually went to quite a famous circus school in Canada when I was a teenager and I was taught juggling and acrobatics there. My father was dead against it and didn't want me to have anything to do with the circus, but he paid for the classes on the condition that I went to university and got myself what he called a proper education. It was ironic really because if I hadn't gone to university I might never have got into street theatre. You see, every vacation I used to travel and I found I could pay for my trips by doing street theatre. That's how I came to the Hat Fair for the first time about ten years ago. I've never had any other job.

Q3

Interviewer: Fantastic! And how do you explain your popularity as a street performer? I mean, your act has been attracting tremendous crowds here in Winchester.

Max: Well, you've seen it. It's a combination of high class acrobatics which are performed without safety equipment and some quite risky stunts.

Q4

So it gives the audience a thrill. But what I think really gets them into it is that I get them involved and I make them laugh. There's a lot of clowning in my act which builds a sort of two-way communication with the audience. They love it. And that's what makes street theatre in general so good. Your audience pay you according to how much they like you. The better your act, the more you get. And if it's no good at all, then you get nothing.

Q5

Interviewer: An instant comment on the quality of your work, in other words.

Max: That's right.

Interviewer: And what are the problems that street performers come up against?

Max: A good question. In a place like Winchester, not many. We're each given a place and a time to perform. As you've seen I attract pretty large crowds and I need plenty of space for jumping around and so on, so narrow streets are no good. Here we're given the main shopping street, which is fine. In other places, if you haven't got permission, you'll get moved on by the police. But I always make sure that I have the right permits. It's just not worth it otherwise. Probably the main difficulty in places like Britain and Canada is actually things like rain or snow. I mean, people just won't stand around watching you if they're going to get cold and wet doing it, will they?

Q6

Interviewer: I imagine not. But what about Winchester? Has the Hat Fair put the town on the map, so to speak? I mean does it attract a lot of visitors from outside?

Max: I'm not the best person to ask that question to. I'm just a street entertainer. I get the impression that the people who come to the Hat Fair tend to be people from the area rather than visitors from outside. What Winchester gets is an amusing party – something they can do which isn't work. It's just plain fun. You know, they gather in the streets and parks and all have a laugh together, either at the performers or at each other. And it's all so good-natured. They unwind and forget about the other pressures in their lives.

Q7

Interviewer: Mighty Max, thank you and I hope the rest of the fair goes well for you.

Max: Thank you.

④

> **Suggested answers**
> Some residents may find it annoying, it interrupts traffic, it may encourage pickpockets and thieving, it may be dangerous, etc.

Extension idea Ask students:

- Do you enjoy watching street performers?
- How much money is it reasonable to give a street performer?
- (if suitable) Have you ever participated in street theatre?

Grammar
The passive

❶

> **Answers**
> *Suggested phrases to underline:* **b** is passed around **c** they're being laughed at **d** was taught **e** we're given, you'll get moved on

❷ Point out that often speakers have more than one motive for using the passive, and that the motives may be open to interpretation.

> **Suggested answers**
> **2** a **3** b, d, first passive in e **4** a, b, d, first passive in e

❸ Before doing this exercise, go through the notes in the Grammar reference section on page 165 (The passive – form and uses) with the students.

> **Answers**
> **2** My wallet has been stolen! **3** You won't be able to ring me while my mobile is being repaired. **4** Have you heard? I've been given a place on the course! **5** If you'd interrupted the meeting, you would have been arrested.

❹ Give students one minute to do this.

> **Answers**
> People go out in the open air in the early morning; they eat traditional foods; young men swim in the Nile

❺

> **Answers**
> **2** as **3** been **4** to **5** is **6** being **7** by **8** have **9** doing **10** were (*Note: fish* can be singular or plural, depending on the context.)

❻

> **Answers**
> **1** a **2** A large number of contemporary Egyptian traditions are said to have their origins in very ancient times. For example, offerings of fish are believed to have been made to the ancient gods ...

❼ Before doing this exercise, go through the notes in the Grammar reference section on page 166 (The passive with reporting verbs) with the students.

> **Answers**
> **2** It is said that a large number of contemporary Egyptian traditions have their origins in very ancient times. **3** Five thousand people are reported to have joined in the festivities. **4** Our festival is said to have the best fireworks in the world.

❽

> **Answers**
> **2** expected to be chosen **3** said that the festival is **4** is thought to be **5** is considered to be

Extension idea Ask students to write four sentences of their own using *believe, report, say, consider, expect* or *think* in the passive.

Reading Part 2

❶ ***As a warmer*** Ask students what they would expect in a Spanish fiesta and if they have ever been to one.
Note: fiesta is defined in the *Cambridge Advanced Learner's Dictionary* as 'a public celebration in Spain or Latin America, especially one on a religious holiday, with entertainments and activities'.

❷

> **Answers**
> **1** F – there are seven questions and no example **2** T **3** T **4** T **5** F – be flexible and change your mind if you find a better place for a sentence **6** F – read it again to check it reads logically

❸ When students have underlined words and phrases, ask them to compare what they have underlined with a partner and to discuss what they might expect in the spaces.

> **Answers**
> *Suggested phrases to underline:* The owner of a nearby vegetable stall provided the perfect weapons; In the main square; When we awoke ... the next day; people poured into the town for the fight; From there they went ...; Water poured from the rooftops; Nor could I look at or eat another tomato

❹

> **Answers**
> 1 H   2 C   3 F   4 G   5 A   6 B   7 D

❺ *As a warmer* Ask students which festivals described so far in the unit have a long history. (*Answer:* only Sham el Nessim) Ask what are the origins of an important festival in their region.

For a change of pace you could do the photocopiable activity on page 136 at this point.

Use of English Part 3

❶ *As a warmer* Ask students to form the noun for the person from each of these verbs and nouns: direct (director), employ (employer, employee), work (worker), act (actor/actress), interpret (interpreter), translate (translator), visit (visitor), travel (traveller), piano (pianist), chemistry (chemist), science (scientist), magic (magician), politics (politician).

> **Answers**
> 1 owner   2 tourists   3 firemen

❷

> **Answers**
> 2 artist   3 performer   4 collector
> 5 creator   6 participant   7 musician
> 8 politician   9 fisherman   10 cyclist

❸ *Alternative treatment* You can make this a quiz by asking questions such as:

- What do you call someone who serves in a restaurant? (*A waiter/waitress*)
- What do you call someone who is swimming? (*A swimmer*)
- Someone who studies biology? (*A biologist*) etc.

> **Suggested answers**
> waiter, swimmer, biologist, typist, director, conductor, policeman, postman

❹

> **Answers**
> 1 10   2 Read the whole text quickly before answering the questions   3 what type of word (adjective, noun, verb, etc.) you need
> 4 Make sure you have spelled the word correctly
> 5 read the completed text again

❺

> **Answers**
> 1 exciting   2 arrangements   3 activities
> 4 participants   5 impossible   6 visitors
> 7 disorganised   8 traditional   9 usually
> 10 impressive

Speaking Part 3

❶ *As a warmer* Ask students what things they have celebrated recently. Ask them how they celebrated.

> **Answers**
> 1 graduating   2 a sporting triumph   3 a new house
> 4 good exam results   5 an engagement
> 6 the first car   7 a new baby

❷

> **Answers**
> a party with friends, a party with family, a meal, a holiday, buying furniture, going to a restaurant, buying something nice, e.g. new clothes, going for a (long) drive

Recording script   CD2 Track 17

Teacher: Now, I'd like you to talk about something together for three minutes. Here are some important moments in people's lives. First talk to each other about what would be the best way of celebrating each of these occasions. Then decide which two you would be happiest to celebrate. All right?

Nikolai: Well, I think there are two ways of celebrating graduating from university: you have to have a party with your friends who are graduating at the same time and another party with your family. Don't you agree, Antonia?

Antonia: A party with your friends, yes, maybe. I think that the event – I'm not sure what it's called in English – the event when you graduate …

Nikolai: The ceremony?

Antonia: Yes, the graduation ceremony is enough for the family – with perhaps a meal afterwards.

Nikolai: You could be right.

Antonia: And for someone winning an important race, in other words a sporting triumph, I'm not sure. I guess another party would be fine, wouldn't it?

Nikolai: Yes, or perhaps I'd suggest a holiday somewhere really nice.

Antonia:	A holiday?
Nikolai:	Yes, because you work really hard to achieve a sporting triumph and I think you'd probably deserve one.
Antonia:	I think that's a really good idea. How do you think people should celebrate buying a new house?
Nikolai:	Well, people usually have a party don't they, so that people can see where they live.
Antonia:	It's parties for everything, isn't it? Maybe in this case I'd celebrate by going out and buying a nice piece of furniture to put in the house.
Nikolai:	Good idea – and then you could invite your friends to come and help paint the house!
Antonia:	When you pass your First Certificate, will you hold another party?
Nikolai:	Maybe. I think it depends on how I'm feeling. I might just go out to a restaurant with a friend to celebrate that one.
Antonia:	Me too. And I might also go and buy myself something nice …
Nikolai:	As a reward.
Antonia:	Yes, some new clothes or something, you know, because I've studied so hard.
Nikolai:	Yes.
Antonia:	And getting engaged is really a moment to have a party with your family and friends together.
Nikolai:	And your fiancé's family and friends as well.
Antonia:	What about being given a new car?
Nikolai:	That would be wonderful. I'd celebrate by going for a long drive in it.
Antonia:	Me too, and with the music turned up really loud!
Nikolai:	Yes. Shall we move on to the second question?
Antonia:	OK. I think for me the thing I'd be most happy to celebrate would be getting a new car at the moment.
Nikolai:	Really? Why's that?
Antonia:	Because I'm tired of walking and using public transport. A new car would give me a lot of freedom. What about you?
Nikolai:	I'd say graduating from university because then I can start looking for a job and once I have a job I can do other things like buy a car or buy a house, or …

Antonia:	Or even get married.
Nikolai:	Or get married if I can find the right person!
Teacher:	Thank you.

❸ You can also ask which ways of celebrating they enjoy the most.

❹ 🎧

> **Answers**
> 2 F   3 T   4 T   5 F   6 T   7 T

❺ 🎧

> **Answers**
> 2 could   3 suggest   4 idea   5 case   6 depends
> 7 move

❻ Point out that when students don't know the word, they should find other words to explain what they mean.

> **Answers**
> 2 Shall we move on to …   3 Perhaps I'd suggest …
> Maybe in this case …   4 You could be right.
> 5 I think it depends on …

❼

> **Answers**
> 1 F – you do it with a partner   2 F – you have about three minutes   3 T   4 T   5 T   6 F – try to discuss all of them   7 T

❽ Give students three minutes to do this task.

Writing Part 1

❶

> **Answers**
> 1 There is one question you must do   2 120–150 words   3 a letter or an email   4 You must deal with four specific points in the task   5 40 minutes

❷ *As a warmer* Ask students if they invite visitors or friends from other places when there's a festival in their town; ask how their visitors feel or react to the festival.

> **Answers**
> 1 Sam, an English-speaking friend   2 informal
> 3 Things you must deal with: saying the dates of the festival, describing the festival, inviting Sam to visit, agreeing to visit the festival together
> 4 *Students' own answers*

❸ *⊘*

> **Answers**
> ~~bout~~ about, ~~exiting~~ exciting, ~~wich~~ which, ~~begining~~
> beginning, ~~were~~ where, ~~especial~~ special, ~~trough~~
> through, ~~cloths~~ clothes, ~~their~~ there, ~~preffer~~ prefer,
> ~~confortable~~ comfortable, ~~becaus~~ because, ~~now~~
> know, ~~an~~ and, ~~froward~~ forward

❹ If you give the task for homework, remind students that in the exam they would have 40 minutes for it.

⟶ For more on writing emails, you can refer students to page 169 (Writing reference – Part 1).

Sample answer: See the model email in Exercise 3.

Unit 15 photocopiable activity: The college's 100th anniversary

Time: 20–30 mins

> **Objectives**
> ● To practise language skills which are useful for First Certificate Paper 5, including making suggestions, giving opinions, justifying, offering and recommending

Before class

You will need one photocopy of the activity page for each group of three or four students. Cut up the Students' instruction cards before the lesson.

In class

❶ *As a warmer* Ask students: Does / Did your school have a special day when it invites / invited parents and other people from outside to celebrate something? What happened? How was it organised?

❷ Tell students they are going to discuss how to organise an event at this college. Ask them to work in groups of three or four and give them the handout with the Director's questions. They then follow the instructions.

❸ You should also give each student a Student's instruction card. For groups of three, don't hand out the card for Student D.

❹ When students have finished discussing the questions on the handouts, they should change groups and report what they have decided.

❺ *Extension idea* Students return to their original groups.

- Tell them they should write a report for the Director which summarises their decisions and recommendations.
- Tell them that each student should write one section of the report, e.g. Food, Guests, Entertainment, Time and place, etc.
- Students then work alone and write their section.
- They cut and paste their sections onto the same page and together write an introduction.
- The reports can then be displayed on the walls of the classroom and students can read each other's work.

The college's 100th anniversary

❶ Work in small groups. The college where you are studying is 100 years old this year. The Director wants to organise an event to celebrate its 100th anniversary and you have been asked to form part of a committee to organise this event. Look at the diagram of points below which the Director wants you to decide. Your teacher will also give each of you a card with further instructions.

You should:
- discuss and decide together how to organise the event using the diagram below and the instruction card your teacher gives you
- make brief notes about your decisions.

❷ When you have finished, change groups and report what you have decided to other groups.

Director's questions

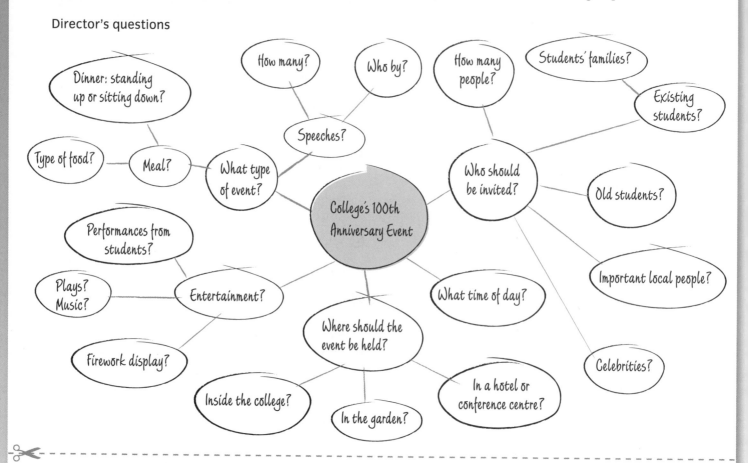

Students' instruction cards

Student A	Student B	Student C	Student D
• You are in charge of the meeting. Make sure everyone has a chance to express their opinions. • Find out if anyone in your group could perform (music, a play, etc.) at the event.	• Suggest an exhibition of students' work at the event. • Find out what work people in your group could exhibit.	• Ask if anyone in the group has been to a similar event in the past. • Find out what happened at the event. • Discuss which things to imitate and which to avoid.	• Find out what food people in your group think is most successful at this type of event. • Should it be prepared by students or by professionals?

Word list

Unit 15

Note: the numbers show which page the word or phrase first appears on in the unit.

ancient *adj* (136) of or from a long time ago, having lasted for a very long time

break out *v* (138) If something dangerous or unpleasant breaks out, it suddenly starts.

chaotic *adj* (138) in a state of chaos (= a situation where there is no order and everything is confused)

chuck *v* (138) to throw something carelessly

cram *v* (138) to force a lot of things into a small space

contemporary *adj* (136) existing or happening now

conventional *adj* (135) traditional and ordinary

flock *v* (138) to move or come together in large numbers

frenzy *n* (138) uncontrolled and excited behaviour or emotion, which is sometimes violent

harvest *n* (136) the time of year when crops are cut and collected from the fields, or the activity of cutting and collecting them, or the crops which are cut and collected

hurl *v* (138) to throw something with a lot of force, usually in an angry or violent way

juggling *n* (135) the activity of throwing two or more balls into the air, repeatedly, often in order to entertain people

lie ahead *v* (138) to be going to happen in the future

load *n* (138) a large amount of things that a person or animal carries

manic *adj* (138) very excited and physically active in a way that is not controlled

move on *v* (135) If the police or other people in authority move you on, they ask you to leave a place.

myth *n* (136) an ancient story or set of stories, especially explaining in a literary way the early history of a group of people or about natural events and facts

raw *adj* (136) (of food) not cooked

scour *v* (138) to search a place or thing very carefully in order to try to find something

sizzle *v* (138) to make a sound like food cooking in hot fat

sour *adj* (138) having a sharp, sometimes unpleasant, taste or smell, like a lemon, and not sweet

squash *v* (138) to crush something into a flat shape

stale *adj* (138) no longer new or fresh, usually as a result of being kept for too long

stall *n* (138) a large table or a small shop with an open front from which goods are sold in a public place

symbolise *v* (136) to represent something

trap *v* (136) to catch an animal using a piece of equipment

triumph *n* (140) a very great success, achievement or victory (= when you win a war, fight or competition), or a feeling of great satisfaction or pleasure caused by this

trundle *v* (138) (to cause something) to move slowly on wheels

upbeat *adj* (138) full of hope, happiness and good feelings

welfare *n* (136) physical and mental health and happiness, especially of a person

Unit 16 Machine age

Unit objectives

- **Reading Part 3:** practising exam technique including studying the questions before approaching the text(s)
- **Writing Part 2:** a review
- **Use of English Part 4:** revision of grammar and vocabulary covered in recent units
- **Listening Part 3:** practice in underlining and listening for the main idea
- **Speaking Part 4:** including round-up of exam technique and ways of gaining time
- **Grammar:** linking words: *when, if, in case, as if, even if, even though* and *whether*; reported speech: grammatical patterns following different reporting verbs; practice of this grammar with Use of English Part 4 task
- **Vocabulary:** types of gadget or device, words and collocations connected with uses of gadgets, confusion between *check, supervise* and *control*, different reporting verbs

Starting off

❶ *Alternative treatment* With books closed, ask students to brainstorm a list of electronic gadgets (e.g. digital cameras) that have become popular in the last ten years.

> **Answers**
> **2** MP3 player   **3** webcam   **4** digital camera
> **5** DVD player   **6** mobile phone   **7** SatNav
> **8** digital TV

❷

> **Answers**
> **2** find   **3** date   **4** give   **5** do   **6** save   **7** wherever
> **8** take, store

❸ You can ask students to write two or three sentences as examples.

> **Suggested answers**
> digital camera: to take good photos easily and store them on my computer   digital TV: to keep up to date with what's going on and to give me more choice of what I watch   DVD player: to give me more choice of what I watch   laptop: to help me do my homework, to save time and effort and to keep in touch with friends   mobile phone: to keep in touch with friends   MP3 player: to listen to music wherever I want   SatNav: to find my way   webcam: to keep in touch with friends and to keep up to date with what's going on

❹ *Extension idea* Ask students to work in pairs and answer these questions: Is there a device or gadget you haven't got, but would like to have? Why do you want it? What would you use it for?

Reading Part 3

❶ Before they start, you can remind students of modal verbs to express certainty and possibility (see Student's Book pages 92 and 161). Elicit sentences about the first photo using modal verbs.

❷ *Alternative treatment* Ask students in groups to brainstorm how much they remember about Reading Part 3, what it consists of and exam technique. Then do the exercise in the book.

> **Answers**
> **1** F – there are 15 questions   **2** T   **3** F – read the questions carefully before the text(s)   **4** T – or think carefully about what they mean   **5** F – 20 minutes   **6** F – answer every question

❸ Make sure students follow the technique in the Exam round-up.

> **Answers**
> **1** C   **2** D   **3** A   **4** A   **5** E   **6** A   **7** D   **8** B
> **9** E   **10** E   **11** B   **12** D/E   **13** D/E   **14** C/D
> **15** C/D

❹ *Extension idea* You can widen the discussion with these questions: do you think many gadgets (like the Tulip Ego) are really fashion accessories? Would you like a gadget which gave you an excuse to hang up the phone? Do you think parents should be able to check where their children are at all times?

Vocabulary

Check, supervise and *control*

❶ ⊙

> **Answers**
> **2** control **3** check **4** supervise **5** control

❷ To do this exercise, students may need to look carefully at how the words are used in context in the text.

> **Answers**
> **1** b **2** c **3** a

❸ Remind students to pay careful attention when using these words in their writing and speaking so as to avoid mistakes.

> **Answers**
> **2** supervise **3** check **4** supervise **5** control
> **6** check

❹ Encourage students to use the target vocabulary when answering these questions.

Grammar

Linking words: *when, if, in case, as if, even if, even though* and *whether*

❶ ⊙

> **Answers**
> **2** ~~if~~ when **3** correct **4** ~~when~~ if **5** correct
> **6** ~~when~~ if

Extension idea Ask students to write three or four sentences of their own, but with *if* or *when* left blank. They then pass them to a partner who decides which word should go in the gap.

❷ ⊙

> **Answers**
> **2** ~~even if~~ even though **3** ~~even if~~ even though
> **4** correct **5** ~~Even if~~ Even though **6** ~~even though~~
> even if

❸ ⊙ Go through the notes in the Grammar reference section on page 166 (Linking words and phrases) with the students.

> **Answers**
> **2** if **3** in case **4** in case **5** in case **6** if

❹

> **Answers**
> **2** when **3** if / when / even if **4** in case **5** even
> though **6** in case **7** if

Listening Part 3

❶ *Extension idea* You can ask: Do you think technology is affecting the way families behave? Do you think it's bringing them closer together, or driving them apart? You can prompt students by asking about the effects of email and messaging, television, mobile phones, etc.

❷

> **Answers**
> **1** five speakers, six alternatives **2** read and
> underline the main idea in each alternative
> **3** the main idea of what each speaker is saying

❸

> **Answers**
> **1** C **2** F **3** E **4** D **5** B

Extension idea After listening, ask students: Which of the five speakers' experience is closest to yours?

Recording script CD2 Track 18

Speaker 1: My parents aren't really at home with computers at all. They use one for doing the accounts – they run a small business – but they often forget to check their email, for example. I told them that they'd build up their business no end if they set up a website. They thought this was so sophisticated that they'd need a lot of new equipment in order to do this. My dad had this idea that we should go shopping for some really powerful machine for me to run the website from and I must say I was pretty tempted. But I had to admit we could do the whole thing with the stuff we've got at the moment. I missed a big opportunity to take advantage of my parents there, didn't I?

Speaker 2: Well, I have to do a lot of my homework using the internet, you know, to research things and so on, so my computer is usually switched on when I'm studying anyway. And last term in our class we had to do quite a few group projects which meant having to chat a lot with each other while we were doing them. When my parents saw me, they got the idea into their heads that I wasn't studying properly. They told me to cut down on the chat. They just don't have any idea how good computers can be for working together. Anyway, I got good marks in my end-of-term exams, which showed them.

Speaker 3: I love computers and if I could, I'd spend most of my free time doing things with them. I mean, I don't just use them for chatting with friends or surfing the internet or things like that. Actually, what I really like is designing things on the computer. I've got a really powerful one which my mum and dad bought me when I passed my exams and I'd like to study design in the future. <u>Anyway my dad found these classes you could do in the summer holidays and said if I was really interested I should go to them and learn to do things properly instead of teaching myself.</u> And my mum even offered to pay for them! They're great!

Speaker 4: My parents have the idea that computers are some sort of magic and that I'm some sort of genius just because I can handle them. You know, I can do lots of things which they just haven't learnt to do. <u>When they went to one of those parent–teacher evenings at school last month, I heard them saying, 'But she's marvellous on the computer!'</u> – you know how parents talk – and I saw the teachers looking at them with one of those patient looks teachers have when listening to parents. You could see they were probably thinking, 'Yeah, just like all the others' and 'Pity about her maths'!

Speaker 5: Well, we've only got one PC in my house and I use it a lot for chatting with my mates. I've got friends all over the world in lots of different countries. The trouble is that both my dad and my mum are hooked on this really crumby computer game. Anyway, I get home from school before they get home from work, so I get to the computer before them. This leads to no end of rows. You know, <u>they ask me when I'm going to log off and give them a chance to use it</u>, and haven't I got anything better to do, and isn't it about time I gave a hand with the housework, and so on. It's really funny actually because you can see they're just itching to get on the computer themselves!

Suggested answers
1 students can use the internet for research; they can easily share their work with other students; they can work on projects together from their homes; they can store and edit their work easily; they can add graphics and other features to their work and present it in a way which looks smart; they can cooperate with students in other colleges and other countries, etc.   **2** they learn research skills, typing skills, creativity, design skills, coordination; they may write more to their friends using email or chat, etc.

Grammar
Reported speech 2: reporting verbs

| **Answers** | | | | |
reporting verb + infinitive	reporting verb + object + infinitive	reporting verb + preposition + noun or verb + -ing	reporting verb + verb + -ing	reporting verb + (that) + sentence
offered to help	advised me to go \n told me to send	complained about (not) having	suggested buying	said they were

Answers
2 of lying   **3** to buy   **4** for breaking   **5** to go   **6** to visit
7 to help   **8** to buy   **9** to visit
10 installing   **11** to buy   **12** to use

Extension idea Perhaps for homework, ask students to write their own example sentence for each reporting verb.

❷ You may want to go through the Grammar reference section (Reported speech 2: reporting verbs) on page 167 of the Student's Book before students start the exercise. Otherwise, they can do the exercise and then check their answers by looking at the Grammar reference section.

❸

Answers				
reporting verb + infinitive	reporting verb + object + infinitive	reporting verb + preposition + noun or verb + *-ing*	reporting verb + verb + *-ing*	reporting verb + (*that*) + sentence
offered to help	advised me to go	complained about (not) having	suggested buying	said they were
agreed to buy	told me to send	accused (Brian) of lying	admitted stealing	
offered to help	asked me to go	apologised for breaking	recommend installing	
promised to visit	invited me to visit			
	persuaded his mother to buy			
	remind you to buy			
	warned me (not) to use			

❹ Point out to students that there may be more than one correct answer. Encourage them to use the Grammar reference section to check their answers.

> **Answers**
> **2** suggested going swimming that / suggested they went swimming that   **3** told me to turn off / told me to switch off   **4** reminded Natasha to post
> **5** of not taking any   **6** to do her best

Speaking Part 4

❶

> **Answers**
> **1** 4 minutes   **2** the same theme as Speaking Part 3
> **3** may be asked the same questions or different questions   **4** your opinion plus an explanation, reason or example   **5** listen carefully, may have to

❷ 🎧

> **Answer**
> Tell me about a machine or gadget you couldn't live without. Why (not)?

Recording script CD2 Track 19

Teacher: Irene

Irene: That's quite a hard question to answer because there are several things which really for me are necessities. If I had to choose, perhaps it would be my mobile phone. I find this really essential because it keeps me in touch with my friends and my family and I can find out where they are and what they're doing at any time. And also if I have any problems or an emergency I can always call someone for help, so for me it would be my mobile phone.

Teacher: Miguel

Miguel: I'm not too sure because I'm using different machines all day long and for almost everything I do. For example, I think I'd find life really difficult without my car to get around in. And I couldn't do any work without my computer. I mean I do everything on the computer. On the other hand, I love listening to the radio and I get all my news from there, so that's another thing I don't think I could give up.

❸ 🎧

> **Answers**
> Irene: mobile phone – to keep in touch with friends and family, to get help with problems or in an emergency
> Miguel: several things: car to get around in, computer for work, radio to listen to news

❹ You can point out that both options – giving one answer or mentioning several possibilities – are equally valid.

> **Answers**
> **1** Irene   **2** Miguel   **3** both Irene and Miguel   **4** both candidates give good answers

Machine age (141)

(5)

> **Answers**
> They used phrases 1 and 2.

(6) Encourage students to practise using some phrases from Exercise 5 when they answer. When they have finished, encourage them to give each other feedback on how well they answered each question, how they could improve their answers, etc. Round up the main points of the feedback with the whole class.

Use of English Part 4

(1)

> **Answers**
> 1 eight   2 five   3 word   4 Contractions
> 5 change   6 vocabulary   7 same   8 number
> 9 given

(2)

> **Answers**
> 1 her homework on her own   2 didn't mean to dial
> 3 are expected to rise   4 to have got lost   5 had the
> system installed by   6 wouldn't have broken out
> 7 can't have borrowed   8 Don would cut down

Writing Part 2 A review

(1) Make sure that students underline the points they must deal with when they read the writing task.

> **Answers**
> 1 *Students' own answers*   2 type of gadget, why you bought it, if it meets your requirements, if you would recommend it to other people   3 *Students' own answers*

(2)

> **Answer**   Yes

Extension idea Ask students to write a plan for the sample review in the book with the contents for each paragraph. (*Answers:* Paragraph 1: new mobile phone – lost previous one, has large keys, large colour screen and flips open; Paragraph 2: easy to use, can hear clearly, bad ring tones; Paragraph 3: not complicated, but good price) Then ask them to write a plan for their own answers and to compare them with other students'.

(3) If you decide to give this task for homework, tell students that in the exam they would have about 40 minutes for it.

→ For more on writing reviews, you can refer students to page 175 (Writing reference – Reviews).

Sample answer: See the model answer in Exercise 2.
As a final fun activity at the end of this course, you can do the photocopiable activity on page 144.

Vocabulary and grammar review Unit 15

Word formation

(1) 2 scientist   3 singer   4 chemist   5 magician
6 geologist   7 manager   8 electrician
9 assistant   10 postman

(2) 2 safety   3 amazement   4 repetition
5 existence   6 truth   7 height   8 addition
9 difference   10 inventions

Grammar

(3) 2 was broken into by   3 were/are reported to have
4 has not been serviced for/in   5 is said to be living
6 the cakes had been eaten

Vocabulary and grammar review Unit 16

Vocabulary

(1) 2 controlling   3 supervised   4 checking
5 supervising   6 check

Grammar

(2) 2 whether/if   3 if   4 even though   5 in case
6 even if   7 when   8 even if   9 in case   10 even though

(3) 2 Mark of being the one who caused the accident / of causing the accident
3 to Maria for not ringing her
4 me to go/come skiing with her
5 to do the photocopies for Trish
6 (me) that she would give me all the money back at the end of the month / to give me all the money back at the end of the month
7 visiting the Musée d'Orsay while they were in Paris / that they visited the Musée d'Orsay while they were in Paris
8 me to buy some eggs while I was out
9 her to walk very carefully because the path was slippery
10 the thieves to drop their guns and put their hands on their heads

Unit 16 photocopiable activity: Reported speech race Time: 30 mins

Objectives
- To use a variety of reporting verbs accurately
- To practise changes needed in reported speech

Before class
You will need one photocopy of the activity page, and perhaps the Rules below as well, for each group.

In class
❶ Divide the class into groups of between three and five players.

❷ Go through the rules with the class and, if necessary, elicit possible answers to the example from square 3, i.e. She promised (that) she would / to give me/him my/his book back the following/next day. Point out that more than one answer may be possible.

❸ When students play the game, you will have to act as referee and, when they disagree or are not sure, tell students when an answer is correct or not.

Alternative treatment Students play the game with three or four teams of two students each, so they can discuss before putting something into reported speech.

Answers
3 ⟶ 10 She promised (that) she would / to give me/him my/his book back the following / next day.

6 ⟶ 12 He agreed (that) his car needed cleaning.

8 ⟶ 11 She explained (that) she had an exam so she would have to stay at home and study.

9 ⟶ 17 She denied that she had written in his/her/my book. / She denied writing in his/her/my book.

13 ⟶ 15 She suggested going to the cinema that night / that they went / should go to the cinema that night.

16 ⟶ 21 He reminded me to lock the door.

19 ⟶ 27 She recommended that we should join the club. / She recommended joining the club (to us).

22 ⟶ 32 They warned me to be careful / that I should be careful if I went walking in the mountains.

24 ⟶ 28 My teacher told me that I should have given him / her the homework the week before / the previous week.

25 ⟶ 29 She admitted that she broke / had broken the plate / breaking the plate.

31 ⟶ 35 He told us not to make any noise.

34 ⟶ 40 He suggested that we / they all went / they should all go fishing that afternoon.

36 ⟶ 37 She told me to drive more slowly / that I should drive more slowly.

38 ⟶ 41 He agreed that the book wasn't his / didn't belong to him.

43 ⟶ 49 He promised (her/him/me/us/them) that when he had finished all his work he would come and visit her/him/me/us/them. / He promised to come and visit her/him/me/us/them when he had finished all his work.

44 ⟶ 47 He denied speaking / having spoken / that he had spoken to Simon.

46 ⟶ 50 They agreed that the film they had seen the week before / the previous week was not / had not been very good.

Rules
Work in small groups. You will need a dice and counters.

❶ Throw the dice in turn. When you land on a square with direct speech, move to a square with reported speech and put what the person said into reported speech. You must decide which is the correct square.

   Example: You land on square 3. The correct square is 10. You must use She promised ... to put 'I'll give you your book back tomorrow' into reported speech.

❷ If the other players agree your answer is correct, stay on the new square. If your answer is wrong, go back to the square you landed on (from square 10 you would go back to square 3).

❸ The winner is the first person to reach Finish.

Reported speech race

1 **START**	**2**	**3** Mary said, 'I'll give you your book back tomorrow.'	**4**	**5**	**6** John said, 'You're right. My car needs cleaning.'	**7**
14	**13** 'Why don't we go to the cinema tonight?' Sonia said to her friends.	**12** He agreed …	**11** Paula explained …	**10** She promised …	**9** I didn't write in your book,' said Sarah.	**8** Paula told me, 'I've got an exam, so I'll have to stay at home and study.'
15 She suggested …	**16** Don't forget to lock the door,' Mark said to me.	**17** 'She denied …	**18**	**19** 'You should join the club,' Marina told us.	**20**	**21** He reminded …
28 My teacher told me that …	**27** She recommended …	**26**	**25** 'It was me that broke the plate,' Susie said.	**24** 'You should have given me this homework last week!' my teacher said.	**23**	**22** 'Be careful if you go walking in the mountains,' my friends said to me.
29 Susie admitted …	**30**	**31** 'Don't make any noise,' Peter said.	**32** They warned …	**33**	**34** 'Let's all go fishing this afternoon!' David said.	**35** He told us …
42	**41** He agreed that …	**40** He suggested that …	**39**	**38** 'You're right, this book isn't mine,' Mike said.	**37** She told me …	**36** Mum said, 'You should drive more slowly.'
43 'When I've finished all my work, I'll come and visit you,' said Frank.	**44** 'I didn't speak to Simon,' said Andy.	**45**	**46** 'That film we saw last week wasn't very good,' Carla said. 'No, it wasn't,' answered Matt.	**47** He denied …	**48**	**49** He promised …
						50 They agreed that … **FINISH**

Word list

Unit 16

Note: the numbers show which page the word or phrase first appears on in the unit.

attract attention *v* (147) to make someone notice you

be up to no good *v* (143) to be doing something bad that you should not be doing

break down *v* (145) If a machine or vehicle breaks down, it stops working.

built-in *adj* (143) If a place or piece of equipment has built-in objects, they are permanently connected and cannot be easily removed.

compatible *adj* (143) Compatible equipment can be used together.

coordination *n* (143) the ability to make your arms, legs and other body parts move in a controlled way

current *adj* (143) of the present time

demand *v* (143) to need something such as time, effort, or a particular quality

device *n* (143) an object or machine which has been invented for a particular purpose

downside *n* (143) the disadvantage of a situation

elsewhere *adv* (143) somewhere different; somewhere else

gadget *n* (144) a small device or machine with a particular purpose

give up *v* (145) to stop owning and using something

goal *n* (143) an aim or purpose

indoors *adv* (143) into or inside a building

link *v* (143) to connect computers so that information can be sent between them

loudspeaker *n* (143) a piece of equipment that changes electrical signals into sounds, especially used in public places so that large numbers of people can hear someone speaking or music playing

overlong *adj* (143) too long

persuade *v* (143) to make someone do or believe something by giving them a good reason to do it or by talking to them and making them believe it

pinpoint *v* (143) to find out or say the exact position in space or time of something

price tag *n* (143) how much something costs

proud *adj* (146) feeling pleasure and satisfaction because you or people connected with you have done or got something good

resemble *v* (143) to look like or be like someone or something

set targets *v* (143) to decide what you want to achieve by a particular time

signal *n* (143) an action, movement or sound which gives information, a message, a warning or an order

substantial *adj* (143) large in size, value or importance

suit *v* (143) to be right for a particular person, situation or occasion

switch on *v* (143) to turn a piece of equipment on

track *v* (143) to follow a person or animal by looking for proof that they have been somewhere, or by using electronic equipment

turn into *v* (143) to change and become someone or something different, or to make someone or something do this

Vocabulary and grammar

❶ **Complete each of the sentences below by choosing the correct alternative (A, B, or C) for each gap.**

0 There's no ....B........ in my suitcase for your clothes as well!

A place   B (room)   C area

1 What's that thing .... that you use to open bottles?

A called   B named   C entitled

2 There isn't enough .... for all of us in our flat so we're looking for a bigger one.

A place   B rooms   C space

3 Let's put the TV in the .... between the sofa and the window.

A place   B room   C space

4 Last Saturday's demonstration in the town .... passed off peacefully.

A place   B square   C location

5 Many people go to parties on 31st December to .... the New Year.

A celebrate   B commemorate   C hold

6 The immigration officer .... all my passport details very carefully when I returned from holiday.

A controlled   B supervised   C checked

7 When I'd finished the job, my boss .... my work to make sure it didn't contain any mistakes.

A supervised   B checked   C controlled

8 She passed the exam .... she didn't study very hard.

A even though   B even if   C in case

9 I'd never give up work .... I had lots of money.

A even though   B even if   C in case

10 Take the spare front door key .... you get home before me.

A even though   B even if   C in case

❷ **Complete the following sentences by putting the verb in brackets into the correct tense.**

0 If I ....*'d had*.... (have) my mobile phone with me yesterday, I *would have been* (able to) contact you.

1 I wish I .... (be) kinder to him when I .... (see) him last week.

2 Millie .... (not have) an accident if she .... (drive) more carefully.

3 It was a disastrous evening. If I .... (not be) late, we .... (not miss) the beginning of the film.

4 What .... you .... (do) if a lion .... (come) into the camp last night?

5 If only I .... (not stay) up all night celebrating. It was a stupid thing to do!

❸ Complete the second sentence so that it has a similar meaning to the first sentence, using the word given. Do not change the word given. You must use between two and five words, including the word given.

0 I feel sick because I ate too much chocolate this morning.

SO

If I ....*hadn't eaten so much*.......... chocolate this morning, I wouldn't feel sick now.

1 We didn't really enjoy our visit to the city because there wasn't much time to explore.

MORE

If we .... to explore, we'd have enjoyed our visit to the city.

2 They couldn't have won the competition without the support of their team.

THEY

If .... the support of their team, they couldn't have won the competition.

3 I regret buying a new computer.

WISH

I .... a new computer.

4 It is known that birds can fly enormous distances..

ABLE

Birds are known .... enormous distances.

5 What was the reason Dad wouldn't allow us to have a pet when we were younger?

LET

Why .... have a pet when we were younger?

6 Smoking is forbidden in all public buildings.

ALLOWED

Nobody .... in any public building.

7 Someone is coming to install our new kitchen next week.

HAVING

We're .... next week.

8 We won't be able to cook while they are installing the kitchen.

IS

We won't be able to cook while .... installed.

9 People say that the computer was invented over 150 years ago.

TO

The computer is .... invented over 150 years ago.

10 It looks as if the dog has been injured in a fight.

BEEN

The dog seems .... in a fight.

❹ **Use the word given in CAPITALS to form a noun that fits each gap.**

0 Most .....*visitors*..... to the Rio de Janeiro carnival say it is an   VISIT
unforgettable experience.

1 Traffic is now considered to be the main cause of .... in   POLLUTE
most cities.

2 I don't understand anyone who wants to be a .... It's an   POLITICS
impossible job.

3 Sean's .... of how email actually works was very helpful.   EXPLAIN

4 All my .... with my parents are about money.   ARGUE

5 The .... of Julia's wedding dress took up a page of the email.   DESCRIBE

6 Many of our .... are away on holiday at the moment, so the   EMPLOY
office is very quiet.

7 Mandy is an antiques .... and her house is full of beautiful   COLLECT
old things.

8 We have a team of .... trying to develop a car which runs   SCIENCE
on hydrogen.

9 Only three of the .... managed to finish the race.   COMPETE

10 Students' .... had a meeting with the headteacher to discuss   REPRESENT
the problem.

❺ **Complete the sentences by writing the correct reporting verb in the past tense.**

0 Anne reluctantly ...*admitted*.... to me that she'd told a lie and said she was sorry.

1 Ruth's boss .... her of stealing some money.

2 Donna .... for interrupting us, but said she had some important news.

3 Pete .... to the manager about the poor service in the shop but nobody seemed to
care.

4 Because I was so busy, Ella .... to take our dog for a walk, and I was happy
to accept.

5 Don .... walking as the best way of exploring the city.

❻ **For questions 1–6, complete the second sentence so that it has a similar meaning to the first sentence, using the word given. Do not change the word given. You must use between two and five words, including the word given.**

0 NASA issued an announcement last night saying that their scientists have completed their work on the latest Mars project.

ANNOUNCED

It ...*was announced last night*... that NASA scientists have completed their work on the latest Mars project.

1 I hope no one has stolen my bike because I can't see it anywhere!

BEEN

I hope my bike .... because I can't see it anywhere!

2 They say it's possible to see the Great Wall of China from space.

BE

It is said that the Great Wall of China .... from space.

3 All traffic has been diverted because the main road is under repair at the moment.

BEING

All traffic has been diverted because the main road .... at the moment.

4 The police are looking for a man who someone saw driving a blue BMW last night.

SEEN

The police are looking for a man .... a blue BMW last night.

5 It is believed that people played an early form of tennis 600 years ago.

HAVE

People .... an early form of tennis 600 years ago.

6 They have postponed the match until the end of August.

PUT

The match .... until the end of August.

7 Karen only helps when people ask her to.

IS

Karen never helps .... to.

8 Reports state that James is living on a Pacific island at the moment.

REPORTED

James .... on a Pacific island at the moment.

9 A carpenter is making us a door for our garage.

HAVING

We .... for our garage by a carpenter.

10 If I were you, I wouldn't drive that car until they've repaired it for us.

HAD

If I were you, I wouldn't drive that car until we .... repaired.

Answer key

Progress tests

❶ 1 ... is a really **annoying** person ...
2 ... **so long** / ... **such a long time** ...
3 ... she's **such a** supportive person ...
4 ... were **very young** / ... were **young** ...
5 ... felt very **embarrassed** when he sang ...

❷ 1 so much noise   2 too hot   3 very
4 much better   5 warm enough

❸ 1 luxurious   2 comfortable   3 adventurous
4 spicy   5 longest   6 confusing   7 helpful
8 choice/choices   9 attractive   10 wonderful

❹ 1 **a** gets   **b** does
2 **a** meal   **b** dish
3 **a** travel   **b** trip
4 **a** summed up   **b** made up
5 **a** tactless   **b** nervous

❺ 1 felt   2 was starting   3 used to dream
4 had stopped   5 thought   6 booked
7 had been saving   8 had left   9 was standing
10 were just beginning

❻ 1 have you been travelling   2 has been
3 am doing   4 am learning   5 Do you like
6 have always wanted   7 have been
8 has happened   9 Are you / have you been
travelling   10 love / am loving

❼ 1 as/so many Italian restaurants as
2 eat less meat than
3 worked more efficiently / better than
4 least favourite job
5 one of the easiest dishes

❶ 1 study   2 find out   3 courses   4 opportunity
5 job   6 fun   7 listen to   8 marks   9 took part in
10 occasion

❷ 1 A, C   2 C, D   3 A, D   4 A, C   5 A, D

❸ 1 Sam is **doing research** into ...
2 ... problem **of global** warming ...
3 ... variety **of different** species ...
4 ... birds there are in **the** world?
5 I read recently that **the** Brazilian government ...
6 ... There's **a** fantastic nature programme ...
7 **Cars** are responsible ...
8 ... seeing a whale for **the** first time ...
9 ... survived **on (the) food** they found ...
10 ... environmental science **at university** before ...

❹ 1 I'll probably go   2 I'll be lying   3 I'll have
finished   4 it's going to be   5 I'll enjoy
6 I'll be leaving   7 Will you come   8 I'll be
9 I'm meeting   10 We're going to help

❺ 1 deal   2 go   3 at   4 little   5 out
6 to   7 few   8 no   9 an   10 Unless

❻ 1 if I earned
2 unless you read / if you don't read
3 were you, I wouldn't
4 had/spoke better Italian, he would/could
5 if we didn't have

❶ 1 C   2 C   3 A   4 C   5 A   6 B   7 B   8 A   9 C   10 B

❷ 1 disagreement   2 inexpensive   3 unpaid
4 misunderstanding   5 impatiently

❸ 1 c   2 d   3 f   4 b   5 a

❹ 1 managed to   2 Can   3 could   4 will be able to
5 can

❺ 1 Despite   2 stay   3 take   4 as   5 where

❻ 1 if he could lend him some money   2 she would go
to the beach with me at the weekend   3 I would have
to work overtime that/this weekend   4 what time
the film started   5 the coat was there and ready to be
collected

❼ 1 into   2 what   3 down   4 me   5 Although   6 for
7 must   8 as   9 so   10 there/going

❽ 1 where   2 who/that   3 what   4 whose   5 who

PROGRESS TEST Units 13–16

❶ 1 A 2 C 3 C 4 B 5 A 6 C 7 B 8 A 9 B 10 C

❷ 1 had been, saw
2 wouldn't have had, she'd driven / she'd been driving
3 hadn't been, wouldn't have missed
4 would you have done, had come
5 hadn't stayed

❸ 1 had had more time
2 they hadn't had / had not had
3 wish I hadn't / had not bought
4 to be able to fly
5 wouldn't/didn't *or* would Dad not / did Dad not let us
6 is allowed to smoke
7 having a / our new kitchen installed
8 the kitchen is being
9 said to have been
10 to have been injured

❹ 1 pollution 2 politician 3 explanation
4 arguments 5 description 6 employees 7 collector
8 scientists 9 competitors 10 representatives

❺ 1 accused 2 apologised 3 complained 4 offered
5 recommended/suggested

❻ 1 has not been stolen 2 can be seen 3 is being repaired 4 (who was) seen driving 5 are believed/thought to have played 6 has been put off
7 unless she is asked / except when she is asked
8 is reported to be living 9 are having a door made
10 have had it

Writing reference

Part 1
Exercise 1
1 1 suggest either 5th or 7th November to speak to students 2 give her some ideas about what aspects of her work students would find most interesting 3 tell her a DVD player would be better for showing the short film 4 give number and age range of audience
2 a formal style (similar to the email in the task)
3 aspects of her work students would find most interesting, number and age range of audience

Exercise 2
1 talk about the police's work in fighting crime and how they go about it and about career opportunities in the police force; audience: 100 people aged between 16 and 18 and a few teachers
2 formal

Part 2
Letters
Exercise 1
1 An English friend, Pat
2 what a typical family in your country is like and how family life is changing
3 project, different countries

Exercise 2
1 families close, spend time together, help each other, get together at weekends, young people live with parents until 25 or 30, get married in 30s, have children quite late, just one or two children
2 women now work, men take more responsibility in home, people richer, moving to larger houses in suburbs

Reports
1 formal – it's for your teacher 2 formal style; yes

Stories
Exercise 1
1 When I got up that morning, I thought it would be just another ordinary day …
2 starting with the words
3 other students at the school

Exercise 2
2 no – you should use a range of past tenses to make the story more dramatic 3 yes – it makes the story more interesting to read 4 yes 5 maybe 6 yes
7 maybe

Exercise 3

1 yes **2** no **3** yes **4** yes **5** no **6** yes (surprised, shocked, frightened) **7** yes

Reviews
Exercise 1

1 what it's about, why we would all enjoy it
2 everyone would enjoy, film or book
3 readers of your school's English-language magazine, i.e. other students; in the magazine

Exercise 2

1 first and second paragraphs **2** third paragraph

Articles
Exercise 1

2 d **3** e **4** h **5** c **6** b **7** a **8** i **9** f

Exercise 2

Para 1: c **Para 2:** b **Para 3:** a **Para 4:** d

Essays
Exercise 1

1 Your teacher **2** giving your opinions, All young people should continue at school or college until at least the age of 18

Exercise 2

Para 1: Introduction: the situation in my country now
Para 2: Points in favour:

> **1** *difficult for 16 yr olds to find work* + reason *jobs more specialised and technical*
> **2** *stay at school* + reason *more opportunities in future*

Para 3: Points against:

> **1** *some students – school difficult/boring* + reason *prefer earning money*
> **2** *cause problems for other students* + reason *not motivated*

Para 4: My opinion(s) *stay at school – practical/ technical subjects* + reason(s) *leave too soon – miss opportunities*

Speaking reference

Part 1
Exercise 1

2 f **3** d **4** i **5** g **6** c **7** e **8** j **9** a **10** h

FCE model paper from Cambridge ESOL

Paper 1 Reading
Part 1

1 A **2** B **3** B **4** D **5** B **6** D **7** A **8** C

Part 2

9 F **10** E **11** H **12** A **13** B **14** G **15** D

Part 3

16 B **17** D **18** A **19** B **20** C **21** C **22** A **23** A **24** D **25** B **26** C **27** D **28** C **29** A **30** D

Paper 2 Writing
Part 1

Question 1

CONTENT
Email should include all the points in the notes.

*   Thank James for accepting the invitation.
*   Say which of the two given dates is preferred (not necessary to say why).
*   Give some information about the sports club members (not necessarily their ages or the sports they enjoy).
*   Suggest one or more topics which James could talk about.

ORGANISATION AND COHESION
Clear organisation of ideas, with suitable paragraphing, linking and opening/closing formulae as appropriate to the task.

RANGE
Language relating to the functions above. Vocabulary relating to sport and sports people.

APPROPRIACY OF REGISTER AND FORMAT
Standard English appropriate to the situation and target reader observing grammar and spelling conventions.

TARGET READER
Would be informed.

Question 2

ESSAY

CONTENT
Essay should state which subject(s) candidate thinks are most important for young people to study at school. It is acceptable to say that all subjects are equally important/unimportant.

ORGANISATION AND COHESION
Clear organisation of ideas with suitable paragraphing and linking.

RANGE
Language of describing, explaining and expressing opinion.
Vocabulary relating to subjects studied at school.

APPROPRIACY OF REGISTER AND FORMAT
Consistent register suitable to the situation and target reader.

TARGET READER
Would be informed.

Question 3

STORY

CONTENT
Story should continue from the prompt sentence.

ORGANISATION AND COHESION
Storyline should be clear. Paragraphing could be minimal.

RANGE
Narrative tenses. Vocabulary appropriate to the chosen topic of story.

APPROPRIACY OF REGISTER AND FORMAT
Consistent register suitable to the story.

TARGET READER
Would be able to follow the storyline.

Question 4

REVIEW

CONTENT
Review should:
- describe the music on the CD
- explain what the candidate thinks about it
- say whether candidate would recommend it to others.

ORGANISATION AND COHESION
Clear organisation of ideas, with suitable paragraphing and linking.

RANGE
Language of describing, explaining and giving opinion.

APPROPRIACY OF REGISTER AND FORMAT
Consistent register suitable to the situation and target reader.

TARGET READER
Would be informed.

Question 5a

SET TEXT

CONTENT
Article should give opinions about the ending of the book, explaining how the candidate feels about it.

ORGANISATION AND COHESION
Clear organisation of ideas, with suitable paragraphing and linking.

RANGE
Language of giving opinion and expressing feelings.
Vocabulary relating to how the story ends.

APPROPRIACY OF REGISTER AND FORMAT
Consistent register suitable to the situation and target reader.

TARGET READER
Would be informed.

Question 5b

SET TEXT

CONTENT
Essay should describe how the characters of Jane and Lizzie Bennett are different and explain why their relationship is strong.

ORGANISATION AND COHESION
Clear organisation of ideas, with suitable paragraphing and linking.

RANGE
Language of describing, explaining and giving opinion.
Vocabulary relating to character and relationships.

APPROPRIACY OF REGISTER AND FORMAT
Consistent register suitable to the situation and target reader.

TARGET READER
Would be informed.

Paper 3 Use of English

Part 1

1 C   2 D   3 B   4 C   5 A   6 D   7 C   8 B   9 C
10 A   11 C   12 C

Part 2

13 as   14 at   15 in   16 which   17 than   18 more
19 to   20 were/are   21 because   22 of   23 so
24 most

Part 3

25 limited   26 advisable   27 headache   28 dependent
29 unhealthy   30 helpful   31 encouragement
32 carefully   33 probability   34 unfortunately

Part 4

35 be **requested** to show (them) / produce
36 **wish** (that) I had/'d visited
37 I look/check it **up** in
38 **whether** she/Sophie had had OR
   her/Sophie **whether** she had had
39 was (completely/totally) **unaware** of
40 are not / aren't **as** many
41 too far **away**
42 difficulty/difficulties **in** understanding the

Paper 4 Listening

Part 1

1 B   2 A   3 C   4 C   5 A   6 B   7 C   8 A

Part 2

9 natural history   10 Room Managers / room managers
11 hotel (for example)   12 Japanese   13 Team Leader /
team leader   14 information desk   15 orange
16 11,200 / eleven thousand two hundred   17 weekend
(off/free)   18 15(th) December / (the) fifteenth of
December / December 15(th)

Part 3

19 E   20 C   21 A   22 F   23 D

Part 4

24 A   25 B   26 C   27 A   28 B   29 A   30 B

Paper 4 Recording script

CD3 Track 2 (Instructions to candidates)

CD3 Track 3

You'll hear people talking in eight different situations.
For questions 1–8, choose the best answer, A, B or C.

One.

On a train, you overhear a man talking on a mobile
phone.

Why will he be late?

A because of the bad weather

B because of an unexpected meeting

C because of his car breaking down

Did I say I'd be there by seven? ... Well, there's been a
change of plan. I'm on the train now, but I can't come
straight to you because I've got to call in at the office and
see someone about a company car ... I'm sorry, I know
it'll make me late, but this evening's the only time he's
available. I'll meet you at the restaurant ... Yes, I know it's
raining, but get a taxi there and go straight inside. Then
you won't get wet.

Two.

You overhear a woman in a café telling her friend about
her holiday.

What did she do?

    A   She borrowed a video camera.

    B   She hired a video camera.

    C   She bought a video camera.

M: So, did you enjoy the holiday, though?

W: Yes, it was fantastic. You'll have to come round one
   evening and watch the video Jeff made. It's really good.

M: I didn't know you had a video camera.

W: No, well we've been planning to get one for years, but
   they're still really expensive and what with Jeff only
   working part-time, we just couldn't afford it. Then we
   thought of just renting one for the fortnight, but then in
   the end my neighbour said we could have hers, as she
   didn't need it for a while. It cost us quite a lot, actually,
   because she gave us an enormous shopping list of
   things she wanted from Spain and we couldn't charge
   her for them really, in the circumstances. But at least
   we got the camera.

Three.

You hear a radio programme about dealing with stress.

What is the woman advising people to do?

A try an unfamiliar activity

B do an energetic activity

C find an interesting activity

I had a very stressful job and it was very difficult to relax
until I found something that completely involved me and
where I could try hard to see an improvement. I had two
small children, and no time for myself. I tried reading
various self-help books but one day a friend suggested
Latin American dance classes – I used to go to classes at
university ... Now I go as often as I can, and I love it. My
dancing has got better – and I've got much fitter too. But
it doesn't matter what you do – my friend goes to book-
binding classes in the room next door!

Four.

You overhear two friends talking about a job interview.

How did the young man feel about the question he was asked?

A embarrassed that he didn't have any hobbies

B annoyed at being asked a personal question

C surprised by the way the question was phrased

Paul: You know that interview I went for at the bank.

Anna: Yeah?

Paul: Well, they asked me what my hobbies were.

Anna: Oh, you're joking! But that's just so predictable. Whatever did you say?

Paul: Well, I told them. People don't call them hobbies any more. I mean, listening to music's not a hobby unless you're crazy about one band or something, and playing football at the weekend, you know, that's more a way of life. No, I told them that they should ask people about their interests.

Anna: Exactly. So, did you get the job?

Paul: No, I didn't actually.

Five.

You hear a woman talking about an experience she had when travelling.

What happened?

A She missed a ferry she intended to catch.

B She was given wrong information about ferries.

C All ferries were cancelled that day.

We had such a mess up trying to get back from Ireland. We were on the west coast and we were supposed to come back from Rosslare, the port in the south. And when we got there they'd cancelled the ferry. Brilliant. And the next one wasn't going until something like 9 o'clock that night so they told us we should drive up to Dublin and get another ferry from there. There was one at 4 o'clock. So we raced up the coast and arrived just in time to see it disappearing out of the harbour.

Six.

You hear a man talking on the radio about a film.

Which aspect of the film did he find confusing?

A the speed of the dialogue

B the development of the plot

C the number of characters

The problem with thrillers like this is that you spend most of the film wondering what's going on and if you miss a few lines of dialogue at the beginning you'll probably never catch up. It's only right at the end that it starts to make sense. So you actually enjoy it after you've seen it rather than at the time. The film jumps from one part of the world to another, which doesn't help, and several of the main actors look very similar which was really a mistake.

Seven.

You overhear three young people, Jane, Susan and Nick, planning a party.

What is Jane's responsibility?

A decorations

B food and drink

C invitations

Jane: Hi, Nick. Hi, Susan.

Nick: Hello, Jane. Hey, what have you got there?

Jane: Decorations.

Nick: Oh, I thought that was my job and you were sending out the ...

Jane: Yes, sorry, Nick. I saw them and liked them. Do you like them?

Nick: Well ...

Susan: They're lovely, Jane.

Jane: Thanks, Susan. So, how's the food and drink going?

Susan: Oh, fine. Lots of ideas. I'll manage very well, I think.

Nick: At least Susan is making progress.

Jane: Hang on. You're the only one who's still got it all to do.

Nick: Decorations aren't so easy as invitations, Jane.

Jane: Maybe, but you don't know the trouble I took over them.

Eight.

You hear a woman talking about living on her own.

What does she say about it?

A It's not the first time she has lived alone.

B It gives her plenty of time for housework.

C She prefers sharing with other people.

I lived on my own when I was twenty-six and hated it. I was scared and lonely. So I went back to sharing a flat but it was a nightmare, I felt I was in someone else's house. Now I wouldn't dream of living with someone else. I love the freedom I have, to stay up till 6 am if I want to and leave the washing-up. But the only downside is the worry of something going wrong, like the washing machine breaking down, because I've got to deal with it.

CD3 Track 4

You'll hear an interview with Ayesha Surrenden, who is responsible for staff in a museum. For questions 9–18, complete the sentences.

Interviewer: Hi, I'm Brad Taylor and this is the job-finder programme, where we look at job opportunities for young people in the region. This week, I'm joined by Ayesha Surrenden, who's the personnel manager at the City Museum. Ayesha, welcome.

Ayesha: Hi.

Interviewer: Now, it's a pretty big place the museum, isn't it?

Ayesha: Oh, yes, there's all sorts of things on display from paintings, obviously, through sculpture, costume, ceramics, a bit of everything. And we get people from all over the world coming to view the exhibitions in the natural history section, which is really famous. It would take days to see everything properly.

Interviewer: So there are lots of job opportunities?

Ayesha: That's right. At the moment, the museum is looking for more people to work as what are called Room Managers. Now these are not the people who put up the works of art and keep them clean, but they are more than just the old-fashioned security guards that you used to get in museums. These people are there to offer a friendly service to visitors in each room, as well as keeping an eye on the exhibits.

Interviewer: So you have to know a bit about art?

Ayesha: If you have an interest in art, that's good, but it's certainly not a requirement for the job, and you don't need to have worked in a gallery or museum before either. What's much more important is to have some sort of experience in dealing with the public, maybe working in a hotel for example. Because you'll be handling questions from members of the public, especially foreign visitors.

Interviewer: So languages are important?

Ayesha: Yes, any European language would be useful. Lots of people know some French or Spanish these days, but we would be specially keen to hear from anyone who's studied Japanese. We've got Chinese and Russian speakers on the staff, and we can make sure these people are on duty if we know we have a group coming.

Interviewer: So it's quite a varied job?

Ayesha: Yes, you'll be given a specific area of the museum to look after as part of a group of five people under a Team Leader, and you'll be expected to make sure that everything is running smoothly within that area. You could find yourself looking after a party of overseas schoolchildren or approaching people to ask them to observe the gallery's rules, such as not touching the art works. And, to add variety, you'll spend some time each week working at the information desk in the museum as what we call a 'meeter and greeter'. Then there's a restaurant and a shop in the building too. So you could be called on to help out in those places if there's a problem. And you'll look good too: all gallery assistants are provided with a very smart uniform, not the traditional black or brown type either, but an orange one. It was designed specially for us by a leading fashion house.

Interviewer: And is the job well paid?

Ayesha: Basic pay starts at £11,200 annually, but this can rise to £14,500 with experience, and there's also a staff canteen with very low prices. Because the gallery is open seven days a week, twelve hours a day, you work on shift, although you are guaranteed every third weekend off, and you get paid extra for working on national holidays, which is sometimes necessary. And another good thing is that all staff also receive a leisure card offering free entrance to most other galleries and museums in the country.

Interviewer: Right, that can't be bad. So how do you apply?

Ayesha: Well, anyone interested should call or write in for an application form. The office is actually closed from 20th December until 2nd January – it's our annual holiday – so the closing date for applications is 15th December and a series of interviews will be held on 8th January.

Interviewer: Ayesha, thank you.

Ayesha: Thanks, Brad.

CD3 Track 5

You'll hear five different people talking about their favourite teacher. For questions 19–23, choose from the list A–F what each speaker says. Use the letters only once. There is one extra letter which you do not need to use.

Speaker 1

The school I went to was a very old-fashioned one so our teachers were quite strict and were always forbidding us to do things. I liked the Latin teacher best because she was incredibly enthusiastic about her subject and I always enjoyed her lessons and tried not to make too many mistakes. I remember studying Virgil's *Aeneid* with her, but we didn't read certain parts about Dido and Aeneas's love affair – they were considered unsuitable for young girls! It seems funny now. In the library, there was a locked cupboard and only teachers were ever supposed to read the books inside it. One day, I felt incredibly worldly-wise when the Latin teacher let me explore its contents.

Speaker 2

Today I make my living writing music, and when I was at school it was the only subject I was interested in. But because I was bad at other school subjects the music teacher believed I was hopeless at that too and never encouraged me. He even wrote to my parents that I was 'a below average student'! Luckily, Mr Hayes, the English teacher, who I liked better than the others, recognised my enthusiasm for music, although he knew little about the subject himself, and persuaded me to write my own musical compositions and play them in our drama classes – I loved that and felt I was making progress. I'm sure I would have gone on to music college after I finished school anyway, but those classes really gave me confidence.

Speaker 3

Mrs Winter was my favourite teacher although I never had lessons from her at school. When my parents wouldn't allow me to apply for a place at drama school, she persuaded them to change their minds. She read through the more amusing scenes from *Romeo and Juliet* with me in her sitting room. It wasn't fun though. I had to give a short performance before I could be accepted at drama school. Mrs Winter's standards were terribly high and, however hard I tried, she always said I could do it better! And when I'm performing on stage today, I still make use of things I learnt from her.

Speaker 4

When I was younger, I used to be a keen swimmer and once I was nearly chosen for a place in my country's Olympic team. My swimming coach, who was the teacher I liked more than any other, also happened to be my father! The difficult thing about having Dad as a coach was that I could never get out of a training session. Even when I broke a finger, he encouraged me into the pool with my hand in a plastic bag and made me practise my leg movements! It was laughable really. Eventually I got bored with swimming but Dad was determined to make a champion out of me. He's still disappointed that I gave it up.

Speaker 5

My teachers probably hated having me in their class. I was always playing tricks on them and trying to get the other kids into trouble. A girl once burst into tears in an English class, saying I was ruining her education by being so noisy! And if I didn't like a teacher I just missed their lessons. But I always went to Miss Ford's classes because she didn't mind us having a laugh sometimes. In between the jokes, we got a lot of serious work done without realising it. Her method of teaching opened up the world of study for me and I'd definitely call her my favourite teacher.

CD3 Track 6

You'll hear an interview with Peter Jones, who works at an animal hospital. He's talking about how he recently rescued a baby seal. For questions 24–30, choose the best answer, A, B or C.

Interviewer:	Peter Jones works for an organisation that rescues sick or injured animals who normally live in the sea. He told me about how he found his latest patient, a baby seal, called Pippa.
Peter:	I expect you know that seals feed on fish.
Interviewer:	Mmm.
Peter:	When they're babies, they can get into trouble really easily. If they're out to sea, for example, they can get caught in fishing nets, and fishermen sometimes bring them in to us.
Interviewer:	Right.
Peter:	But if they're close to the shore and they're injured, they usually come out of the sea themselves and then lie on the beach. They look rather like a large rock and unfortunately, people often walk right past them.
Interviewer:	How did you find out about the seal you rescued recently?
Peter:	She's called Pippa ... that's what we named her ... We got a phone call and when we got the call I did what we always do first. I asked the caller some questions to make sure that she was really injured ... sometimes you get calls about baby seals and when we arrive to collect them, we find out that they're simply asleep on the beach.
Interviewer:	So there's nothing wrong with them at all ...
Peter:	Exactly. But I could tell from this conversation that Pippa had been in a fight – probably with another baby seal, and I

Answer key (157)

needed to collect her quickly because she was still moving.

Interviewer: What do you mean?

Peter: Well, there are things that can make a rescue operation difficult and this is one of them ... by the time you've got all the equipment ready and got there, you go to the spot where you think the seal'll be and, of course, it isn't any more. When we arrived at the beach we had to follow the marks she'd made in the sand in order to find her. We were lucky that it wasn't dark and it was a pretty small area of beach.

Interviewer: So did you transport her in a special way?

Peter: There are certain things that we had to do first ... before we picked her up ... we looked at her cuts and took her temperature to check for any fever. We thought she might have been injured for some hours and be thirsty, so we gave her some water as well. Then we took her to our animal hospital where we checked her for any illness that might be dangerous to other sea animals.

Interviewer: How do animals react to being taken into a hospital – you must get a bit of resistance!

Peter: I think people expect us to get hurt. They think the animals are going to try and attack us or something. Occasionally, I've had a bit of a struggle to pick an animal up or get it to go where I want it to, but generally it's the opposite ... they're shaking with fear and we have to reassure them that we aren't going to hurt them.

Interviewer: Was Pippa like that?

Peter: Yes, and what we do on arriving at the hospital, and it's the same with any animal, we always put them in an area by themselves to start with as this seems to make them calmer. Pippa actually had quite an affectionate personality but we do have to be careful – if you put animals together straight away they can bite each other or something. We can also get close to them and treat them more easily. Pippa wasn't that badly injured so ...

Interviewer: Just some cuts and bruises?

Peter: Yes, we checked her every four hours and she was soon ready to move into the 'general' area of the hospital. Pippa was only a two-week-old pup so we started by feeding her milk and then we moved her on to fish around five to seven days after that, which is the normal time ... about three weeks old. Pippa was quite thin when we first got her but she soon put on weight and made a quick recovery.

Interviewer: Well, I'm sure we're all glad to hear that ...

Acknowledgements

I'd like to give my warmest thanks to the editors for their help, advice, guidance, enthusiasm, feedback and ideas throughout the project: Susan Ashcroft and Nicholas White for their painstaking and detailed input; Niki Donnelly and Sara Bennett for their organisation and support; Alison Silver for her expertise, advice, encouragement, enthusiasm and meticulous hard work; Sophie Clarke (production controller), Michelle Simpson (permissions controller), Hilary Fletcher (picture researcher), John Green (audio producer), Tim Woolf (audio editor) and Ruth Carim (proofreader). Special thanks also to the design team at Wild Apple Design.

My thanks also to my students at the British Council, Valencia, from 2006 to 2007, who good-humouredly worked through and trialled materials, pointed out faults and suggested improvements.

Very special thanks to my family, Paz, Esteban, and Elena, for all their help and encouragement.

I dedicate this book to Paz with love and admiration for her courage through difficult times and her huge enthusiasm and support.

Thanks also to: Juan Barrios and Jenny Aquino for photo 3 on page 8, Olga Stankova for photo 4 on page 8 of her husband, Lubor Stanek and daughter Pavla Stankova, Elena and Esteban Brook-Hart and Bianca Selva for photo 1 on page 129 of the Student's Book.

Guy Brook-Hart
Valencia, Spain, January 2008

The author and publishers are grateful to the following for reviewing the material: Alison Silver, UK; Jane Coates, Italy; Nick Witherick, UK; Kevin Rutherford, Poland, Laura Matthews, UK; Christine Barton, Greece; Petrina Cliff, UK; Gill Hamilton, Spain; Rosalie Kerr, UK; Alison Maillard, France; Anne Weber, Switzerland; Fiona Dunbar, Spain; Rosemary Richey, Germany; Simon Vicary, Italy; Tonie de Silva, Mexico.

The author and publishers would also like to thank: Helen Naylor for writing the four Progress tests; Kate Woodford for editing the definitions for the items in the Word lists; Cambridge University Press for the definitions in the Word lists. Used by permission of Cambridge University Press.

Recordings produced by John Green, TEFL Tapes, edited by Tim Woolf, recorded at The Audio Workshop, London.

Illustration: Heather Allen p. 99

Cover design by Wild Apple Design Ltd.

Designed and typeset by Wild Apple Design Ltd.